THE END OF CHRISTIANITY

THE END OF CHRISTIANITY

ALBERTUS PRETORIUS

WIPF & STOCK · Eugene, Oregon

THE END OF CHRISTIANITY

Copyright © 2022 Albertus Pretorius. All rights reserved. Except for brief quotations in critical publications or reviews, no part of this book may be reproduced in any manner without prior written permission from the publisher. Write: Permissions, Wipf and Stock Publishers, 199 W. 8th Ave., Suite 3, Eugene, OR 97401.

Wipf & Stock
An Imprint of Wipf and Stock Publishers
199 W. 8th Ave., Suite 3
Eugene, OR 97401

www.wipfandstock.com

PAPERBACK ISBN: 978-1-6667-8998-0
HARDCOVER ISBN: 978-1-6667-9872-2
EBOOK ISBN: 978-1-6667-9873-9

Contents

Chapter		Page
Foreword		ix
Introduction		1
1.	The Various Flavors of Christianity	8
	Differences in the Time of the New Testament	8
	Contemporary Christian groupings	11
	Doctrinal Differences	13
	Christianity is Losing Ground	22
	Ignorance Regarding Key Christian Doctrines	34
	Theology: a Pseudoscience	39
2.	The Bible: a Collection of Uninspired Writings	46
	Conventional Views Regarding the Bible	46
	The Biblical Authors were Fallible People	52
	Contradictory and Improbable Rendering of History	58
	Misquotations of Old Testament Texts by the New Testament	73
	Contradictory Descriptions of God and his Will for Mankind	76
	Fundamentalism and Anti-Evolutionism	100
	The two Faces of Fundamentalism	112
	Flat-Earth Theology	116
	Conclusions	120

	3. Theological Absurdities	124
	Original Sin	124
	Morality and Religion	130
	The Trinity	156
	Redemption	159
	Resurrection, the Last Judgment and Life Everlasting	165
	Prayer	184
	Satan and Demons	194
	Conclusion	205
4.	Religion Explained	207
	Initial Explanations	207
	Personification	210
	Dreams	215
	Altered States of Consciousness	216
	Supernaturalism	226
	Human Needs Satisfied	230
	Oracles	237
	Rituals and Ceremonies	244
	Summary	246
	Bibliography	249

List of Illustrations

The Theological Seminary, Stellenbosch	2
Venus of Willendorf	51
Charles Darwin who first formulated the theory of evolution in 1859	101
Professor Johannes du Plessis	114
Pope Francis	145
Tomas de Torquemada	150
Grave on a hilltop	172
Karl Marx	208
Sigmund Freud	209

List of Tables

Percentages of the Populations of the Following Countries During 2015 which may be Regarded as Nonreligious	27
Importance of Religion and Crime Rate per Country	133
Importance of Religion and Homicide Rate per Country	136

FOREWORD

This book is the result of a lifetime of study – theology, philosophy, history and psychology.

It is with a certain measure of trepidation and hesitation that this book is being presented to the world. I am very conscious of the fact that I am contradicting the beliefs of many people who hold firm religious views and whose faith is something dear to them. I have seen countless cases where a religious faith helped people to find meaning in life and to find guidance in the struggle between good and bad and right and wrong. Many people have found emotional and social support in their religious communities.

This book cannot but undermine those beliefs and I feel sorry for those people who might go through an intellectual and emotional struggle when they consider the evidence presented in this book.

However, it cannot be helped. I feel compelled to disclose the results of my investigations, ruminations, and own struggles and in the process unmask certain superstitions and even religious hypocrisy and fraud. If I don't do it, I won't be true to myself.

Albertus Pretorius, February 2022

INTRODUCTION

Ever since scholars such as Thomas Paine, Friedrich Nietzsche, Ludwig Feuerbach, Karl Marx, and Sigmund Freud started to attack Christianity and religion in general, a fierce battle erupted. No winner has, as yet, emerged from this debate and an unofficial stalemate was declared. Christian theologians declare that atheists (and agnostics) cannot prove their point of view conclusively, namely that God doesn't exist. Atheists and agnostics contend that the burden of proof rests on Christians to demonstrate that God really does exist, which they can't do, either. The consensus seems to be that neither side can prove their claims definitely and finally with logical arguments.

In the meantime, churches in the western world are losing members at an alarming rate. There are various reasons for this state of affairs, but it will be shown in this book that the main reason is that more and more people are gaining the insight that Christianity is simply a sophisticated (and irrelevant) form of superstition. In previous ages, the Bible was regarded as the Word of God, but research has shown that it contains numerous contradictions, irrational ideas and mistakes, with the result that its credibility as a source of reliable knowledge about the world and humanity is highly suspect; it has, at most, historical value as a record of what people believed in the past.

The dogmas of Christianity, which purportedly are based upon the teachings of the Bible, contain many incredible notions that are incompatible with contemporary insights regarding cosmology, history, psychology, medicine and ethics.

It will also be shown that religion played an important part in the lives of people in past ages and that there are various explanations for the existence of religious beliefs. Sophisticated people of the twenty-first century are increasingly gaining the insight that we do not need religion to lead happy, fulfilling and moral lives.

I know Christianity intimately from the inside out since I was a zealous minister of religion for most of my adult life. I studied theology at the Theological Seminary of the Dutch Reformed Church of South Africa in the university town of Stellenbosch.

The Theological Seminary, Stellenbosch (established in 1859)

Throughout my career as minister of religion I had difficulties with certain parts of Holy Scripture. I found it impossible, for example, to compose sermons about the miracles Jesus was supposed to have performed. I found it utterly unbelievable that anybody could walk on water, change water into high-quality wine, revitalize decom-posing corpses or feed a multitude of people with only a few fishes and a few pieces of bread.

Although the Bible often depicts Satan as an evil personage, I could never include him in any of my sermons; I always regarded him as a mere personification of all that is bad, wrong, and evil.

After my last sermon I received a certificate declaring me to be a retired minister of religion who was of sound doctrine and exemplary behavior (although that was definitely no longer true regarding the beliefs I held). It was a relief to slide into retirement. I just could not continue preaching a Gospel I didn't believe in anymore. Slowly, but surely, I developed a set of new beliefs and convictions – and this book is the result.

This book is in a certain sense a prophetic book. I will try to show why people will increasingly conclude that Christianity, despite its beautiful and useful aspects, is a hollow edifice without any real foundations and that it is destined to collapse. I will show that theology is a pseudo-science, in the same league as other pseudosciences such as astrology and palmistry. I will show that most Christian doctrines cannot any longer be entertained by rational and sane human beings, due to their inherent inconsistencies, contradictions and absurdities and the fact that they are at odds with established scientific insights. Christianity is already disappearing in many parts of the world, especially in Europe and the English-speaking countries.

In this book, various quotations will be given from the Bible, together with comments thereon. Certain traditional Christian doctrines will be explained by quoting from three Protestant creeds, the Belgic Confession, the Heidelberg Catechism and the Westminster Confession. These creeds are supposed to provide an authoritative rendering of the message(s) of the Bible, although it will be shown that this is not necessarily the case.

I often mention the findings of various scientific disciplines in this work. I have great respect for rigorous scientific investigation. Our knowledge of the world and ourselves has been growing exponentially during the last two centuries and we can regard that knowledge for the most part as reliable since the technology that was developed upon this knowledge does work, usually without any hitches.

Our modern civilization is built on and sustained by the marvels of engineering, medicine, agriculture and the technology of other scientific disciplines. Many Christians seem to be suspicious of science and scientists, but they, nevertheless, rely on these scientific inventions to lead normal lives.

The late Christian philosopher Herman Stoker wrote a few decades ago that scientific knowledge is not simply a description of phenomena. It is systemized knowledge that endeavors to understand, to explain and to evaluate. It seeks relationships in order to combine knowledge into a system or a finished whole, called a theory.[1] This description of scientific knowledge still holds good today – despite the fact that Stoker was a Christian.

No scientist will contend that science provides all the answers. Science has its limits. It can only pronounce on phenomena that can be observed by our senses, either directly or indirectly by means of sophisticated instruments, such as radio telescopes, fMRI scanners or electron microscopes. Scientists gather knowledge by means of experiments or observations; they measure, count, weigh and test. But they cannot tell us what the origin of the universe is, what type of behavior is right or wrong or what the meaning of life is. When we come to those topics, we are dealing with philosophy.

In this book, much will be made of scientific insights, but in essence, this book is about philosophy, the love of wisdom. The teachings of the Bible and the dogmas of Christianity will be scrutinized and evaluated according to their logical content and rationality and philosophical and scientific criticism will be levelled against all the irrational ideas and concepts propagated by Christians.

It has to be stressed that in my analysis of the Christian faith, I take the text of the Bible rather seriously. Each author of a biblical book tried to convey a certain message to his readers. It may be assumed that those biblical authors were serious about their convictions and that they were convinced that they really spoke on behalf of their God – just as there were various other pagan oracles in the ancient world. But it is possible to step, as it were, into their frame

---

[1] Stoker, *Beginsels en Metodes*, 135–36.

of mind and conclude what really prompted them to write what they wrote. With the knowledge we have of the world in which these authors lived we may reconstruct what really happened and why they constructed myths and presented certain legends and fantasies as fact. The pious deceptions played upon humanity by prophets and apostles will thereby be exposed and explained.

* * *

I predict with confidence that Christianity is destined to become extinct, due to the knowledge explosion through the internet, although respect for Jesus of Nazareth as a wise teacher will probably remain.

The spread of Christianity during the first few centuries was made possible by the availability of Holy Scriptures and other literature – the Old Testament of the Jews, the letters of the apostle Paul and other early Christian authors, various Gospels, some of which did not make it into the Bible, and the extensive writings of the church fathers. Other religions in the Roman Empire did not have that advantage and became extinct.[2] Philosophy enjoyed much respect in antiquity and the books of various philosophers were copied and disseminated on a large scale. The corpus of Christian literature gave Christianity an elevated status, similar to the most respected philosophical schools of the time.

The Protestant Reformation of the sixteenth century was made possible by the invention of the printing press. Martin Luther started the Reformation in 1517 and his ideas could be spread through the printed word after Gutenberg had invented his printing press half a century earlier. More people had access to published works in Luther's time than during the Middle Ages when books still had to be copied by hand. This development caused may people to turn their backs on many of the superstitions held by the Medieval Church.

---

[2] Ehrman, *Misquoting Jesus*, 19.

The downfall of communism and the dismantling of the Berlin Wall in 1989 became possible through the Xerox machine and television. The anti-communist underground in Poland, East Germany and elsewhere under the Soviet yoke distributed pamphlets with their ideas, which were multiplied on clandestine copying machines, while television programs from West Berlin with news regarding the failures of communism could be picked up in the whole of East Berlin. That led to the demise of communism and the dissolution of the Soviet Union and the Warsaw Pact.

The internet, which revolutionized the distribution of knowledge, became available during the nineties of the previous century. The mass of information, which thus became accessible to the world's population, will cause a similar reaction as the Reformation of the sixteenth century and the peaceful revolutions, which swept communist regimes away. It becomes clearer and clearer every day that the orthodox Christian faith is built upon a number of fictions and fantasies; it is like a house of cards that will, inevitably, be blown away by the winds of change. The days are passing when certain preachers are able to build vast religious and financial empires and to influence people to adore them as saints.

Christianity is destined to wither away and make way for rational thought, the insights of science and a moral way of living without a religious foundation.

Through the ages, Christianity was built upon various different world views. In antiquity, when the various biblical books were written, a primitive world view was prevalent. People thought of the earth as the center of the universe. They experienced the world as being flat. God or the gods lived somewhere on mountain tops or in the sky beyond the stars, while hell or the abode of the dead was thought to be below the surface of the earth. The world was populated by all sorts of spiritual beings – gods, angels, demons and the spirits of the ancestors.

This world view was superseded since the Renaissance by a more modern world view in which scientific discoveries played a major role. Christianity managed to adapt to a certain extent to this new world view in which the earth was seen as a tiny speck in a vast universe without a center. No space could be found inside this universe for heaven and hell and these were thought to occupy higher dimensions of space and time, outside the physical universe. The idea was accepted that natural phenomena have natural causes and that everything in the universe was ruled by the laws of nature – except, perhaps, in exceptional cases where God intervened and performed miracles. Most contemporary Christians seem to be stuck in this world view.

It will be shown that even this modernized world view of Christians cannot be entertained any longer and is nothing but an outdated superstition. A superstition is described as a "belief, half-belief, or practice for which there appears to be no rational substance."[3] It will be shown that all theistic religions – Christianity, Judaism and Islam – amount to systems of pious superstitions, which cannot be entertained anymore in the light of all the available evidence.

The book contains much that promises to keep theologians, philosophers and scientists busy, but it is also aimed at the layperson who is interested in religion, philosophy and science.

---

[3] Encyclopaedia Britannica, "Superstition".

CHAPTER 1

THE VARIOUS FLAVORS OF CHRISTIANITY

Differences in the Time of the New Testament

When people call themselves Christians it is not always clear what they mean. There is a large number of denominations consisting of main-stream churches, various sects and even syncretistic groups where ideas from Christianity and other religions have been thrown together and combined. There are a number of theological "schools", each with its own characteristic doctrines and teachings. In addition, Christianity is also characterized by a number of "movements", each with its own emphasis on certain ideas, purportedly taken from the Bible.

This diversity compels one to ask: who are the "real" Christians? Are there any "real" Christians? Which group is on the right track – if any? Why are there so many groups that see each other as opponents and even as adversaries and enemies?

The New Testament book of Acts is supposed to present a historical account of how Christianity started and developed after the ascension into heaven of Jesus Christ. The impression is created that early Christianity was a unified movement which started on the day of Pentecost with the outpouring of the Holy Spirit on the apostles and a number of other followers of Jesus. The trials and tribulations of the Jerusalem congregation are sketched in the first few chapters of this book and then Paul arrives on the scene in chapter 9 where his conversion to Christianity is described. The rest of Acts is devoted to

Paul's missionary travels, as well as his contacts with the Jerusalem congregation.

In the following chapters it will be demonstrated that parts of the book of Acts are simply fiction or fantasy, which are contradicted by details given in Paul's own letters about his life and work.

It is, however, clear that the followers of Jesus never formed a unified movement. There was, for instance, the Jewish Jesus movement. These people never thought of themselves as belonging to a new religion and they continued to worship in the Jerusalem temple, just as the other Jews of their time (Acts 2: 46 and 5: 12). They were called the "sect of the Nazarenes" in Acts 24: 5. Then there were also those who followed the teachings of the apostle Paul who actually created a new religion, and who broke away from the Jewish religion. They were called "Christians" in Antioch, the city where Paul was a preacher before he embarked on his missionary travels (Acts 11: 26).

In addition, there were at least two other early movements that had links with the followers of Jesus and Christianity – the followers of John the Baptist and a number of Gnostic sects.

We read in the Gospels that John had a number of disciples, some of whom later became disciples of Jesus (Matt 14: 12). Paul encountered some of John's followers during his missionary travels (Acts 18: 24–25 and 19: 1–5). A group of these followers of John survive today in northern Iraq and northern Iran. They are known as Mandaeans and they follow the teachings of John, together with some Gnostic ideas.[4]

The origin of the Gnostic movement(s) is unknown, although Simon Magus – of whom we read in Acts 8: 9–24 – was one of the influential figures. This movement, which consisted of a number of unrelated groups, combined certain teachings of Jesus with elements from Neoplatonist philosophy and the Persian religion of Zoroastrianism. According to them, a person could be saved from this

---

[4] Thomas, *Israelite Origins*.

sinful material world by gaining knowledge (*gnosis*; Greek: γνῶσις) of his spiritual home with God.[5]

It is possible that Christians were warned against this movement in 1 Tim 6: 20–21 –

> "O Timothy, take good care of that which is given to you, turning away from the wrong and foolish talk and arguments of that *knowledge* which is falsely so named; through which some, who gave their minds to it, have been turned away from the faith" (*emphasis added*).

Within the version of Christianity introduced by Paul, there also existed more than one variety. Paul's own letters are rather rational and he tried to convince his readers of his views with arguments from the Old Testament. The writings attributed to John – the Gospel and three letters – have their own distinct flavor, which tend to be speculative and seem to a certain extent to be influenced by Gnosticism and Greek philosophy. The last book in the Bible, Revelation, is one of a kind and contains visions and prophecies and was influenced by pagan astrology.[6]

A number of extra-biblical gospels have come to light during past decades. Some of them show clear Gnostic influences and, therefore, never made it into the Bible. Others contain pure fiction and they endeavored to fill the gaps in our knowledge about Jesus. It took a long time before there was consensus about which books should be regarded as having divine authority and should be included in the New Testament.[7]

---

[5] Encyclopaedia Britannica, "Gnosticism".
[6] Malina, *Genre and Message of Revelation*.
[7] Armstrong, *The Bible*.

The second century Roman scholar, Celsus, who wrote a tractate against the Christians, had this to say about the disunity of the Christians in his day (as quoted by his critic, Origen):

> "Christians at first were few in number, and held the same opinions; but when they grew to be a great multitude, they were divided and separated, each wishing to have his own individual party: for this was their object from the beginning."[8]

It is clear, therefore, that early Christianity never formed a unified and homogenous movement and that remained the case throughout the ages. There were at all stages groups who fought each other and condemned their opponents as heretics and apostates.[9] During the first few Christian centuries there were various competing forms of Christianity – orthodoxy (which won the day), Arianism, Nestorianism, Pelagianism, Ebionism and so forth. The number of competing varieties only increased as the centuries passed.

Contemporary Christian Groupings

Christianity today is a religion with many faces and denominations. The Center for the Study of Global Christianity at Gordon-Conwell Theological Seminary estimated that 34,000 denominations existed in 2000, rising to an estimated 43,000 in 2012. These numbers have exploded to the present number from $\pm 1,600$ in the year 1900.[10]

Some Christian groupings are large, e.g., the Roman Catholic Church, Orthodox Churches, various Protestant churches such as the Lutherans, Baptists and Reformed or Presbyterian churches, and the

---

[8] Origen, *Contra Celsum*, III: 10.
[9] Ehrman, *Misquoting Jesus*, 152.
[10] The Way? "How Many Christian Denominations Worldwide?"

Anglican community. A large number of smaller denominations and sects exist.

Within Christianity, there are various movements, which are not restricted to certain denominations. There are, for instance, pentecostalists, fundamentalists, pietists, charismatics, and evangelicals. There are, likewise, various theological "schools". One finds Roman Catholic, Lutheran, Reformed, Charismatic, Pentecostalist, Pietistic, Liberation and Liberal or post-modern theologies; they all differ regarding key aspects of the Christian faith.

The Roman Catholic Church denomination is the largest Christian group in the world today with more than a billion followers constituting about half of the world's Christian population. There are approximately 800 million Protestants in the world and approximately 260 million people worldwide are Orthodox Christians. About 279 million people (12.8% of the world's Christian population) regard themselves as Pentecostalists, 304 million (14%) are charismatics, and 285 million (13.1%) are Evangelicals, or Bible-believing Christians. These last three categories overlap in many instances.[11]

When I was a young minister of religion, fresh from theological seminary, I thought that only my church was on the right course and that most other churches were heading in the wrong direction. In many a sermon, I criticized the charismatic movement, Pentecostalism, the Roman Catholic Church and various other heresies (as I saw them). As the years passed on, I came to the conclusion that my own church had many flaws, that its doctrines were not above criticism and that many questionable practices were tolerated. When I started preaching about the wrongs of apartheid, which in those days was seen as the will of God, some members of my congregation reported me to the secret Security Branch of the Police.

---

[11] Pew Forum, "The World's Christian Population".

All these groups call themselves Christians, followers of Jesus Christ. They all read the same Bible and pray to the same God. Yet, they are divided and their teachings diverge on many points. This begs the question: which one of them is on the right track? Which denomination or movement interprets the Bible correctly? Which denomination or movement is most faithful to the teachings of Jesus and the apostles?

As will be shown, there are various dogmatic or doctrinal differences between these groups. If they all rely on the same Bible, one cannot but conclude that the message of the Bible cannot be very clear and may be interpreted in diverse ways. If that is true, then it also means that no group within Christianity may regard itself as the "real" Christians.

Doctrinal Differences

Differences between Christians

Christian theologians, churches, denominations, movements and ordinary Christians have deep-rooted differences regarding quite a number of doctrinal issues. They differ regarding the following aspects:

- Protestant churches are of the opinion that Christians should base their faith only on the teachings of the Bible. The Roman Catholic Church and Orthodox churches also rely on tradition as part of God's revelation to man and adherents of Pentecostal and charismatic groups believe that God is still communicating with believers as he did in biblical times when he spoke to prophets, apostles and others. There is, in other words, no unanimity regarding the source(s) of the Christian faith.
- Christian groups differ from each other regarding which books to include in the Bible. The Roman Catholic Church regard the

so-called apocryphal books of the Old Testament as deuteron-canonical and they are included in the Biblical text used by this denomination. Other groups consider the First Book of Enoch to be part of Scripture.

- Pentecostals and charismatics rely very much on the direct guidance of the Holy Spirit in the lives of believers and they believe that God still makes use of people with a prophetic gift to communicate with his children; other Christians believe that the guidance of the Holy Spirit is only to be found in Scripture.
- The doctrine regarding the Triune God: exactly how do we have to understand the idea that there is only one God but three divine Persons – Father, Son and Holy Spirit? Are they distinct Persons or only different names for the same divine entity? Although the "official" position of most Christian groups is that the Trinity consists of three distinct divine Persons, united in one Godhead, the popular idea held by many ordinary Christians amounts to a merger of the three Persons.
- How are we to understand the relationship between the divine and human natures of Christ? Did Christ hide his divine nature while on earth or was he only apparently a human being? The "official" view held by most Christian denominations is that Christ had two distinct natures – a divine nature (which was hidden while he was on earth) and a true human nature with all its limitations. Many ordinary Christians often do not understand this distinction and they explain the many miracles attributed to Jesus on account of the idea that he was, after all, "God Almighty".
- The traditional Protestant position is that a sinner can only be saved by having faith in Jesus Christ; the Catholic and Orthodox view is that a person's life style and good deeds play a role in determining his/her destination in the afterlife.

- Some churches administer infant baptism, while others declare this to be a heresy and insist that only believing adults may be baptized. Those who support infant baptism argue that there are a number of instances mentioned in the Bible where whole households – children included – were baptized by the apostles. Their opponents declare that a person may only be baptized if he has made a conscious decision for Christ.
- There are churches that maintain that one cannot be saved without having being baptized, while others do not support this idea. It has to be noted that the Bible nowhere mentions that the disciples/apostles of Jesus were ever baptized, while the unbaptized criminal crucified with Jesus received the promise of paradise directly after his death on that same day.
- Some churches declare that only baptism by immersion is valid – just as Jesus was baptized in the Jordan by John the Baptist. Others point out that Jesus was not baptized in the name of the Father, the Son and the Holy Spirit and that this example does not count, while the first Christian baptism took place in Jerusalem where thousands of people were baptized, which could only have happened by the sprinkling of water because there were no pools or rivers in ancient Jerusalem where immersion could take place.
- The Lord's supper or Eucharist: how must we understand the bread and the wine? Do these really miraculously change into Jesus Christ's body and blood – while still looking and tasting like bread and wine – or are they only symbols of his flesh and blood as Protestants contend?
- Catholic and Orthodox churches maintain that there are seven sacraments; Protestants recognize only two sacraments.
- Catholic and Orthodox churches venerate a host of saints of which the most important is Mary, the mother of Jesus, whom they even call the "mother of God"; in 1950 the Pope officially

declared that Mary did not die but descended directly into heaven, just as Jesus did. Protestants think that this amounts to idolatry because they find no justification for this belief in the Bible.
- Protestants accuse Catholics of leaving Jesus on the cross, due to the fact that Catholic churches all have crucifixes depicting Jesus' execution. Protestants contend that the Gospels tell us clearly that Jesus was taken off from the cross, was buried and was resurrected – and therefore it is wrong to depict Jesus as if he never left the cross.
- Some Protestant churches declare that only those people who are chosen by God will inherit eternal life, but there are also those who maintain that one's eternal destination is totally dependent upon one's own choice for or against God and Christ.
- Some denominations believe that all men are born as sinners and that all deserve eternal punishment, unless they are born again; others believe that sin and evil does not exist in a new-born child and that the bad examples of others lead that child to fall into sin and wrongdoing.
- Most churches congregate on Sundays, the first day of the week, but there are also those who believe that we have to obey the Ten Commandments in this respect and congregate on the seventh day of the week, that is, on a Saturday.
- Certain charismatic churches support the so-called "prosperity theology", according to which believers may expect that God bless them with earthly riches; if they fail to gain this prosperity it is a sign that they lack faith. Mainline churches declare this position to be a distortion of the message of the Bible.
- There is no unanimity in Christianity regarding the role and place of women. There are those who advocate the position

that the Bible prohibits women from holding offices in the church, while there are also those who hold exactly the opposite view.
- Some churches are organized hierarchically. That means that there are bishops, archbishops and other church leaders who have the authority to make decisions of behalf of the whole believing community. Other churches are more democratic and each congregation is managed by a board consisting of elders and deacons who are chosen by the members of the congregation. Both these incompatible positions are being justified from the same Bible.
- An extreme example of the hierarchical position is to be found in the Roman Catholic Church, which teaches that the pope as spiritual leader of the church is able to make infallible pronouncements – as declared by the First Vatican Council in 1870. Protestants reject this position and contend that there is absolutely no Scriptural support for this idea and that there are many instances where popes in the past held wrong and even heretical points of view.
- The Roman Catholic Church teaches that people who die go to Purgatory, a place or state of purification before they can be admitted into heaven. Protestants declare that there is no basis for this doctrine in the Holy Scriptures and that when God forgives the sins of a sinner all his/her guilt has been taken away so that he/she is ready to enter heaven without having to go through a purification process after death.
- According to Roman Catholic teaching, it is possible for one person to help a deceased loved one to leave Purgatory sooner by performing certain good deeds, such going on a pilgrimage, giving alms to the needy or to buy indulgences. Protestants reject this idea.

- There is a wide divergence of views regarding the second coming of Christ and judgment day. Some Christians maintain that the end will be preceded by a glorious millennium during which believers will reign with Christ on earth. Others find no Scriptural foundation for this point of view.

It is abundantly clear that there is much confusion within Christianity regarding many key doctrines. One cannot but ask: Whom must we believe? Which church or movement is correct? Who understands and obeys the Bible most faithfully? The fact that Christians cannot agree on a large number of doctrinal issues may be the reason why so many people – especially in the Western world – turned their backs on religion. They seem to reason that if Christians cannot agree amongst themselves on a number of important topics, then none of them can be taken seriously.

History has shown that it is possible to prove almost any point of view while quoting verses from the Bible – ethical, theological and political. There were those who justified all sorts of positions from the Bible – apartheid, racism, communism, capitalism, socialism, anti-Semitism, fascism, slavery, the denial of human rights to minorities and women, polygamy, a flat earth, so-called "scientific creationism", a crackdown on homosexuals and witches and a prohibition on premarital sex – to mention but a few.

As will be shown in chapter 2, there are deep-rooted differences regarding the acceptance of scientific theories and findings within Christianity. So-called "scientific creationism" is an endeavor to prove from the Bible that the biological theory of evolution is evil and false. There are also those, on the other hand, who declare that we cannot misuse and abuse the Bible as if it were a scientific manual and that there is nothing in the Bible to contradict the theory of evolution.

The result of all these doctrinal differences and differences in style is that churches and church leaders criticize and attack each other, try to steal the other's followers and make outrageous claims about their own superiority. For example: during January 2017 the late Pastor T B Joshua, a well-known spiritual leader from Nigeria and leader of the Synagogue Church of All Nations, declared that there are too many pastors in Malawi and that that was supposed to be the reason why there is so much poverty in that country! In addition, many of the pastors are, according to him, "fake pastors and prophets."[12] The trouble is that Joshua has received much criticism in turn due to his own practices and views, including a claim that he can cure people who suffer from "homosexual demons" and HIV through prayer.[13] Joshua pronounced various "prophecies" over the years, including the prediction that the president of Malawi, Peter Mutharika, would die before 1 April 2016 – which never happened.[14] He also predicted that Hilary Clinton would become the next president of America – which also, of course, did not happen.[15]

Only one conclusion can be drawn from this state of affairs: the credibility of many a Christian leader is close to zero. Which one of them can we believe when they start attacking and vilifying each other?

Differences with Other Religions

Knowledge about religions other than Christianity is much more available to Christians than ever before. The printed media, television and the electronic media brought the world's religions into closer contact with each other. It became clear to many Christians that many Muslims, Buddhists, Judaists and adherents of other religions are happy, mature and balanced people, that they are leading morally

---

[12] News24 Wire, 12.01.2017.
[13] Mail Online, 12.01.2017.
[14] The Telegraph, 13.03.2016.
[15] Punch, 13.11.2016.

exemplary lives and that they are very sincere about their religious beliefs.

Most westernized countries uphold the principle of religious freedom. That means that any inhabitant of a given country is entitled to belong to the religious organization of his or her choice or even not to adhere to any religion. This places the various religions on the same legal footing and creates the assumption that all religions are more or less equal.

This poses the following questions: on which basis does Christianity claim to be the only valid and true religion? Who dares to say that only the Christian Bible contains God's will for mankind? How can we be sure that other religions, besides Christianity, do not also provide valuable insights into the nature and will of God?

During 2016 and again during 2019 a television series was screened on the History Channel in which the well-known actor Morgan Freeman featured, namely *The Story of God*. He interviewed numerous adherents and spiritual leaders of all the main religions on earth. This series suggested that all religions are legitimate paths to reach God.

This religious pluralism led many Christian theologians to conclude that the work of missionaries in the past, where they tried to convert adherents of other religions to Christianity, was ill-founded and actually arrogant. These theologians propose that Christians ought rather to enter into dialogue with people from other religions in order to find common ground and to promote mutual respect.

This religious pluralism also led many Christians to declare that no religion can be relied upon to provide a road map for life since they differ so much between themselves. If these different religious views clash and they cannot agree on certain key points, then the conclusion may be reached that they are all wrong and deluded. The people who came to this conclusion often also point out that horrific crimes have been perpetrated in the name of religious fanaticism:

- The many religious wars that have been fought through the ages, even in our own time;
- Muslim extremists who commit suicide with explosives strapped to their bodies in a bus or on a busy street to take as many "infidel" victims with them as possible;
- The fact that certain Muslim countries prohibit the practice of any other religion within their borders and that people who transgress these prohibitions are punished harshly, even put to death;
- The torching of the great library in Alexandria, Egypt, by fanatical Christians in AD 391 because it was suspected of housing heretical and blasphemous books, thereby destroying a large number of irreplaceable books from antiquity;
- The Holy Inquisition of the Roman Catholic Church, which sentenced many suspected heretics or witches to death after extracting confessions from them under torture;
- Many Roman Catholic clerics, and even the pope, who closed their eyes to the horrors of Nazi Germany during the Second World War and who helped Nazi criminals to escape justice after the war;
- Roman Catholic bishops who protected pedophile priests until the public outcry against this practice forced the pope to crack down on the culprits;
- Many Protestants who also persecuted suspected witches;
- Fundamentalist Christians who have bombed abortion clinics in the belief that they are defending God's honor; and
- Christian missionaries who forcibly took children away from their pagan parents to raise them as Christians, pftern with the help of civil authorities.

The list is actually endless. These practices forced many people from Christian countries to conclude that all forms of religion are bad and unhealthy and have to be avoided.

Christianity is Losing Ground

Statistics

Christianity is, without doubt, the largest religion in the world. The possibility exists that Christianity will lose this position in favor of Islam, sometime in the future. The Christian religion is slowly, but surely, losing ground.

It is estimated that there are about 2,18 billion Christians world-wide, roughly a third of the world's population. Christianity seems to grow only in Africa and the Far East.[16] On the other hand, Europe and North America, which used to be Christian continents in previous centuries and where every adult person was assumed to be a believer – with the exception of Jews and heretics – are nowadays more secularist or humanist than Christian.

World-wide, Christianity is growing slower than Islam, the fastest growing religion. Between 1970 and 2010 Islam has gained 4,23% of the world population, while Christianity only gained 2,10% during the same period.[17]

America is a case in point. Alex Jones wrote in 2012:

> "Is Christianity in decline in America? When you examine the cold, hard numbers it is simply not possible to come to any other conclusion. Over the past few decades, the percentage of Christians in America has been steadily declining. This has espcially been true among young people... [and] there has been a mass exodus of teens and young adults out of U.S.

---

[16] Fairchild, "Christianity Today".
[17] Wikipedia, "Irreligion".

churches. In addition, what 'Christianity' means to American Christians today is often far different from what 'Christianity' meant to their parents and their grandparents. Millions upon millions of Christians in the United States simply do not believe many of the fundamental principles of the Christian faith any longer. Without a doubt, America is becoming a less 'Christian' nation."[18]

The proportion of Americans that consider themselves to be Christians has been steadily declining. Back in 1990, 86 percent of all Americans called themselves Christians. By 2008, that number has dropped to 76 percent. In a survey by the Pew Research Center during 2020, only 63% of adults in the United States identified themselves as Christians.[19]

Meanwhile, the number of Americans who reject religion entirely has soared. According to data from the U.S. Census Bureau, the number of Americans with "no religion" more than doubled between 1990 and 2008. Fifteen percent of all Americans in 2008 said that they have "no religion". That is up from 8 percent in 1990[20]. In 2015, that number has again risen to 33%.[21]

A Pew research report in 2015 in which 35 000 people were polled found that 30% of Americans never or seldom attend religious services. This is up from 27% in 2007. Almost 23% of Americans in 2014 had no religious affiliation and did not find religion to be an important aspect of their lives – up from 16% in 2007. Only 63% of those polled were absolutely certain that God exists – compared to

---

[18] Jones, "The Shocking Decline of Christianity".
[19] Pew Research Center, "Measuring Religion".
[20] Jones, "The Shocking Decline of Christianity".
[21] Wikipedia, "Irreligion".

71% in 2007. The overall picture is that Americans are steadily becoming less religious.[22]

The Canadian organization Atheist Republic reported in July 2021:

> "The annual Values and Beliefs poll conducted by Gallup shows a significant decrease in religious influence on US society. Now, only 16 percent of Americans claim that the impact of religion is increasing in society. The last notable significant increase in Americans' perception of religious influence on society came after the catastrophe of the 9/11 attacks. Disasters aside, religion is slowly decreasing its societal power in a slow yet steady trend in America. In April 2020, the same Gallup poll showed that 58 percent of adult Americans believe that religion is losing its influence, and that number is up to 82 percent this year. In 2020, for the first time in 80 years, the number of churchgoers plummeted to a level below 50 percent, down to 47 percent."[23]

Atheist Republic also reported in June 2021 some findings of the American Worldview Inventory 2021:

> "They found that Millennials have gone farther in cutting ties with traditional Christian views and normative biblical teachings than previous generations. Just 16% of Millennials and 26% of Gen X believe that they will go to Heaven if they accept Jesus as their savior, compared to approxi-mately half of the generation before them. Moreover, 43% of Millennials

---

[22] Pew Research Center, "US Public Becoming less Religious", 3, 4, 143, 149, 152.
[23] Atheist Republic, 12.07.2021.

stated they either don't know, don't care, or don't believe God exists compared to 28% of Boomers."[24]

These reports by Atheist Republic show conclusively that younger people in America are turning their backs on religion, and especially Christianity, in increasingly greater numbers.

Professor Hans Küng, the late well-known Swiss-German theologian, characterizes the Catholic Church world-wide, but especially in the Western World, as "gravely ill" and "terminally ill". The church is losing members at an alarming rate and fewer and fewer young men report for training as priests. Dwindling parishes are being merged and there are not enough priests to minister effectively to the remaining congregations. The church is bleeding dry – and few bishops acknowledge that this dangerous situation exists.[25]

John Humphreys quotes the results of a survey done by the polling organization YouGov in Britain. Of those polled, 25% declared themselves to be agnostics or atheists. On the other hand, only 22% believe in a personal God. The percentage of people who prayed regularly or fairly regularly amounts to 24%. Those who never pray or hardly ever pray are 74% of those polled. Only 11% attend a place of worship at least once a month,[26]

If trends continue, the number of non-believers in Britain is set to overtake the number of Christians by 2030. It was found that Christianity is losing more than half a million believers every year, while the numbers of atheists and agnostics are rising by almost 750,000 annually.[27]

South Africa also has a sizable percentage nonreligious people, although the numbers are lower than in the countries

---

[24] Atheist Republic, 10.06.2021.
[25] Küng, *Can we Save the Catholic Church?* 14–42.
[26] Humphrys, *In God We Doubt*, 112–15.
[27] Martin, "The Year Britain will Cease to be a Christian Nation".

mentioned above. South Africa had 15,1% of its population calling themselves nonreligious in 2001 – slightly below the world average, which was estimated at 16% at that time. According to the census figures of 1996 and 2001 for South Africa, the number of nonreligious persons rose in this time from 4,6 million to 6,8 million. This is an increase from 11,7% in 1996 to 15,1% in 2001.[28] It can be assumed that this figure has again increased since 2001. An international survey conducted in 2011 and 2012 claimed that only 64% of South Africans regarded themselves to be religious.[29]

A survey done by the online News Service, News24, during April 2017 under its readers in South Africa posed the following question to which five possible responses were supplied: "What is the best thing about Easter long weekend?" Only 37.6% of the respondents marked "the religious significance". Those who preferred "time off from work" and "family time" amounted to 55,8% of the total. Very few votes were given to "pickled fish" and "Easter eggs".[30] Although this survey may not be representative of the population of the country as a whole it, nevertheless, demonstrates a trend away from religion and Christianity.

A South African professor in theology recently told me that fewer and fewer students are studying theology with the goal of entering the ministry in South Africa. He foresees that in a few years' time, when a large number of middle-aged ministers will reach retirement age, there will simply not be enough young people to replace them. In addition, the intellectual abilities of theological students have steadily declined over the years with the result that students who are studying at present are less bright that students of a generation ago. This all bodes ill for the future of the church.

---

[28] Statistics South Africa, *Census 2001*, 24.
[29] News24, 10.08.2012.
[30] News24, 18.04.2017, "What is the Best Thing About the Easter Long Weekend?"

In addition, the ability of congregations in South Africa to pay the salaries of their ministers is also declining – especially after the Corona virus of 2020 and thereafter wreaked havoc in the country's economy. More and more congregations will, therefore, only be able to afford part-time ministers and that means that many a minister of religion will be compelled to pursue another (part-time or full-time) job for which he or she is not always adequately trained. The lack of pastoral care in these congregations will only hasten their dissolution and demise.

According to the annual Yearbooks of the Dutch Reformed Church (Nederduitse Gereformeerde Kerk), a substantial number of congregations were forced to dissolve and to combine with neighboring congregations during recent years. This trend seems to continue.

This state of affairs may be one of the reasons why brighter students prefer to take courses at university that will lead to better job security instead of preparing for the ministry.

Large percentages of the populations of the following countries during 2015 may be regarded as nonreligious:

Country	Percentage
Norway	78%
Czech Republic	67,8%
Sweden	±65,5%
Cuba	64%
Vietnam	±63,5%
Denmark	±61,5%
Switzerland	57%
Netherlands	±56,1%
Albania	52%
United Kingdom	±52%
Japan	51,8%
Azerbaijan	51%
China	±50,5%
Estonia	49%
France	48,5%

Russia	48,1%
Belarus	47,8%
South Korea	46,5%
Serbia	45%
Finland	±44%
Hungary	42,6%
Ukraine	42,4%
Iceland	42%
New Zealand	41.9%
Latvia	40,6%
Belgium	35,4%
Germany	34,6%
Chile	33,8%
USA	33%
South Africa	32%

There is a clear trend in these statistics.[31] The countries with the highest percentages of people with no religious affiliations are either affluent and sophisticated former Protestant countries in Europe and the English-speaking world, or former/current communist countries where atheism used to be part of the state ideology.

Churches in Europe are losing members in ever-increasing numbers. A good case in point is the Protestant congregation in the university town of Leyden in the Netherlands. The largest and oldest church building of the town, the church of Saint Peter (Pieterskerk), a 600-year-old gothic basilica, is no longer used for religious purposes; it now serves as a conference center, wedding venue, banqueting hall, exposition center and concert hall. It is being managed by a trust called the "Stichting Pieterskerk Leiden".[32] This trend is to be found in many a European town or city.

The time of the year when this trend towards secularism becomes most visible is at Christmas. This feast is meant to celebrate

---

[31] Wikipedia, "Irreligion".
[32] Stichting Pieterskerk Leiden.

the birth of Jesus Christ – although nobody knows on which date he was actually born. Nevertheless, very little of Jesus Christ has remained in contemporary Christmas. It is a time of partying, drinking, eating, being idle, giving presents and visiting friends and family. The urban scene is dominated by multi-colored Christmas trees, glittering stars and other shiny decorations. It is the time of the year when retail business reaches a peak as everybody is focused on consuming the maximum amount. Of Jesus Christ very little is left, the bearded figure of Father Christmas is the focus of attention and that is a clear symptom of the way the Western World is progressing.

Scientists without Religion

A survey done among members with e-mail addresses of the Royal Society, the most prestigious body of scientists in the English-speaking world, revealed that 78,8% of the members did not believe that a personal God exists. A meta-analysis done in 2002 found that there is a strong correlation between unbelief and IQ or educational level. That means that more intelligent people and better educated people tend not to believe in God.[33]

The 517 members of the US National Academy of Sciences disclosed in a survey that only 7% of these scientists reported that they believed in a personal God. Of the rest, 72.2% were atheists and 20,8% called themselves agnostics.[34]

Greg Graffin, a lecturer in biology at UCLA, sent a questionnaire to fellow biologists regarding their religious beliefs. Of the 149 who responded, only 13 (±9%) believed in a God who intervened in the world. Of his respondents, 88% rejected the notion of immortality.[35]

---

[33] Dawkins, *The God Delusion*, 102.
[34] Stenger, *The New Atheism*, 75.
[35] Graffin and Olson, *Anarchy Evolution*, 41, 45.

Hill conducted a study under American graduates regar-ding their religious beliefs and he concluded:

> "The results indicate that some, but not all, religious beliefs are altered by higher education. Most notably, respondents become slightly more skeptical of the super-empirical if they attend and graduate from college. The effects are often exaggerated for college graduates and those attending elite universities."[36]

Christianity is Disappearing

Christianity is by no means dead. It is, after all, the largest religion in the world. There are, though, clear signs that Christianity is disappearing from many countries. In 1910 about 35% of the world's population were Christians. This figure has dropped in a century to 32%. In 1910, 66,3% of the world's Christians lived in Europe. This figure has decreased to 25,9% in 2010.[37] This trend is due to spread to the rest of the world as well. It may, though, be a slow process.

It has to be pointed out that the phenomena of atheism or agnosticism would have been unthinkable during the Middle Ages. People were burned at the stake merely for being suspected of harboring heretical notions. The Inquisition of the Roman Catholic Church is still remembered today as a very dark blot on the history of Christianity. The rise of rationalism during the seventeenth century and the accumulation of scientific knowledge, inevitably, forced the Church to rethink these practices – although they are clearly prescribed by the Bible (see chapter 2). When these persecutions were halted, people became free to think for themselves and to embrace ideas that ran counter to the superstitions contained in the Bible.

---

[36] Hill, *Faith and Understanding*, 533–51.
[37] Pew Research Center, "Global Christianity".

It must be remembered that the worldview of the authors and first readers of the Bible was a primitive one. For them, the world was flat. Heaven was somewhere above and hell was below the surface of the earth. Earth was the center of the cosmos. The universe was, according to this worldview, filled with living creatures as well as gods, spirits, ghosts, angels and demons that all played a part in events on earth. The scientific revolution that started during the Renaissance altered this world view. We now see that earth is a tiny speck in a huge universe in which there is no place either for heaven or for hell. Many people, though, still believe in spirits, angels and demons, although these beings don't seem to interfere with everyday life so much anymore. Many Christians still believe in miracles when God somehow or other is supposed to interfere with the usual operation of the laws of nature.

Western civilization has in the meantime largely moved into the so-called post-modern period. According to post-modernism, there may be various ways in which the truth about the world and ourselves may be seen. Everything is part of a bigger whole and all phenomena are parts of bigger systems where every part has an influence upon the rest. In this way of thinking and seeing the world, there is no place anymore for the primitive worldview of the Bible and the belief in all sorts of spiritual beings. In other words: the message of the Bible – and religion in general – simply does not appeal to sophisticated people of the present age anymore.[38]

Although Christianity is growing in the Third World and it is clear that Islam is gaining ground faster, it is also evident that the fastest growing religious trends in the world today are those of atheism, secularism, agnosticism, naturalism, humanism and rationalism. Christianity is doomed in the long run – and so are Judaism and Islam. Superstitions and outdated ideas die hard but the increase in the levels of education throughout the world will help to

---

[38] Craffert, *Die Nuwe Hervorming*, 67–87.

sweep the superstitions of Christianity, Judaism and Islam away. Gerald Benedict remarks, quite correctly, that "the demographics of belief indicate a marked trend to atheism and agnosticism."[39]

Hypocrisy

Many people turned their backs on the church and religion due to the perceived hypocrisy of bishops, priests, pastors and other church officials. Grayling and Küng both point out that the Roman Catholic Church forbids abortions or the use of contraceptives. A large number of members of this denomination, nevertheless, do use contraceptives or undergo abortions. This church teaches a strong anti-sex morality, but a large number of homosexual and heterosexual priests have been defrocked after it came to light that they were guilty of pedophilia – something that was denied and covered up for a long time.[40]

This initial failure to discipline priests guilty of sexual abuse of minors led to police investigations in Germany and other countries – much to the consternation and embarrassment of the Catholic hierarchy.[41]

It was recently reported that the Polish archbishop of Krakow decreed that no priest may be alone with a minor. That is due to the fact that nearly one out of every three cases of sexual abuse against children in Poland involved a clergy member.[42]

All these developments prompted the late Willem de Klerk, a well-known theologian and author in South Africa, to declare that Christianity is experiencing a "crisis" due to the fact that God is

---

[39] Benedict, *The God Debate*, 37.
[40] Grayling, *The God Argument*, 44–45; Küng, *Can we Save the Catholic Church?*
[41] Küng, *Can We Save the Catholic Church?* 25–28.
[42] Atheist Republic, 21.01.2022.

disappearing from the world. In many cases, people still participate in religious rituals without believing in the message of the church.[43]

It is actually sad and tragic to see how churches and theologians are – sometimes desperately – struggling to stay relevant. They try their best to prove that the message of the Bible – whatever it is – may be severed from the primitive world view of past ages and may be integrated into the post-modern views of contemporary society. In the process, they alienate less sophisticated, less educated and confused church members – people who got stuck in the world views of previous ages and who still interpret the Bible literally.

These modern theologians twist and turn the contents of the Bible in such a manner in an endeavor to render it meaningful for people of the twenty-first century. But these theologians also do not seem to be able to convince post-modern people that the Bible's message has any relevance and they do not realize that it won't help to update Christianity because Christianity – in whatever form – cannot be updated or defended anymore.

It may even be said that their mental gymnastics to translate the message of the Bible – whatever it is – into contemporary language result in an intellectual construct that often differs very little from humanism, agnosticism or even atheism. But they do not convince many people. People of our time just do not find it necessary to take religion seriously, to be saved from their sins, to worship a God whose existence cannot be proved and to belong to a moribund church or religious organization. The efforts of these post-modern theologians do not impress them in the least. If these theologians want to be honest and credible, they must abandon their efforts to bolster Christianity or religion in general and rather abandon religion altogether.

---

[43] De Klerk, *Die Vreemde God,* 13–15.

Ignorance Regarding Key Christian Doctrines

It was already shown that there exists much confusion between all the various Christian groups regarding key doctrines. There are, though, also quite a number of other issues on which most Christians are supposed to agree. But there seems to be much ignorance amongst ordinary Christians and even ministers of religion regarding many of these key Christian doctrines.

The doctrines of Reformed churches are contained in the so-called formularies of unity, namely the Heidelberg Catechism, the Belgic Confession and the Canons of Dordt. When theological students of these churches are admitted to the ministry, they have to sign a declaration that they accept these creeds as a faithful rendering of scriptural "truths". If a minister should publish or propagate any ideas that contradict the contents of these creeds then it is regarded as a heresy and that minister may be disciplined.

I have heard many sermons by colleagues from which it appeared that they do not quite understand what the official church doctrine is. More than once, I heard a minister say from the pulpit that the relationship between Christ and believers is like the relationship between a father and his children. Wow! That means that God the Father is actually the grandfather of believers because Christ is supposed to be his Son!

The Canons of Dordt contain a lengthy explanation of the doctrine of predestination, a key reformed or Calvinist doctrine. Many of my former colleagues admitted to me that they have no inkling what the doctrine of predestination really entails and that they are too afraid to preach anything connected to this doctrine because the danger exists that they will only confuse their parishioners.

Ministers of the Dutch Reformed Church eagerly call themselves "reformed", but they unfortunately do not always know what this means and I have seen many cases where they were easily swayed by the ideas of charismatic and fundamentalist theologians, under the impression that these ideas are in accordance with the reformed creeds. Many ordinary members of the Reformed Churches are constantly being bombarded with ideas from every conceivable Christian movement or group through the mass media. If their ministers are not always sure what the official views of their church regarding a number of doctrines and issues are, then it is to be expected that these lay mem-bers will experience much more uncertainty and confusion.

Since the advent of the internet there are literally thousands of sermons available to be downloaded. A large number of these sermons are of questionable quality, but they are, nevertheless, often adopted by preachers in the Reformed Churches when they cannot find anything to tell their congregations on a Sunday. This also leads to doctrinal confusion on the pulpit and in the pews of congregations throughout the country.

There is a large number of black churches in South Africa. Bengt Sundkler, a Swedish missionary, published his study of these churches in 1948 under the title "Bantu Prophets in South Africa" (reprinted in 2004). He found that there are many break-away churches from the mainline churches amongst the black people in South Africa, where Christian views and elements from traditional African religious cultures are combined into a syncretistic mixture. The leaders of these churches usually model their leadership on the pattern of either traditional witch doctors or tribal chiefs.[44] The same pattern seems to be repeated in other parts of Africa. That means that many black people practice a religion that may be a combination of Christianity and traditional religions.

A similar situation exists in America. The Barna Research Group conducted a survey of so-called born-again American

---

[44] Sundkler, *Bantu Prophets*.

Christians in 2000 to test their insights into a number of biblical principles. They found the following:

- Only 44% of born-again Christians believe that moral truth is absolute;
- 38% are unsure how to regard moral truth;[45]
- 85% believe the Bible is totally accurate in all of its teachings;
- 68% believe that the Bible teaches that God helps those who help themselves (this idea is nowhere to be found in the Bible);
- 24% believe that Jesus committed sins when He lived on earth (according to 2 Cor 5: 21 and Heb 4: 15, he never committed a sin);
- 53% believe that the Holy Spirit is a symbol of God's presence, but is not a living entity;
- 30% believe that Jesus Christ did not return to life physically after He was crucified;
- 26% believe that whatever is right for your life or works best for you is the only truth you can know;
- 24% believe lying is sometimes necessary;
- 47% believe Satan is not a living being but is a symbol of evil;
- 31% believe that if a person is generally good or does enough good things for others, they will earn a place in heaven for themselves;
- 29% believe that all people experience the same outcome after death, regardless of their beliefs;
- 35% do not believe that a failure to consciously accept Jesus Christ as Savior will condemn somebody to hell;
- 10% believe in reincarnation;

---

[45] Barna and Hatch, *Boiling Point*, 80.

- 27% believe that God is ultimately responsible for allowing suffering in one's life; and
- 30% believe that all religious faiths teach the same basic principles.[46]

Barna and Hatch conclude:

> "The Church is rotting from the inside out, crippled by abiblical theology. (. . .) Let's acknowledge that we are in a state of spiritual anarchy."[47]

These authors also assert:

- "The core values of the Church are a mixture of the world's values and a series of spiritually oriented preferences."[48]
- "Our desire for convenience has changed how we select and engage with our church. Rather than starting with a theological perspective and picking a church that will foster spiritual growth that is consistent with our biblical convictions, most of us select a church that is close to our home and that offers worship services at times that fit our schedule. (. . .) Our longing for stimulating experiences means that we will attend a church that is in vogue, and our first order of business is to take advantage of the satisfying events it has to offer. It becomes vitally important for us to feel good about our church choice and church experiences."[49]
- "The predominant belief is that it doesn't matter what you believe as long as you believe something and feel good about

---

[46] Barna and Hatch, *Boiling Point*, 190–94.
[47] Barna and Hatch, *Boiling Point*, 202.
[48] Barna and Hatch, *Boiling Point*, 88.
[49] Barna and Hatch, *Boiling Point*, 90.

it. (...) Millions of adults say they believe in and worship God, but they have no idea what worship means, who God is, what He stands for ..."[50]

Barna and Hatch provide this diagnosis:

> "Evangelism will become tougher and tougher among adults since a large number of them will have made a first-time decision in the past but have been abandoned after that decision, and thus fallen away from the faith. Reviving their interest in Christianity will prove to be extremely difficult."[51]

Not only are the numbers of Christians dwindling in Europe, South Africa, America and elsewhere, the spiritual strength of the churches in these countries also seems to be waning. The future for Christianity in America truly looks bleak, according to Barna and Hatch – and this also seems to apply to the rest of the Western world.

There may also be another reason why certain Christians in America and elsewhere do not support some orthodox biblical teachings anymore: They have been exposed to newer research findings regarding the origins of the Bible, which contradict the traditional views. When people start to question traditional belief systems – as has happened in Europe – then it does not take long for them to leave the church and abandon their Christian beliefs altogether. This, also, does not bode well for the future of Christianity in America, Europe and elsewhere.

---

[50] Barna and Hatch, *Boiling Point,* 186.
[51] Barna and Hatch, *Boiling Point,* 228.

Theology: a Pseudoscience

Field of study

Students at universities are able to study a large number of sciences. Each scientific discipline has a more or less clear idea of what is being studied and investigated in that subject. For instance: astronomy investigates the cosmos, geography investigates the earth's surface, botany studies plants, economics deals with the world of money, history studies the actions of humans and societies in the past, psychology looks at human behaviour, *etcetera.*

One may, however, also ask: what is the field of study of theology? Is it a science at all? Or is it a pseudo-science, such as astrology, phrenology or palmistry? The fact that it is being taught at certain universities does not automatically qualify it as a science. It must be admitted that the oldest European universities from medieval times started as schools where theology, law and medicine were taught.[52] But that does not mean that the practice and teaching of theology can still be regarded as a scientific activity in our time.

Various disciplines connected to religion are being taught at universities: history of religions, religious studies, philosophy of religion, psychology of religion, sociology of religion, biblical studies, history of Christianity, cultural anthropology, *etcetra*.[53] It is clear, therefore, that there is consensus that religion, as a phenomenon and a human activity, is a legitimate field of study.

The question, though, remains: is theology in itself a science?

Theologians disagree amongst themselves what exactly is supposed to be studied or investigated when they practice and teach Christian theology – just as various denominations and Christian groupings cannot agree on a number of doctrinal issues. The following

---

[52] Encyclopædia Britannica, "University".
[53] Seckler, *Im Spannungsfeld von Wissenschaft und Kirche*, 27.

diverging thoughts regarding the nature of theology as a scientific discipline can be found:

Theology is the Science that Studies God

There are theologians who see their discipline as a field of study in which God is being studied and investigated.[54] These authors seem to have a valid point. The word "theology", after all, means "knowledge about God".

One has to agree, though, that God cannot be an object of study. All the known sciences gather data through experimentation, calculation, observation. analysis and deduction and base their explanations and theories on an analysis and interpretation of these data. It is, however, not possible to perform experiments in which God is involved, to do calculations regarding God or to observe God. It is, therefore, just not possible to have a science that studies and investigates God directly or indirectly.

Theology is the Science that Studies the Bible

Other Christian theologians argue that theology studies the Bible.[55]

This view is problematic. Theologians who study the Old and the New Testaments also have to study the secular history of those times. They also rely on secular sciences such as archaeology and textual criticism; the last-mentioned discipline is needed to reconstruct the original text of the biblical books. Church historians don't find their study material in the Bible; they have to consult all sorts of documents created by individuals and ecclesiastical bodies stored in archives to know what happened in the church through the

---

[54] Pannenberg, *Theology and the Philosophy of Science*, 297, 301; Dreyer, *Poimeniek*, 2; Stone, *The Word of God*, 92.

[55] Hodge, *Systematic Theology*, 15, 21; Kuyper, *Encyclopaedie,* 164, 244; Firet, *Het Agogisch Moment*, 13; Heyns and Jonker, *Op Weg met die Teologie*, 13, 132, 137.

ages. Practical theologians rely to a large extent on the social sciences. Theologians, therefore, do much more than only study the text of the Bible.

Theology is the Science that Studies the Christian Faith

Various theologians propagate the view that theology investigates the Christian faith.[56]

This view is also not without problems. Kuyper pointed out that the study of the Christian faith as a cultural phenomenon cannot be regarded as a science as such; it can only be seen as a topic that can be investigated by practitioners of the history of religions or sociology of religion – just as other religions are also investigated by these sciences.[57]

Heyns and Jonker thought along similar lines.[58]

Theology is the Science that Investigates God's Revelation in Scripture and Creation

König wrote that theology is supposed to investigate God and the whole of creation from the perspective of faith. The study object of theology is, therefore, God and his whole creation.[59] According to Oden, theology is "that knowledge of God witnessed to in Scripture, mediated through tradition, reflected upon by systematic reasoning, and embodied in personal and social experience."[60]

---

[56] Schilling, *The Threefold Nature of Science*, 79–80; Küng; "Paradigm Change in Theology", 32; Ott, *Die Antwort des Glaubens*, 35; Seckler, *Im Spannungsfeld von Wissenschaft und Kirche*, 18, 19, 31; Metz, *Glaube in Geschichte und Gesellschaft*, 44, 50–52; Van Huyssteen, *Teologie*, 2–3; and Muller, *The Study of Theology*, 185.

[57] Kuyper, *Encyclopaedie*, 267–68.

[58] Heyns and Jonker, *Op Weg met die Teologie*, 56.

[59] König, *Teologie*, 18, 31.

[60] Oden, *Pastoral Theology*, x.

This point of view means that theology has to take note of the results of all the other sciences – natural sciences and social sciences. That boils down to the fact that theology cannot be distinguished from (Christian) philosophy, which also deals with the whole of reality.

Conclusion

It became clear that theologians give widely differing answers when trying to answer the question: What is the field of study of theology?

If it is not possible to reach unanimity then one has to conclude that theologians don't really know what they are doing and theology, therefore, cannot be regarded as a scientific endeavour. One cannot but agree with Thomas Paine who declared towards the end of the eighteenth century that theology "is the study of human opinions and of human fancies concerning God."[61]

Quite a number of universities have come to a similar conclusion and abolished their faculties of theology. The University of South Africa in Pretoria is a good example. The erstwhile Faculty of Theology has been split up into five separate departments within the School of Humanities.

The University of the Western Cape in South Africa previously had a Faculty of Theology; now it only has a Department of Religion and Theology inside the Faculty of Arts, which caters for Christian and Islamic theology. The University of Cape Town has merely a department of Religious Studies. The University of Leyden in the Netherlands, which previously housed the oldest theological faculty in the country, nowadays provides theological training in the Faculty of Humanities. According to the syllabus, this training amounts to merely the science of religion and the history of religions. The Dutch University of Utrecht only provides courses in the study of the Christian and Islamic religions.

---

[61] Paine, *The Age of Reason*, 26.

The Faculty of Divinity at the University of Cambridge in the United Kingdom provides teaching and research in Theology, Biblical Studies, Religious Studies, and the Philosophy of Religion and Ethics. The University of Princeton in the USA merely has a Department of Religion – not of Theology.

The Methods of Theology

Richard Dawkins provided some good reasons why traditional Christian theology cannot be regarded as a scientific activity.

Christian theology relied traditionally to a large extent on a study of the Bible. Dawkins finds this unacceptable because we should only believe anything if there is sufficient evidence for accepting that belief. There are, however, "three bad reasons for believing anything. They are called 'tradition', 'authority' and 'revelation'." He adds:

> "People believe things simply because people have believed the same over centuries. That's tradition. The trouble with tradition is that, no matter how long ago a story was made up, it is still exactly as true or untrue as the original story was. If you make up a story that isn't true, handing it down over any number of centuries doesn't make it any truer!"

For instance: The Roman Catholic tradition that Mary, the mother of Jesus, never died and was taken up bodily into heaven is an example of such a tradition. It isn't mentioned in the Bible and only became an official doctrine in 1950.

> "But the story was no more true in 1950 than it was when it was first invented six hundred years after Mary's death."

Basing religious belief on authority is also problematic, according to Dawkins:

> "Authority, as a reason for believing something, means believing it because you are told to believe it by somebody important. In the Roman Catholic Church, the pope is the most important person, and people believe he must be right just because he is the pope." [62]

Christians also believe what the Bible says because they trust that the Bible was written on God's authority.

Furthermore: many people, including biblical authors, claim to have received "revelations". There is no way to corroborate or test these revelations for their veracity. Therefore: when theology purports to study the revelations of prophets and apostles then nobody can claim that objective and scientific knowledge has been gained.[63] The revelations and visions contained in the book of Revelations were actually creative stories inspired by pagan astrology.[64] The conclusion is that when certain biblical authors claimed to have received visions and revelations it is not possible to verify their writings and ideas objectively.

From the foregoing it is clear: the phenomena of religious faith and practices may certainly be studied scientifically by trained historians and social scientists. That is the task of the following sciences: history of religions, religious studies, psychology of religion, sociology of religion and cultural anthropology. Theology, on the other hand, as a study of what prophets, apostles and others have claimed to be revelations from God, cannot claim to be a science. This insight is gaining increasingly support in the world of academia.

Summary
All the topics dealt with in this chapter allow only one conclusion:

---

[62] Dawkins, "Good and Bad Reasons for Believing", 18–19.
[63] Dawkins, "Good and Bad Reasons for Believing", 20–22.
[64] Malina, *On the genre and message of Revelation*.

Christianity consists of various competing factions. Each faction or group maintains that it is on the right track and that the others are mistaken in their beliefs. One may ask: How does one choose between these competing factions and points of view? The only rational answer is: all of them must be wrong and misguided. They all rely more or less on the teachings of the same Bible and each of them finds justification for its diverging views from the same sacred scriptures. If the Bible allows so many different interpretations then the Bible itself must be regarded as full of contradictions and an unreliable source of religious knowledge. That will be the topic of the next chapter.

CHAPTER 2

THE BIBLE: A COLLECTION OF UNINSPIRED WRITINGS

Conventional Views Regarding the Bible

The Word of God

There can be no doubt that the Bible was the most influential collection of writings in the history of mankind. Untold numbers of people have found solace, inspiration, and motivation in its pages and Western civilization was decisively influenced by it.

The Bible can be regarded as a monumental literary achievement. The first part, called the Old Testament by Christians, is the product of a rather insignificant ancient people, the Israelites, containing their myths, history, songs, wisdom and oracles. The second part, the New Testament, tells the story of Jesus of Nazareth and how his movement progressed from Judea to the center of the Roman Empire, the city of Rome itself. Other religions have their own sacred writings, but the Bible has been a best-seller for many decades.

Most Christians have always regarded the Bible as the Word of God. They had the impression that God spoke through the various authors of the biblical books – David, Isaiah, Jeremiah, Amos, Paul, John, James and various other anonymous writers. They came to this conclusion on account of the following biblical verses:

- "Every scripture inspired by God is also profitable for teaching, for reproof, for correction, for instruction which is in righteousness, that the man of God may be complete, furnished completely to every good work" (2 Tim 3: 16–17).

- "We have the more sure word of prophecy; whereunto you do well that you take heed, as to a lamp shining in a dark place, until the day dawns, and the day star arises in your hearts: knowing this first that no prophecy of scripture is of private interpretation. For no prophecy ever came by the will of man: but holy men of God spoke, being moved by the Holy Spirit" (2 Pet 1: 19–21).

These biblical pronouncements are, of course, not really convincing since they amount to an invalid circular argument. This argument declares in effect: The Bible is truthful because the Bible says so.

Confessional Creeds

The confessional creeds of Reformed churches, the Belgic Confession, the Heidelberg Catechism and the Westminster Confession of Faith, may be regarded as a good representation of the conventional view regarding the inspiration of the Bible, as held by most Protestant churches. This view represents the Bible as a collection of writings inspired by God or the Holy Spirit in which God revealed himself to mankind. The pronouncements of these creeds, however, do not agree in all respects.

Article 5 of the Belgic Confession states:

Article 5: The Authority of Scripture
"And we believe without a doubt all things contained in them [the books of the Bible].... because the Holy Spirit testifies in our hearts that they are from God, and also because they prove themselves to be from God."

In other words: every word and every sentence in the Bible ("all things contained in them") are to be accepted as being true and authoritative.

The Heidelberg Catechism teaches in Question & Answer 21 that "I hold for truth all that God has revealed to us in his word..."

According to Q & A 22, a Christian has to believe "[a]ll things promised us in the gospel...." We may also know that the triune God "has so revealed himself in his word, that these three distinct persons are the one only true and eternal God." (Q & A 25) Furthermore: in Q & A 31 we are told that God "has fully revealed to us the secret counsel and will of God concerning our redemption" and that Christ "governs us by his word and Spirit ..."

This means that Christians only have to believe God's *promises* in the Bible – not necessarily everything contained in the Bible. God revealed himself in the Bible and believers have to know that Christ governs them through his word. This begs the question: where does the self-revelation of God begin and where does it end in the Bible? Is every bit of history in the Bible part of God's revelation, or not?

Chapter 1 of the Westminster Confession of Faith deals with "holy Scripture". In Section I we are told that God revealed himself in his creation, but especially in the Bible, which contains his will for mankind. Section II assures us that all the books of the Bible "are given by inspiration of God, to be the rule of faith and life." The Holy Spirit is supposed to convince us of "the infallible truth and divine authority thereof...." (Section V). Section VI also reminds us:

> "The whole counsel of God, concerning all things necessary for his own glory, man's salvation, faith, and life, is either expressly set down in Scripture, or by good and necessary consequence may be deduced from Scripture..."

In Section X we are taught that it is "the Holy Spirit speaking in the Scripture."

To summarize: the Bible contains God's self-revelation and the Holy Spirit spoke through the Bible. This collection of books contains everything we need to know how to serve God and how we may be saved from our sins.

Thus: according to the Belgic Confession and the Westminster Confession, everything in the Bible is infallibly true. The Heidelberg Catechism only requires of Christians to believe God's promises and his self-revelation, wherever those are to be found in the Bible.

The problem is: what exactly did God reveal to us in his word? Every statistic and historical detail, or only who and what he is, how he must be worshipped and how we are to be saved from our sins? It is clear that these confessional creeds do not quite agree with each other.

This disagreement was the cause for much confusion and strife within Christianity. There are those, who may be called fundamentalists, who insist that everything contained in the Bible – history, wisdom, poetry, parables, sermons, prophecies *etcetera* – must be interpreted literally and must be accepted as infallibly true. They seem to get support from the Westminster Confession and the Belgic Confession. There are also those who think that we may agree that the Bible contains statements, which are not historically true or may clash with certain scientific insights, but that the message of the Bible regarding God and what he expects from his people may be accepted as trustworthy and their view seems to be supported by the Heidelberg Catechism.

Theological Liberalism

There are also those who do not accept the doctrines contained in the confessional creeds at all and who treat the Bible as they would treat any other example of ancient literature. According to them, the contents of the Bible may be critically analyzed, although the Bible is also recognized as the foundational collection of documents of Christianity. The Bible is not God's word, but the reports of certain humans regarding their experiences with God. This movement is known as theological liberalism or modernism.[65]

---

[65] König, *Die Evangelie is op die Spel*, 206–07.

The confessional creeds or the biblical texts quoted above do not stipulate exactly how the inspiration by the Holy Spirit was supposed to have happened. One may presume, though, that the Holy Spirit must have guided the biblical authors so that they did not commit errors of any kind while composing their parts of Scripture.

But here one must ask: does the Bible really contain the characteristics of a collection of writings that was inspired and guided by the Holy Spirit? It will be shown that this cannot be the case. When the contents of the Bible are scrutinized, it will become clear that a literal interpretation leads to all sorts of absurdities, that there are many historical and geographical errors in the Bible and that the key ideas of various biblical books contradict each other in essential aspects.

In other words: the Bible shows all signs of being an all too human piece of work with countless errors. Only one conclusion can be made: there is no sign of divine inspiration – despite the fact that the Bible itself proclaims that it is an inspired collection of books. Many people have already made this conclusion and they regard the Bible as an interesting, yet irrelevant, relic from ancient times.

Why so Late?

A very pertinent question in this regard must be asked: if the Bible is really God's word, his revelation to mankind, why did it take so very long in the course of human history before he got to the point of revealing himself? According to the very first few chapters of the Bible the first humans, Adam and Eve, are supposed to have known God and communicated with him. We know that this cannot be true.

The first humans, many thousands of years ago, seem to have had a primitive form of religion in which they held all sorts of superstitions, believed in spirits and other supernatural beings and saw certain natural phenomena, such as the sun, moon, stars, thunder storms, fertility and death as signs of a transcendent reality.⁶⁶

Gerald Benedict points out that "fertility goddess cults" are probably "the earliest religions of which we have evidence in the form of artifacts and artwork." He adds that early forms of religion deified "most, if not all aspects of nature." This type of religion is usually called "animism" since all aspects of nature were seen as being animated by spirits.⁶⁷

Venus of Willendorf: A statuette, presumably of a fertility goddess, of ±22 000 BC found in Lower Austria near the city of Krems. It is carved from an oolitic limestone and tinted with red ochre. It is at the Vienna Natural History Museum, Austria.

But these early human beings certainly did not worship the God of the Bible. The earliest parts of the Bible only came into existence a few centuries before Christ in Palestine and they were only gradually incorporated into a collection of sacred writings after the Jews returned from exile in Babylonia during the sixth century BC.

During the subsequent years a number of other writings were added to this collection, which became the so-called Old Testament. During the second century AD, Christians started collecting the

---

⁶⁶ Hancock, *Supernatural*.
⁶⁷ Benedict, *The God Debate*, 15, 17–18.

writings of apostles and certain Gospels and thereby compiled the New Testament.[68]

The Israelites only started to worship and acknowledge the existence of a single God at a fairly late stage in their history, about 2 600 years ago, during the reign of King Josiah[69]. If we keep in mind that the first modern humans of the species *homo sapiens* appeared ±200 000 years ago[70], then one must surely ask: why on earth did God – if he exists – take so long to reveal himself and guide the process of creating the Bible? Why did he not reveal himself much earlier? If he really was interested in being worshipped by mankind, then why did he wait for more than 98% of human history to make contact?

We must also ask: why did he confine his initial contact with mankind only to an insignificant people, the Israelites? If he really was interested in being worshipped by all of mankind, then he certainly could have done a far better job of revealing himself worldwide.[71]

Granted, writing was only invented about 5 000 years ago and God's revelation perhaps needed writing to be communicated to a wider public – apart from oral traditions. But that means that God waited for almost 50% of the time after the invention of writing to initiate real contact with the Israelites. Why so long?

The Biblical Authors were Fallible People

Imperfect People
Every book in the Bible was written by one or more human authors.

---

[68] Armstrong, *The Bible*.
[69] Armstrong, *A History of God*.
[70] Encyclopaedia Britannica, "Cro-Magnon"; Rousseau, *Die Groot Avontuur,* 146, 295, 301; McCarthy and Rubidge, *The Story of Earth*, 290–92.
[71] Cunningham, *Decoding the Language of God*, 206.

In certain cases, we know who these people were – amongst others, David who wrote certain Psalms, Isaiah, Jeremiah, Amos and other prophets who wrote prophetical books, the Gospel of Luke and the book of Acts who were penned by the same author (Luke?), Paul who wrote a number of letters and Revelation, which was authored by the visionary, John of Patmos.

In many cases we do not know today who the authors were. Many writings are anonymous. In this vein, there is no indication of who were responsible for the books of Judges, Ruth, 1 and 2 Samuel, 1 and 2 Kings, 1 and 2 Chronicles or the epistle to the Hebrews. Other writings were coupled through the ages to the names of various authors. It was accepted for a long time that the first five books of the Bible were written by Moses. It is certainly possible that certain portions may have originated from him, but he could not possibly have been responsible for the references to –

- Kings who ruled long after his time over Israel and of whom he could not have had any knowledge (Gen 36: 31; Num 24: 7; Deut 17: 14–20; Deut 28: 36);
- The fact that the Canaanites lived in the country of Palestine a long time (Gen 12: 6 and 13: 7); or
- His own end on earth (Deut 34).

It has to be pointed out that the language used in the first five books of the Bible date from the post-exilic era. The parts that may, perhaps, have originated from Moses must initially have been in an antique version of Hebrew, which were transmitted by editors, centuries afterwards into a contemporary variety of the language. The song of Deborah (Judg 5) and other songs, however, were retained in an ancient and primitive form of Hebrew.[72]

---

[72] Encyclopædia Britannica, "Hebrew language".

In the same vein the four Gospels are ascribed to certain authors, namely Matthew, Mark, Luke and John. There is, though, no certainty that this is correct, since the names of the authors are nowhere mentioned in these books.

However – the fact remains that people of flesh and blood compiled the various books of the Bible through the ages. They were certainly not sinless and perfect people. They wrote in three languages: Hebrew and Aramaic in the Old Testament and Greek in the New Testament – and they often made grammatical errors, which sometimes cause problems in understanding and interpreting them.

The Biblical Authors had Restricted Insights

We must never forget that the authors of the various biblical books lived in times that differ radically from the 21st century. They knew nothing about –

- Scientific knowledge regarding the earth, the starry skies, life forms on earth and modern medicine;
- The technology of the 21st century; and
- Democracy as a form of government and other political and social institutions – such as human rights – which are accepted in our time as a matter of course.

The world view from which the Biblical authors had their point of departure was a primitive world view and every Bible student must keep that in mind. The Biblical authors, for instance, believed that the earth is flat and situated on pillars (1 Sam 2: 8), while the heavens are also supported by pillars (Job 26: 11). These pillars or foundations rest on a body of water under the earth (Ps 24: 2). Paul thought that there were three heavens (2 Cor 12: 2); the first one was most probably the heaven of clouds, the second heaven was the starry heaven and the third heaven the dwelling place of God and the angels beyond the stars. It was also believed that the dwelling place of the dead was a physical place below the surface of the earth (Num 16: 31–33; 1 Sam 28: 13–15).

We are in our time convinced that this primitive world view is no longer tenable or viable. Nobody in his right mind can any longer deny that the earth is a solid sphere, rotates on its own axis and revolves with the other planets around the sun.

The authors of the Bible did not realize that slavery was an evil institution and therefore no Biblical author ever condemned this practice. Paul merely admonished slave owners to treat their slaves humanely and justly – he nowhere gave an indication that it was desirable to free them (Eph 6: 5–9; Col 4: 1; Philem 1: 17).

Copied from Pagan Sources

When the Jewish elite were taken into exile in Mesopotamia after the destruction of Jerusalem by the Babylonians, they came into contact with the most advanced civilization of their time. They could not help but to take note of the myths of the Sumerians and Babylonians and some of these myths made it into the book of Genesis, albeit in a revised and edited form. Where these pagan myths included a whole pantheon of Gods, the Jews rewrote them to include only their national God, YHWH.

In Genesis 1 and 2 we find the Jewish creation myths with parallels to the pagan prototypes. It is clear though, that the Jewish compilers of these chapters emphasized that the pagan deities, the sun, moon, stars and other natural phenomena, were their God's creations. The story of Noah (Gen 6–9), who survived a cosmic flood together with his family and a number of animals in a huge ship, also has its pagan counterparts.[73]

The story of the Tower of Babel (Gen 11) must have been a product of the exile in Babylon. The Jewish exiles were suddenly exposed to dozens of foreign languages where they were settled and

---

[73] Feiler, *Where God was Born,* 168–70.

worked and they most probably wondered how this multiplicity of languages originated. They seem to have linked this to the Babylonian ziggurats, huge pyramids built of mud bricks, on which some of them may have been put to work. There must have been confusion between workers who could not understand each other and this phenomenon was most probably reworked into the myth of the Tower of Babel.[74]

We only have Unreliable Copies

Before the printing press was invented in the fifteenth century, all books had to be copied by hand to produce new copies. The result was that every copy that was duplicated, either by an amateur or a professional scribe, contained any number of copying errors. Every subsequent copy made of that copy contained the errors of the previous manuscript, as well as a number of new errors.

In the light of this, the remark at the end of Revelation makes sense. One finds there a warning that nobody may add or take away anything from the contents of this book (Rev 22: 18–19). This warning is primarily aimed at scribes who were to make copies of the book and who could, perhaps, alter the contents of the book by committing careless mistakes.

The result of all these copying errors is that we have a number of ancient manuscripts of the New Testament (the oldest dates from the third century AD) that differ from each other. By comparing these manuscripts, academicians have succeeded to a certain extent in reconstructing the original text of the New Testament. There remains, nevertheless, uncertainty regarding many texts or passages.

Before the discovery of the Dead Sea Scrolls in 1947, the oldest available manuscripts of the Hebrew Scriptures dated from the tenth or early eleventh centuries AD. With the discovery of the Dead Sea Scrolls researchers suddenly had copies of biblical books from the

---

[74] Feiler, *Where God was Born*, 196–98.

time before Christ. These ancient copies differed in important respects from the traditional texts and different copies of the same Scriptures also differed amongst themselves.[75] This means that it is often impossible to reconstruct the original Hebrew Scriptures as the various authors wrote them originally.

Modern editions of the Hebrew Scriptures and the Greek New Testament contain alternative readings in the footnotes on account of the fact that the ancient copies of the biblical books often differ from each other. There is not a single page in these Bibles without numerous footnotes containing possible alternative wordings.

It is, therefore, an indisputable fact that we often do not know what Isaiah, Paul, John or other biblical authors originally wrote.[76] In other words: we simply have no guarantee that we possess the supposedly inspired writings of the prophets, poets and historians of the Bible anymore; we only have copies of dubious accuracy. When fundamentalist Christians maintain that every word and every sentence in the Bible is infallibly true, one must ask: where can we find an absolutely accurate and errorless edition of the Bible? Such an edition just does not exist because there is doubt about the exact and correct wording of thousands of texts.

Ancient and Foreign World

Many readers of the Bible during the twenty-first century just cannot understand the message of the Bible anymore. The biblical writers lived in an ancient and primitive era without all the technological marvels of our age.

The result of this is that is that the message of the Bible, namely that sinners can be saved by believing that Jesus Christ died for them on the cross, just does not appeal to many young people

---

[75] Shanks, *The Dead Sea Scrolls*, 19–21.
[76] Ehrman, *Misquoting Jesus*.

anymore. It is, therefore, not surprising that Christianity is losing ground in the modern Western world.

> *A young student told me that he thinks that the Bible has to be rewritten or updated. He knows that the Bible came from an agricultural and pre-industrial background, which is unintelligible to today's younger city dwellers. They cannot understand the idioms of the Bible, cannot identify with the characters in the Bible and have no idea why people believed in spirits, demons and supernatural forces as an explanation for illness and psychological disorders. According to him, the Bible has, therefore, to be updated.*

Contradictory and Improbable Rendering of History

Historical and Geographical Errors

When one compares the Bible's rendering of historical events with extra-Biblical sources, then it appears that the Biblical authors often had it wrong. The position of fundamentalists, namely that every sentence in the Bible is infallibly true, just cannot be maintained.

There are so many historical errors and contradictory reports of certain events that it will take a thick book to point them all out. Here we will only deal with a few examples, which will amply demonstrate the point which we wish to make, namely that the Bible contains numerous historical and geographical errors.

In Genesis 2–4 Adam and Eve are presented as the first human beings. They and their offspring were farmers; they had to tend a garden with fruit trees and their sons were respectively a stock farmer and a tiller of the soil. Paleontology tells us that the first modern humans appeared about 200 000 years ago. Agriculture only started about 10 000 years ago.[77] If Adam and his family really lived and were

---

[77] Mithen, *Prehistory of the Mind*, 248.

agriculturists, they could only have lived during the last 10 000 years – that is, long after the appearance of the first examples of *homo sapiens*. One has to conclude that Adam and Eve were mythological figures, not historical figures. Their story or myth has the function to explain how humans were created, where evil had its origin, why women had to suffer during childbirth, why humans had to toil for a living and why humans are afraid of snakes.

We read in Genesis 6–8 that God sent a world-wide flood because mankind became so evil and wicked with the result that these horrible humans – except Noah and his family – had to be wiped out. We are told that God was sorry that he had made mankind (Gen 6: 6). One may ask: If he really is omniscient, then he must have known that mankind would turn out to be a disappointment; why did he then create people in the first place? After the flood it transpired that Noah and his offspring were not really the upright men the Bible held them to be (Gen 6: 9), due to the fact that Noah succumbed to the temptation of producing wine and becoming intoxicated. He passed out naked on his bed, which caused one of his sons, Ham, to make fun of him. Although it was Ham who was guilty, Noah cursed his grandson, Canaan, without providing an explanation for this switch (Gen 9: 24–25).

We are told in Gen 7: 19 and 20 that the flood in the time of Noah was so severe that even the mountains disappeared under the water. One can only wonder: where did all this water come from? There is only so much water on earth in the oceans, rivers, lakes and clouds and locked up in the ice of the arctic regions and on mountain tops. Van den Heever mentions that the sea contains about 1,322 million cubic kilometers of water. To cover the mountain tops an additional 4,4 billion cubic kilometers of water would have been needed. There was definitely not enough water available to cover the mountains. One may also wonder: where did all this water drain away after the flood had subsided? In other words: the biblical story of the flood cannot be based on any historical event. There might, perhaps, have been a local flood somewhere, but definitely not a world-wide deluge.[78]

One may also ask: how did all those animals, birds and insects from all the corners of the earth manage to reach "the floating zoo that was Noah's ark?"[79] Did the ark contain penguins and polar bears from the arctic regions, kangaroos from Australia, gorillas from Africa, anacondas from South America, tigers from India, spiders from China and lemurs from Madagascar? Was the ark big enough to contain so many species? Where did Noah store food and clean water for all of them? How did he prevent fighting between the different species? How did he and his few family members manage to feed thousands of animals daily and clean the ark out regularly? When all these problems are taken into consideration one is tempted to sympathize with poor Noah who took to the drink after he had successfully delivered all the animals to their original habitats after the end of the flood.

Anyway, the world has not improved since this cleansing of the evil elements of the human species and, therefore, one may ask: what was the point of the flood, if God didn't achieve anything worthwhile or lasting?

It is noteworthy that fundamentalist Christians use this flood – that certainly never happened as described – to explain all sorts of geological phenomena on earth, including the creation of the Grand Canyon in America. If they are asked where all that water came from, they are at a loss for an explanation.

We read of camels in connection with the stories of the patriarchs (Gen 24: 61–4 and 37: 25). This is an anachronism, since camels were only domesticated between 1 100 BC and 800 BC – centuries after the time of the patriarchs.

---

[78] Van den Heever, *Wat Moet ons met ons Kerk Doen?* 80.

[79] Benedict, *The God Debate*, 86.

When the sons of Jacob went to buy grain in Egypt, they met their brother, Joseph, who – unknown to them – was elevated to the status of prime minister and minister of agriculture after they had sold him as a slave. He ordered his servants to put his brothers' money back into the sacks of grain they bought (Gen 42: 35 and 33: 1). From the context it is clear that bags with coins were meant. The trouble with this story is that money in the form of coins was only invented at about 700 BC – quite a number centuries after this episode.[80]

We find in Exodus repeatedly that Moses brought messages from God to the Pharaoh, the Egyptian king. This seems improbable. A Hebrew, even if he was a leader of the slaves, would never have made it past the palace guards. If he did manage to get an audience with the king and required of him to free the Hebrew slaves, it would certainly have cost him his head.[81]

On account of the archaeological record, investigators are unanimous that the Exodus never happened as described in the Bible. There was no mass influx of former Hebrew slaves from Egypt who conquered the Promised Land and devastated a number of cities. There is only one explanation for the existence of the people of Israel: they were Canaanites who were already living in the country and who gradually acquired a separate identity by worshipping YHWH, their own national God.[82]

Callahan points out that there is simply no way the biblical reports of the Israelite's stay in Egypt, the Exodus and the conquest of Palestine by the Israelites can be coordinated with known Egyptian history.[83]

---

[80] Callahan, *Secret Origins of the Bible*, 123.
[81] Callahan, *Secret Origins of the Bible*, 139.
[82] Armstrong, *The Bible*, 15; Finkelstein and Silberman, *The Bible Unearthed*, 48–122,
[83] Callahan, *Secret Origins of the Bible*, 131, 148.

There may, perhaps, be some kernels of truth in the story of Moses and the Exodus. The name Moses (Hebrew: מֹשֶׁה – *Mosheh*), for instance, suggests an Egyptian origin, since various Egyptians had names ending on "–mose", such as Ahmose or Tutmose. According to Ex 2: 10, the Egyptian princess gave him this name with the explanation that she had drawn him from the water, since the name Moses is seemingly related to the Hebrew word 'mashah', which means 'to draw out'. This is not possible, because the Egyptian princess certainly did not know a single word of Hebrew.[84]

Even Abraham Malamat, professor emeritus of Jewish history at the Hebrew University of Jerusalem and defender of the historical accuracy of the Bible, had to admit:

> "In the past, the debate over the Exodus often focused on when it could have happened. Much of this debate, unfortunately, ignored what I call the 'telescoping process' – the compression of a chain of historical events into a simplified and brief account of Biblical historiography – especially of Israel's proto-history. Complex events were com-pressed into a severely curtailed time span by later editors viewing the events in retrospect. The Bible presents a relatively brief, streamlined account of the Exodus, a 'punctual' event, as opposed to a 'durative' event, which could conceivably involve two or more exoduses or even a steady flow of Israelites from Egypt over hundreds of years."[85]

In other words: events that may have happened over several centuries were compressed in the biblical narrative into a single event. So much for historical accuracy!

---

[84] Callahan, *Secret Origins of the Bible*, 132.
[85] Malamat, "Let my People Go", 22.

The Ten Commandments are to be found in Ex 20 and Deut 5. In both cases, we are told that Moses received the stone tablets with the commandments directly from God while the wandering Israelites were camping at the foot of Mount Sinai after they had escaped from Egypt. When one reads these commandments carefully it becomes clear that the two versions, which are supposed to contain the same text, differ from each other in a few aspects. One must, therefore, ask: which one of the two versions is the original?

It is also apparent that the Ten Commandments couldn't have been proclaimed in the desert during the exodus; they rather reflect a sedentary existence with agricultural activities that partly depended upon slave labor, which only became possible inside the Promised Land. They were, after all, warned not to be jealous of their neighbors' houses, slaves or animals and they were also supposed to rest on the Sabbath from all their (agricultural) work together with their animals and slaves. The Israelites who escaped from Egypt were supposed to be former slaves and during the exodus they definitely did not possess slaves themselves. Therefore, the Ten Commandments could only have been formulated long after the Israelites got settled in Palestine where landowners acquired slaves and animals – certainly not during the exodus.

The first chapter of the book of Numbers contains a list of the adult men of military age of the twelve tribes of Israel who supposedly left Egypt en route to the Promised Land, Palestine. A total of 603 550 men was counted. The tribe of Levi was not included because they were not supposed to do military service. If one assumes that the Levites made up one-twelfth of the total, then the number of adult men amounts to 653 846. If one assumes that there were an equal number of women, then the total number of adults were 1 307 692. If one, in addition, assumes that there were on average two children per household, then the total number of Israelites who supposedly left Egypt was 2 615 384. That number is comparable with the number of inhabitants of the City of Tswane (Pretoria) in South Africa where

2 921 488 people resided according to the census of 2011. The provision of clean water and sanitation to the people of Pretoria is a major and sophisticated undertaking. How would Moses and the other leaders of the Israelites have been able to provide these services to 2,6 million people or more for 40 years in the Sinai Desert? That must have been a totally impossible task. Such a large migration of Israelites just could not have happened.

The Israelites are reported to have avoided trekking through the kingdom of Moab on their way to the Promised Land (Num 20: 14–21). If this information is correct, then it can perhaps be used to date the Exodus, since the kingdom of Edom only came into existence during the 1200's BC. This date, though, creates serious difficulties for placing the start of the Exodus within the framework of Egyptian history.[86]

The tribe of Dan is mentioned in the Bible as one of the tribes of Israel and their ancestor was supposed to be a son of the patriarch Jacob (Gen 49: 16–8). Recent archaeological evidence, however, strongly suggest that the members of this tribe were the descendants of a Greek garrison placed there by the Egyptians to guard Egypt's borders of the time and that they, in time, joined the Israelite confederation.[87]

Many more examples of improbable reports from the Old Testament can be mentioned. It is clear, though, that we don't find an accurate rendering of history in the books of Genesis and Exodus. The same applies to the rest of the Old Testament and the same also applies to the New Testament.

Luke writes that the birth of Jesus coincided with a census that was ordered by the emperor Augustus and which happened when Cyrenius (Latin: Quirinius) was governor in Syria (Luke 2: 1–2). The only census in those regions in the time of Quirinius, of which

---

[86] Callahan, *Secret Origin of the Bible*, 156.
[87] Karasavvas, *Only Eleven Tribes of Israel?*

historical sources report, happened a whole decade after Jesus had been born.[88]

Matthew 14: 3 and Mark 6: 17 record that Herod Antipas, the tetrarch or ruler of Galilee, married his sister-in-law, Herodias, the divorced wife of his half-brother Philip. We are also told that John the Baptist criticized him for this sin. However, Herodias was not the ex-wife of Philip, but of Herod Archelaus, his half-brother and ruler of Judea after the death of their father, Herod the great.[89]

The description of geographical details in the Bible is also not always accurate. According to Acts 27: 27, Paul and other castaways drifted 14 days on end during a storm in the Adriatic Sea (Greek: Ἀδρίας – *Adrias*) before being washed up on the island of Malta. A glance at a map of the Mediterranean in New Testament times will immediately reveal that the Adriatic Sea is situated between Macedonia and Italy and is far removed from the island of Malta. The boat on which Paul sailed from Crete to Malta, never came near the Adriatic Sea.

The Bible Contains Inconsistencies and Contradictions

It sounds crass to state that there are inconsistencies and contradictions in the Holy Bible, but any thorough investigation will affirm this statement and it is necessary that any serious student of the Bible should be aware of this fact. Even the well-known conservative reformed theologian in South Africa, Professor Adrio König, admitted that the Gospels contain many inconsistencies and contradictions regarding the stories of Jesus' birth, his sayings, the date of his death and the accounts of his resurrection.[90]

---

[88] Rylaarsdam, "Biblical Literature".
[89] Josephus, *Jewish Antiquities*, XVIII/V/4.
[90] König, *Ek Glo die Bybel*, 145–46, 150, 255–69.

It is impossible to give a full description of all the inconsistencies and internal contradictions contained in the Bible, since there are so many. In the pages that follow, only a selection of such instances is given; these will, however, prove the point that the biblical account of historical events often cannot be relied upon.

These inconsistencies and contradictions occur often where different Biblical books describe the same history. If one compares the books of Samuel and the books of Kings on the one hand with 1 and 2 Chronicles on the other hand it soon becomes apparent that they often differ and contradict each other.

Two examples will suffice: In 2 Sam 8: 4 we read that David looted 1 700 war horses in his battle with king Hadad-Eser of Soba. According to 1 Chr 18: 4, he actually looted 7 000 war horses. According to 1 Kgs 7: 15, Solomon erected two bronze pillars in front of the temple with a height of 18 cubits. We read, on the other hand, in 2 Kgs 25: 17 that the pillars were 21 cubits high, while 2 Chr 3: 15 reports that the pillars were 35 cubits high.

In Ex 6: 2–3 we read the following:

> "And God said to Moses, I am Yahweh: I let myself be seen by Abraham, Isaac, and Jacob, as God, the Ruler of all; but they had no knowledge of my name Yahweh."

This is in direct contradiction with Gen 15: 7 where God revealed his name to Abram and Gen 27: 7 where Isaac blessed his son in the name of the Lord. God also revealed his name to Jacob at Bethel (Gen 28: 13).[91]

Exodus 9: 2–3 assures us that all the animals of the Egyptians, including their horses, died of the plague during one of the ten Egyptian plagues. In spite of that, according to Ex 14: 7, Pharaoh

---

[91] Callahan, *Secret Origins of the Bible*, 134–35.

shortly thereafter suddenly had enough horses for 600 chariots to pursue the fleeing Israelites.

Numbers 22–24 tells the story of Balaam, the soothsayer from the Euphrates, who was called upon by king Balak to curse the Israelites. In Num 22: 20 we are told that God gave him the order to go on his mission, but in verse 22 one can read that God was angry because Balaam started on his journey. It is difficult to reconcile these conflicting statements. After having blessed the Israelites, instead of cursing them, Balaam went back to the Euphrates (Num 24: 25). When the Israelites waged war on the Midianites, they also slew Balaam, who miraculously reappeared from the far-away Euphrates. The reason given for his death is that he enticed the Israelites to worship pagan gods (Num 31: 8 and 16), although he is depicted in Num 22–4 as a worshipper of YHWH. One can only conclude that there was sloppy editing work done when these chapters in Numbers were compiled and the inconsistencies were not evened out.[92]

We read in Josh 11: 22 –

> "So Joshua took the whole land, according to all that Yahweh spoke to Moses; and Joshua gave it for an inheritance to Israel according to their divisions by their tribes. The land had rest from war."

After peace had been assured, Joshua divided the country between the tribes of Israel (Josh 12–19). Yet, in the first chapter of Judges, the book following Joshua, it is reported that it was decided that the tribe of Judah should declare war on the Canaanites, as if there were no peace and the country had not yet been taken.

In Judg 1: 8 we are told that the tribe of Judah captured the city of Jerusalem, killing the inhabitants and burning the place down. Yet, in Josh 15: 63 it is reported:

---

[92] Callahan, *Secret Origins of the Bible,* 162–63.

"And as for the Jebusites, the inhabitants of Jerusalem, the children of Judah could not drive them out: but the Jebusites dwell with the children of Judah at Jerusalem unto this day."

But, when one reads 2 Sam 5: 6–7, it is reported that David captured Jerusalem, which was still in the hands of the Jebusites, the original inhabitants. So – when did Jerusalem actually become Israelite territory? Did it happen during the time of Joshua or of the Judges or did it happen when David conquered the city a few centuries later?

The battle between the young David and the giant Goliath is well known. Less well-known is the fact that the Bible contains two different accounts of the slaying of Goliath. According to 1 Sam 17: 4–49, David slew Goliath, while 2 Sam 21: 19 reports that a certain Elhanan killed the giant.

The second chapter of the book of Ezra contains the results of a census of those Jews who returned from exile. It is stated in verse 64 that there was a total of 42 360 souls. However, when all the numbers of the different families are added up the total amounts to only 29 818. Nehemiah mentions the same total of returned people as Ezra in chapter 7 of his book. When the numbers of the listed families in his book are added up, a total of only 31 089 is found.

Only two of the Gospels contain a Christmas story – Matthew and Luke. Both have totally different narratives and it is not possible to reconcile them. Three of the four Gospels have reports regarding Jesus' resurrection – Matthew, Luke and John. The details of these reports differ widely.

Both Matthew and Luke insist that Jesus' mother, Mary, was a virgin when he was conceived (Matt 1: 23 and Luke 1: 34). She was supposed to have been miraculously impregnated by the Holy Spirit and, therefore, Jesus could not have had a biological father. Moreover, Mary was only engaged to her later husband, Joseph, when she fell pregnant. Both these Gospels seem to forget this rather inconvenient fact when Jesus' parents and family are mentioned and he is repeatedly called the son of Joseph, the carpenter:

- "Isn't this the *carpenter's son*? Isn't his mother called Mary, and his brothers, James, Joses, Simon, and Judas?" (Matt 13: 55).
- "And his *father* and mother were full of wonder at the things which were said about him" (Luke 2: 33).
- "And every year his *father* and mother went to Jerusalem at the feast of the Passover" (Luke 2: 41).
- "[A]nd his mother said to him, Son, why have you done this to us? See, your *father* and I have been looking for you with sorrow" (Luke 2: 48).
- "All testified about him, and wondered at the words of grace which proceeded out of his mouth, and they said, 'Isn't this *Joseph's son*?'" (Luke 4: 22) (*emphasis added*).

The contradictory genealogies of Jesus contained in Matt 1 and Luke 3, both explain Jesus' ancestry from King David through his father, Joseph. That means that Joseph must, in fact, have been his biological father.

In addition, the fact that Jesus became a popular teacher and that the crowds greeted him as their king when he entered Jerusalem on the back of a donkey a few days before his execution (Mark 11: 1–10), suggest that he could not have been born out of wedlock and that his parents must have been married. After all, we read in Deut 23: 2 –

> "One whose father and mother are not married may not come into the meeting of the Lord's people, or any of his family to the tenth generation."

It is generally accepted that the Gospel of Mark is the oldest of the four Gospels. It is, after all, the shortest of the four. It is, furthermore, clear that the Gospels of Matthew and Luke are in a certain sense expanded re-editions of the Gospel of Mark. More or less the whole of the text of Mark is contained in the two other Gospels, but there are numerous additions. Some of these additions in Matthew and Luke originate from the same source and these parts agree almost totally in both these Gospels. This source, called "Q" from the German word for "source", namely "Quelle", contained only certain parables and sayings of Jesus. In addition, both Matthew and Luke utilized other sources – probably mainly oral traditions that came from people who witnessed the ministry of Jesus.[93]

Matthew and Luke changed the text of Mark in many cases (compare for instance Mark 8: 29 with Matt 16: 16 and Luke 9: 20). There are, therefore, in certain cases three variations of the same story. Sometimes these variations amount to contradictions between the three Gospels. For example: according to Mark 10: 46–52 Jesus opened the eyes of only *one* blind man in Jericho, but Matt 20: 29–34 relates that there were *two* blind men whose sight was restored.

According to Matt 5: 3, Jesus taught: "Blessed are the poor in spirit, for theirs is the Kingdom of Heaven." Luke's rendering of Jesus' words differs markedly: "Blessed are you poor, for yours is the kingdom of God" (Luke 6: 20). There is a profound difference between people who are poor, that is, people without money and belongings, and those who are poor in spirit (whatever that means).

Mark 5: 23 tells us that the daughter of Jairus was on the point of death when her father begged Jesus to come to her aid. Matthew 9: 18, though, assures us that she had already died when her father reached Jesus.

When we compare the words with which Jesus instituted the Eucharist in Mark 14: 22–26, Matt 26: 26–29, Luke 22: 15–20 and I Cor 11: 23–25, glaring discrepancies become apparent. It is also remarkable that John contains no report of the institution of the Eucharist; according to him, Jesus simply had a meal with his

---

[93] Mack, *The Lost Gospel*.

disciples on the eve of his execution (John 13: 2). On the other hand, John reports a long speech by Jesus to his disciples on this occasion, which was omitted by the other Gospels (John 13–17).

We read in Luke 23: 39–43 –

> "One of the criminals who was hanged insulted him, saying, 'If you are the Christ, save yourself and us!' But the other answered, and rebuking him said, Don`t you even fear God, seeing you are in the same condemnation? And we indeed justly, for we receive the due reward for our deeds, but this man has done nothing wrong.' He said to Jesus, 'Lord, remember me when you come into your kingdom.' He said to him, 'Most assuredly I tell you, today you will be with me in Paradise.'"

In contrast with this, Matt 27: 44 and Mark 15: 31 inform us that *both* criminals insulted Jesus – not only one. Who can be believed? Luke, or Matthew and Mark?

When one compares Matt 27: 5 with Acts 1: 18, one finds two different stories about the suicide of Judas.

There are also profound differences between the first three Gospels and the Gospel of John. John, for instance, differs from the other three Gospels regarding the day of the week on which Jesus was crucified. Matt 27: 62, Mark 15: 42 and Luke 23: 55–56 claim that Jesus was crucified on a Friday (the day before the Sabbath), while John 19: 31 reports that he was crucified on the Saturday. The Greek text of John explicitly states that the crucifixion took place ἐν τῷ σαββάτῳ (*en to sabbato* – on the Sabbath). Many translations of this text tried to harmonize the Gospels by rendering this expression as "Preparation" instead of "Sabbath".

Mark 15: 25 informs us that Jesus was crucified at the third hour (09:00). According to Matt 27: 45 and Luke 23: 44, Jesus was already hanging on the cross at noon ("the sixth hour"). John 19: 14, on the other hand, tells his readers that Pilate only passed judgment on Jesus at the "sixth hour" (12:00) before he was led away to be executed. So – when was he really crucified?

The Gospels preserve various purported words of Jesus while he was hanging on the cross. They do not agree with each other. The synoptic Gospels (Matt 27: 55; Mark 15: 40; Luke 23: 49) inform us that some women who followed Jesus, including his mother, were looking from afar, while his disciples had already fled when he was arrested (Matt 26: 56; Mark 14: 50). Therefore, there was nobody to record or remember what his last words were and the Gospel writers must have invented at least some of his dying words. John, on the other hand, tells a different story. According to John 19: 25–7, the women who followed Jesus and "the disciple he loved" were standing so close to his cross so that he could talk to them before he died.

When we compare the inscriptions on the cross above Jesus from the four Gospels, we find four different versions:

- The superscription of his accusation was written over him, 'THE KING OF THE JEWS'" (Mark 15: 26).
- "They set up over his head his accusation written, 'THIS IS JESUS, THE KING OF THE JEWS'" (Matt 27: 37).
- "An inscription was also written over him in letters of Greek, Latin, and Hebrew: 'THIS IS THE KING OF THE JEWS'" (Luke 23: 38).
- "Pilate wrote a title also, and had it put on the cross. There was written, 'JESUS OF NAZARETH, THE KING OF THE JEWS'" (John 19: 19).[94]

One may, therefore, ask: what was really written on the cross? The

---

[94] The usual translation of the expression "of Nazareth" is incorrect. The Greek word used is Ναζωραῖος (*Nazoraios*) – which means "Nazarite". It has nothing to do with the village of Nazareth.

Gospels contain the inscription in Greek, although it must originally have been in Latin, the language of the Roman authorities and Pontius Pilate. One can only guess what his exact words were, although there seems to be unanimity that Jesus was executed due to his claim to be the king of the Jews.

Luke does not seem to be certain when Jesus became the Messiah. According to Luke 2: 11, the angel told the shepherds that Jesus, who is the Christ (Messiah), was born in Bethlehem. We are informed, though, in Acts 10: 36-38 that Jesus only became the Messiah when he was baptized by John. When Peter addressed the crowd in Jerusalem on Pentecost, he declared that God made Jesus the Messiah only when he died on the cross (Acts 2: 36).

In Acts 9 we are told how it happened that Paul became a Christian. We are also told that he immediately went to Jerusalem after his conversion to meet the apostles. His own account of what happened is to be found in Gal 1: 11–23 and it tells quite a different story, including the fact that he spent three years in Arabia before eventually travelling to Jerusalem.

Paul informs us in Gal 2 of a meeting he attended in Jerusalem with the apostles of Jesus. His version of this meeting differs markedly from the report we find in Acts 15.

We must conclude on account of the foregoing that the history, as given in the Bible, is by no means complete or reliable. The claim of Christian fundamentalists that the Bible must be absolutely true and correct in all respects, including its rendering of history, cannot be maintained against the background of these clear facts.

Misquotations of Old Testament Texts by the New Testament

In certain cases, the authors of the New Testament referred to events in the Old Testament – and confused two separate episodes with each other and in this manner gave a wrong rendering of history or simply got their facts wrong. In other cases, they twisted the words of the Old Testament to fit their own ideas.

According to Acts 7: 16, Abraham bought a grave from a certain Hamor. We read, on the other hand, in Gen 23: 7–18 that Abraham actually bought the grave from somebody else, namely Ephron, the Hittite, while Josh 24: 32 reports that it was, in fact, Abrahams' grandson Jacob who bought a grave from Hamor.

When Jesus was confronted by the Pharisees when his disciples plucked some heads of grain on the Sabbath, he answered them:

> "Have you no knowledge of what David did, when he had need and was without food, he, and those who were with him? How he went into the house of God when Abiathar was high priest, and took for food the holy bread, which only the priests may take, and gave it to those who were with him?" (Mark 2: 25–26).

Jesus referred to an incident described in 1 Sam 21: 1–6. It turns out that David did not do what Jesus said he did when Abiathar was high priest. The high priest at that time was actually Abiathar's father, Ahimelech.

The authors of the books of the New Testament frequently quoted from the Old Testament to prove some or other point. They usually took their quotations from the Greek translation of the Old Testament – a translation that was not always entirely correct. Quotations from the Old Testament in the New Testament, therefore, do not always agree with the original Hebrew text of the Old Testament.

Compare, for instance Matt 1: 23 with Isa 7: 14. In Isaiah reference is only made of a certain unidentified "young woman" or "maiden" (Hebrew: הָעַלְמָה – *ha-almah*) – and certainly not a virgin!

– who would become pregnant shortly thereafter. The Septuagint, the ancient Greek translation of the Old Testament, changed this word into παρθένος (*parthenos* – virgin). Matthew quoted the inaccurate Greek text of Isaiah and applied it to Jesus' mother Mary to "prove" that Jesus' miraculous birth from a virgin was foretold by Isaiah – which certainly was not so.

Take a look at Amos 9: 11–12:

> "In whose day will I raise up the tent of David who is fallen, and close up the breaches of it; and I will raise up its ruins, and I will build it as in the days of old; who they may possess the remnant of Edom, and all the nations who are called by my name, says Yahweh who does this."

Compare this with Acts 15: 16–17, where Amos is quoted:

> "After these things I will return. I will again build the tent of David, which has fallen. I will again build its ruins. I will set it up: That the rest of men may seek after the Lord; all the Gentiles who are called by my name, says the Lord, who does all these things."

Amos predicted that Israel would prevail over its old enemy, the Edomites. Acts omits the reference to Edom and transforms the old prophecy into a prediction that the gentiles would become Christians.[95]

We find the following mistake in Matthew:

> "Then that which was spoken through Jeremiah the prophet was fulfilled, saying, 'They took the thirty pieces of silver, the price of him who was priced, whom some of the children of

---

[95] König, *Die Evangelie is op die Spel*, 27.

Israel did price, and they gave them for the potter's field, as the Lord commanded me'" (Matt 27: 9–10).

The words quoted by Matthew are not from the prophet Jeremiah, but from Zechariah (Zech 11: 12–13).

It has already been shown that Moses could not have been the author of the first five books of the Old Testament, the Pentateuch, although some portions may perhaps stem from him. Nevertheless, Jesus often referred to him as the author of those books, containing God's law (*e g* Matt 8: 4; 12: 5; 19: 8; 22: 26; 23: 2 *etcetera*). That means that Jesus accepted uncritically the view of his day that Moses wrote the whole law – which has since been proven to be wrong. We cannot, also, use the utterances ascribed to Jesus as proof that Moses was, in fact, the author of the Pentateuch.

Contradictory Descriptions of God and his Will for Mankind

Inconsistencies and Inaccuracies

If the Bible really were the word of God, the vehicle for his self-revelation to mankind, one could have expected that the Bible would provide us with a consistent description of how he is and what he expects from mankind. That is, however, not the case. The various parts of the Bible present us with widely divergent views regarding God and the behavior he expects from us.

One sometimes encounters the point of view that it has to be granted that the Bible contains historical inaccuracies, but that the religious or theological contents are reliable. This is, for instance, the stance of Adrio König who wrote:

> "There are serious problems regarding our understanding of the Bible. We must have the courage to acknowledge this honestly. We will also not get good solutions to all problems.

> But this does not need to undermine our trust in the message of the Bible. (. . .) Not everything in the Bible has authority anymore today. The pronouncements of the Bible, for instance regarding slavery or the clothing of women do not apply any more – those are issues of the past and our 'common sense' helps us to distinguish which issues are at stake" (*own translation*).[96]

König tried bravely to bolster the authority of the Bible. But one must ask: how do we know what the real "message" of the Bible is? How do we distinguish or separate this "message" from the cultural background of the Biblical authors? Who is able to decide where the border between these two is to be found? What are we to do when different parts of the Bible give conflicting "messages"? No two Bible students will find the same "message" in a particular biblical passage and that is the reason why different Christian groups and various theologians cannot agree on a large number of doctrinal issues, as has been shown in the previous chapter. And – how reliable is our "common sense"?

In the paragraphs that follow, it will be shown with some of examples that there is little consistency in the "messages" of different parts of the Bible.

Genocide
The most glaring discrepancy in the Bible is that God purportedly ordered Moses, Joshua and the Israelites on various occasions to exterminate all the people in Canaan due to their paganism when the Israelites ended their forty-year trek through the desert and started to conquer the Promised Land. All the inhabitants had to be slaughtered, their animals killed and their cities destroyed by fire (Num 21: 1–3, 22: 34 and 31: 15–18; Lev 27: 29; Josh 3: 10, 6: 17, 8: 24–26 and 10:

---

[96] König, *Ek Glo die Bybel*, 25.

10–14, *etcetera*). That was a blatant case of a divine sanction for genocide or ethnic cleansing.

Yet, we get this testimony of Moses' character in Num 12: 3 – "Now the man Moses was more gentle than any other man on earth." One can only exclaim in incredulity: How is that possible? How could the Israelites start their campaign of the wholesale slaughter of their pagan enemies under the leadership of this supposedly gentle person?

Michel Onfrey remarks that God invented "total war". He adds: "Clearly, scorched earth, fire, and wholesale slaughter of populations are not a recent invention."[97]

That is the same God who supposedly also gave the Eighth Commandment: "You shall not murder" (Ex 20: 13) and who condemned all forms of homicide, violence and retaliation (Gen 9: 6; Num 35: 30–34; Matt 5: 38–47 and 15: 19–20 *etcetera*). How on earth can we trust a supreme being who so blatantly contradicts himself?

Keith Ward tries to soften this problem by declaring that God did not really command the extermination of the pagans; that was only how the Israelites believed what God would have commanded them to do.[98] This sounds like a reasonable argument, but it boils down to the point of view that we may decide on our own what God said and what he didn't say. That will, inevitably, lead to total arbitrariness regarding biblical exegesis.

Thomas Paine was vitriolic in his criticism:

> "People in general know not what wickedness there is in this pretended word of God. Brought up in habits of superstition, they take it for granted that the Bible is true, and that it is good; they permit themselves not to doubt of it, and they carry the ideas they form of the benevolence of the Almighty to the book which they have been taught to believe was written by

---

[97] Onfrey, *In Defence of Atheism*, 177.
[98] Ward, *Is Religion Irrational?* 146.

his authority. Good heavens! it is quite another thing, it is a book of lies, wickedness, and blasphemy; for what can be greater blasphemy, than to ascribe the wickedness of man to the orders of the Almighty! (. . .) As to the character of the book [of Joshua], it is horrid; it is a military history of rapine and murder, as savage and brutal as those recorded of his predecessor in villainy and hypocrisy, Moses; and the blasphemy consists, as in the former books, in ascribing those deeds to the orders of the Almighty."[99]

The cruelty meted out to pagans was not confined to the time of Moses, Joshua and the judges. In Zech 14: 12 God promises:

"And this will be the disease which the Lord will send on all the peoples which have been warring against Jerusalem: their flesh will be wasted away while they are on their feet, their eyes will be wasted in their heads and their tongues in their mouths."

Ps 137: 8–9 says the following regarding Babylon; "Daughter of Babylon, doomed to destruction, he will be happy who rewards you, as you have served us. Happy shall he be, who takes and dashes your little ones against the rock."

Isaiah 13: 14–6 foresaw the following fate for Babylon: "Everyone who is found shall be thrust through; and everyone who is taken shall fall by the sword. Their infants also shall be dashed in pieces before their eyes; their houses shall be rifled, and their wives ravished."

Do Christians recognize this bloodthirsty deity as their God of love? How can they serve and love this God who approved of the killing of small children?

---

[99] Paine, *The Age of Reason*, 70, 72–73.

The Road to Salvation

The different parts of the Bible describe the road to salvation differently.

Protestants usually follow Paul who taught that we can only be saved by having faith in Jesus Christ, who died on the cross to pay for all our sins. In Gal 2: 16 he wrote that "a man is not justified by the works of the law but through the faith of Jesus Christ." He added:

> "Because by the works of the law, no flesh will be justified in his sight. For through the law comes the knowledge of sin. (...) We maintain therefore that a man is justified by faith apart from the works of the law" (Rom 3: 20, 28).

When we investigate the Old Testament, a different picture emerges. The Old Testament gave very little attention to the afterlife, but it is adamant that the only way to please God is to obey his laws and to worship Him as the only God.[100]

Jesus had the same message. When a rich young man approached him with the question, "Good teacher, what good thing shall I do, that I may have eternal life?", Jesus instructed him to obey the whole law, to sell all his belongings and donate the proceeds to charity (Matt 19: 16–22). Jesus also taught: "Not everyone who says to me, 'Lord, Lord,' will enter into the Kingdom of Heaven; but he who does the will of my Father who is in heaven" (Matt 7: 21).

James, the brother of Jesus, didn't agree with Paul:

> "What good is it, my brothers, if a man says he has faith, but has no works? Can that faith save him? and one of you tells them, 'Go in peace, be warmed and filled;' and yet you didn't give them the things the body needs, what good is it? Even so

---

[100] Boshoff ed., *Geskiedenis en Geskrifte*.

faith, if it has no works, is dead in itself. Yes, a man will say, 'You have faith, and I have works.' Show me your faith without your works, and I by my works will show you my faith. You believe that God is one. You do well. The demons also believe, and shudder. But do you want to know, vain man, that faith apart from works is dead?" (Jas 2: 14–20).

Luke, who wrote the book of Acts, composed some speeches by the apostles in which the meaning of the death of Jesus was explained (Acts 3, 4 and 13). These speeches don't contain the idea that people have to believe that Jesus died on the cross to save them from their sins. Luke declared that Jesus' death had to bring people to the point where they realized that they were sinners – in contrast to Jesus, who was innocent – and that they needed God's forgiveness.[101]

According to Revelation 14: 4–5, the people who managed to enter heaven were those who abstained from fornication, lies. and other iniquities.

We also read in Rev 20: 13:

"The sea gave up the dead who were in it. Death and Hades gave up the dead who were in them. They were judged, each one according to his works."

Rev 22: 14–15 inform us:

"Blessed are those who do his commandments, that they may have the right to the tree of life, and may enter in by the gates into the city. Outside are the dogs, the sorcerers, the sexually immoral, the murderers, the idolaters, and everyone who loves and practices falsehood."

In other words: Revelation does not teach that faith in Jesus

---

[101] Ehrman, *Misquoting Jesus,* 167.

Christ is the determining factor whether or not one enters heavenly bliss; a person's crimes and sins, or lack thereof, during life on earth determine his/her eternal fate.

Protestants usually condemn Catholics for teaching that man can be saved by performing good works. If Protestants really wish to follow the whole Bible, then they will also have to agree that Catholics may have a valid point. It is, anyway, abundantly clear that the teachings in the different parts of the Bible regarding man's redemption contain glaring contradictions.

Bible students struggle with a dilemma regarding the first letter of John. At the beginning of his letter John teaches us: "If we say that we have no sin, we deceive ourselves, and the truth is not in us" (1 John 1: 8). In contrast with this, John also declares:

- "Whoever remains in him [God] doesn't sin" (1 John 3: 6).
- "Whoever is born of God doesn't commit sin, because his seed remains in him; and he can't sin, because he is born of God" (1 John 3: 9).

It is a mystery how these totally contradictory ideas could occur in the same supposedly God-inspired epistle. How is it possible that we are told that *all* people are sinners, yet a few pages later we learn that those who are born again do not sin anymore and even cannot sin anymore?

The Example of Jesus and his Parents
The Ten Commandments teach us to honor our parents (Ex 20: 12). Yet, Jesus gave this advice to his followers:

- "He who loves father or mother more than me is not worthy of me; and he who loves son or daughter more than me isn't worthy of me" (Matt 10: 37).

- "If any man comes to me, and doesn't hate his own father, mother, wife, children, brothers, and sisters, yes, and his own life also, he can't be my disciple" (Luke 14: 26).

This advice runs directly counter to the injunction of the Ten Commandments that we have to honor and respect our parents.

When Jesus, his disciples and his mother attended a wedding, the following happened: "When the wine ran out, Jesus' mother said to him, 'They have no wine.' Jesus said to her, 'Woman, what does that have to do with you and me? My hour has not yet come.'" One cannot but conclude that Jesus gave a rather rude answer to his mother; he certainly did not treat her with respect (if reported correctly). He was not an admirable example in this regard.

Jesus' Resurrection and Ascension

How is the resurrection of Jesus Christ to be regarded? Was it really a case where a person who died from his horrible wounds and serious loss of blood managed to cheat death and was resurrected about 60 hours afterwards, which is a basic tenet of orthodox Christian belief? Or is this only a story, which was in line with cultural beliefs of the days in which the New Testament was written where myths of dying and resurrected deities – for instance, ancient Middle Eastern and Greek gods such as Baal, Melqart, Adonis, Eshmun, Tammuz, Ra and Osiris – were well known?[102]

There is no consistency in the reports regarding the resurrected body of Jesus in the New Testament. Paul wrote that Jesus was resurrected with a "heavenly body" or a "spiritual body" – whatever that means (1 Cor 15: 44–55). Likewise, 1 Pet 3: 18 declares that Christ was "put to death in the flesh, but made alive in the spirit" – in other words, he was not resurrected bodily, only spiritually, although

---

[102] Encyclopaedia Britannica, "Resurrection".

we are not informed how a spiritual resurrection is supposed to take place.

The Gospels, on the other hand, depict Jesus' resurrected body as a material object of flesh and blood. When Jesus appeared to Mary Magdalene and the other Mary, he spoke to them and they grasped his feet (Matt 28: 9). According to John 21: 9–15, Jesus prepared a fire and roasted some fish, which he ate with his disciples – something an immaterial or ethereal spiritual being supposedly cannot do.

The Gospels and Acts also do not agree about Jesus' ascension into heaven. According to Acts, the resurrected Jesus requested that his disciples do not leave Jerusalem. His ascension, accordingly, also took place somewhere in or near Jerusalem (Acts 1: 4, 12). Luke also informs us that the disciples stayed in Jerusalem and that Jesus led them from there to Bethany, a village about three kilometers from Jerusalem, whence he ascended into
heaven (Luke 24: 33, 50).

The oldest manuscripts of Mark do not contain a story about Jesus' appearances to his disciples after his resurrection and of his ascension; we are only told that his grave was empty. An angel at the empty grave, nevertheless, told the women who came to the grave to tell the disciples that Jesus would meet them in Galilee – not Jerusalem (Mark 16: 5–7). Matt 28: 16, on the other hand, states that Jesus appeared for the last time to his disciples on a mountain in Galilee, far to the north from Jerusalem.

John contains no report of Jesus' ascension. He does tell us, though, that Jesus had a last meeting with the disciples at the sea of Tiberias – far from Jerusalem and also not on a mountain in Galilee (John 21: 1).

These discrepancies and contradictions, together with the cultural background of the times, make these reports of Jesus' resurrection and ascension highly suspect and they have a clear mythological slant. One can only conclude that the various stories of

Jesus' resurrection and ascension cannot be taken seriously; they are definitely not based on any real historical events.

Bishop Tom Wright, who vociferously argued that Jesus really did get resurrected, nevertheless admits that the Jews from the Old Testament never believed that the Messiah would be killed and, therefore, the Old Testament doesn't contain any allusions to the resurrection of the Messiah.[103] If this is true, then Paul had it wrong when he wrote:

> "For I delivered to you first of all that which also I received: that Christ died for our sins according to the Scriptures, that he was buried, that he was raised on the third day according to the Scripture." (1 Cor 15: 3–4).

Similarly, John 20: 9 argues that the disciples didn't understand the Scriptures when they discovered the empty grave. John fails, though, to inform us which Scriptures were meant. According to Luke 24: 27, the resurrected Jesus explained to two of his followers on the road to Emmaus what the Scriptures supposedly had foretold about his death and resurrection. We are, unfortunately, left in the dark about which passages in the Old Testament purportedly predicted his resurrection.

The truth is actually that the Old Testament is silent about the resurrection from the grave of the Messiah. It has been claimed that in Acts 2: 25–27 that Ps 16: 10 foretold the resurrection of Jesus. This is a fallacy. David, the poet of this Psalm, merely expresses his faith that God will not let his soul perish in Sheol, the realm of the dead. The Messiah is nowhere mentioned or implied.

Celsus, the second century Roman scholar who was critical of Christianity, did not find the reports of Jesus' resurrection to be credible. He argued that –

---

[103] Wright, "The Self-Revelation of God", 199.

> "[I]f Jesus desired to show that his power was really divine, he ought to have appeared to those who had ill-treated him, and to him who had condemned him, and to all men universally. (. . .) But when he might have produced a powerful belief in himself after rising from the dead, he showed himself secretly only to one woman, and to his own boon companions".[104]

It seems as if Celsus has a valid point and one may verily ask: Why did Jesus purportedly appear only to his followers and not also to the high priest and the members of the Sanhedrin or to Pontius Pilate? If he had done so, nobody would have been able to doubt his resurrection.

Prophecies never Fulfilled

There are a number of prophecies in the Bible that were never fulfilled and where the prophets were led by wishful thinking about the future. A number of examples – by no means an exhaustive list – is discussed below:

According to Gen 2: 17, God promised the first pair of humans: "Of every tree of the garden you may freely eat: but of the tree of the knowledge of good and evil, you shall not eat of it: for in the day that you eat of it you will surely die." This was actually a lie, because they did not fall dead when they ate fruit from the forbidden tree.

The prophet Nathan told King David on behalf of God: "Your house and your kingdom shall be made sure for ever before you: your throne shall be established forever" (2 Sam: 7: 16). It is clear from the subsequent history that this promise was not fulfilled. The dynasty of David came to an end when Jerusalem was sacked by the Babylonians in 586 BC. No descendent of David ever sat on a throne in Jerusalem after that.

---

[104] As quoted by Origen, *Contra Celsum*, II: 63, 70.

Another similar prophecy is to be found in Isa 9: 5–6. We are given the assurance that the child, whose birth is announced, will be a great king:

> "Of the increase of his government and of peace there shall be no end, on the throne of David, and on his kingdom, to establish it, and to uphold it with justice and with righteousness from henceforth even forever."

Christians generally regard this to be a prophecy regarding Jesus, who was supposed to be a descendent of David. The trouble is, though, that Jesus never sat on a throne and ruled over Israel. Christians respond to this problem by arguing that Jesus Christ is an eternal king and that his throne is in heaven. But that is not what Isaiah meant with his prophecy. He clearly had a very human monarch in mind who would sit on a throne in Jerusalem – which never happened. In other words: Isaiah had it wrong with his prophecy.

In Isaiah 11 it is foretold that a great king would rule in righteousness in Israel, sometime in the future. The remnants of the people of Israel, who were exiled after the fall of Samaria in 772 BC, would return to the Holy Land and enjoy peace under this future king. Christians regard this as another prophecy regarding Jesus Christ's reign as eternal king in heaven. Isaiah is, however, explicit that his prophecy deals with the real people of Israel, not very long after his own time – not some hypothetical future millennium. History tells us, though, that those Israelites who were taken away in exile by the Assyrians just vanished. They were simply assimilated by the nations where they were placed and they never returned to Palestine.[105] This prophecy of Isaiah was, therefore, also never fulfilled.

A similar prophecy is to be found in Ezek 37: 21–22:

---

[105] Jones, *In the Blood*, 142.

> "And say to them, these are the words of the Lord: See, I am taking the children of Israel from among the nations where they have gone, and will get them together on every side, and take them into their land: And I will make them one nation in the land, on the mountains of Israel; and one king will be king over them all, and they will no longer be two nations, and will no longer be parted into two kingdoms."

Ezekiel was active as a prophet during the exile of the Jews in Babylonia – long after the northern Israelite tribes were taken away in exile after the fall of Samaria. His expectation that all the tribes would be reunited into a single kingdom never came to pass.

Jeremiah 23: 5–6 contains a prophecy with more or less the same contents. He predicted that a descendent of David would secure the safety of both Judah and Israel. No such descendent of David ever ruled – especially not Jesus.

The fate of Damascus was contained in this prophecy: "Behold, Damascus is taken away from being a city, and it shall be a ruinous heap (Isa 17: 1)." Damascus is perhaps the oldest inhabited city in the world and it still exists (although it contains many ruins due to the civil war that ravaged the country of Syria).

Isaiah 19: 5 predicted that the Nile in Egypt would dry up – which has not yet happened.

Ezekiel 29: 11–12 promised the country of Egypt on behalf of God:

> "I will make the land of Egypt an utter waste and desolation, from the tower of Seveneh even to the border of Ethiopia. No foot of man shall pass through it, nor foot of animal shall pass through it, neither shall it be inhabited forty years."

This threat never came to pass and it may be classified as another case of wishful thinking.

Jesus promised his followers: "Truly I say to you, there are some of those here who will not have a taste of death, till they see the Son of man coming in his kingdom" (Matt 16: 28). Jesus warned his disciples in Matt 23: 36 regarding Judgment Day: "Truly I say to you, all these things will come on this generation". According to Matt 24: 34, Jesus gave a similar promise: "Truly I say to you, this generation will not come to an end till all these things are complete." When Jesus was interrogated by the high priest and asked whether he was the Messiah, he answered: "I am: and you will see the Son of man seated at the right hand of power, and coming with the clouds of heaven" (Mark 14: 62).

On account of these utterances, one may conclude that Jesus expected Judgment Day and the establishment of a theocracy in Palestine to come about in his own lifetime. Many centuries and many generations have passed since Jesus spoke these words and, yet, Judgment Day hasn't arrived. His own generation certainly didn't experience Judgment Day. Numerous biblical scholars through the ages have struggled to explain these erroneous promises and predictions of Jesus away, but to no avail.

Although technically not prophecies, the utterances in Prov 11: 18–19 and 12: 21 run contrary to everyday experience:

- "The wicked earns deceitful wages, but he who sows righteousness reaps a sure reward. He who is truly righteous gets life. He who pursues evil gets death."
- "No mischief shall happen to the righteous, but the wicked shall be filled with evil."

It is a fact of life that all sorts of people experience accidents, disasters and misfortune. Whether one is an honest and gentle person or a wicked and criminal thug, this plays no role in these "acts of God". The good suffers just as much as the bad during floods, droughts, volcanic outbursts or pandemics.

Exactly the opposite wisdom is, anyway, to be found in Eccl 7: 15 –

> "All this have I seen in my days of vanity: there is a righteous man who perishes in his righteousness, and there is a wicked man who lives long in his evil-doing."

Many more examples of unfulfilled, misguided and inaccurate prophecies and threats in the Bible can be mentioned. These examples, though, clearly demonstrate that many a biblical prophet made predictions, which were never fulfilled and which were proved wrong by the subsequent history. In other words: these prophecies could never have been inspired by an all-knowing, truthful and reliable God.

The Old Testament Laws

Christians mostly read the New Testament when they read the Bible. Large parts of the Old Testament seem to be out of touch with reality or outdated and they receive little attention. After all, we read in Gal 3: 13 that Jesus Christ fulfilled the Law (of the Old Testament) in our stead and that he freed us from the obligation to hold the law. Therefore, we are no longer to be judged on Judgment Day whether or not we kept the Old Testament laws. What will only matter, is whether we relied in faith on Christ's atonement for our sins on the cross (John 3: 15–16).

But this is not quite the whole story. Christians are also obliged to obey the law in order to show their love and gratitude towards God for his grace and salvation through Christ. Jesus explicitly taught that his followers are obliged to keep the law in its entirety if they wanted to enter the Kingdom of Heaven (Matt 5: 17–20, Matt 7: 21; Matt 19:17; Luke 10: 26–28). The Heidelberg Catechism teaches the same in Questions and Answers 86 and 91.

It is, therefore, clear that Christians are still supposed to obey the laws of the Old Testament. But it is also true that they, in fact, obey only certain laws and neglect others. Here are some of the laws which no Christian takes to heart anymore:

- "Six days shall work be done, but on the seventh day is a Sabbath of solemn rest, holy to Yahweh. Whoever does any work on the Sabbath day shall surely be put to death" (Ex 31: 15).
- "You may not take any sort of blood as food, and any man who does so will be cut off" (Lev 17: 14).
- "The man who commits adultery with another man's wife, even he who commits adultery with his neighbor's wife, the adulterer and the adulteress shall surely be put to death" (Lev 20: 10).
- "Anyone who curses his father or his mother shall surely be put to death" (Ex 21: 17).
- "He who blasphemes the name of Yahweh, he shall surely be put to death; all the congregation shall certainly stone him: as well the sojourner, as the home-born, when he blasphemes the name [of Yahweh], shall be put to death" (Lev 24: 16).
- Deuteronomy 13: 6–10 requires of Israelites to kill anybody who tries to seduce them to worship pagan gods, instead of worshiping only the God of Israel, even if it is a close relative.
- "And if a man has sex relations with a man, the two of them have done a disgusting thing: let them be put to death; their blood will be on them" (Lev 20: 13).

No civilized country in the world will nowadays tolerate the behavior of anybody who tries to put these laws into prac-tice because it will amount to cold-blooded murder. Most of us live in a world where freedom of religion is treasured, where adultery, homosexual relationships and blasphemy are not illegal and where work on the Sabbath is not prohibited – even if these actions are against God's laws.

In Gal 5: 2–3 the apostle Paul argued that the obligation to undergo circumcision was abolished for Christians. We read, nevertheless, in Acts 16: 3 that he circumcised his pupil Timothy, the son of a Greek father and a Jewish mother, presumably to mollify the apostles and other Jewish followers of Jesus in Jerusalem who still upheld all of Moses' laws.

In our age, it is regarded as morally wrong to discriminate against people due to their gender. Men and women are regarded as equals. The best-known example of Old Testament legislation, the Ten Commandments, regards women as inferior to men and merely the property of their husbands. They are, after all, listed alongside other belongings of their husbands, namely farm animals, houses and slaves:

> "Thou shalt not covet thy neighbor's house, thou shalt not covet thy neighbor's wife, nor his manservant, nor his maidservant, nor his ox, nor his ass, nor any thing that is thy neighbor's." (Ex 20: 17 – King James Version).

But Christians anyway do not obey or respect these laws anymore. This implies that they do not regard these laws as having any authority. With this attitude, Christians actually reject certain parts of Scripture and thereby declare that these parts are not really inspired by the Holy Spirit. This attitude will, inevitably, lead to relativism and chaos. Who is to decide which parts of Scripture are inspired and have to be obeyed and which parts may be discarded or ignored? Every other Christian theologian or preacher will come to a different conclusion in spite of the fact that Jesus expected of his followers to uphold the whole law of Moses, as has been shown above.

It is noteworthy that Jesus did not condemn a woman caught in adultery, although some Jewish elders wanted to stone her – as required by the law, as quoted above (John 8: 1–11). These elders, anyway, did not follow the Old Testament law fully either because the man with whom this woman was caught did not receive the same rough and harsh treatment given to the woman. But neither did Jesus follow the law, because he only warned the woman to sin no more – he did not insist on her death. With this action, Jesus implicitly disregarded a strict Old Testament law, although she was clearly guilty.

There is another incident when Jesus contradicted an Old Testament law. Lev 24: 19–20 (the *lex talionis*) ordered that those who had caused harm to others, had to suffer the same harm:

> "And if a man does damage to his neighbor, as he has done, so let it be done to him; wound for wound, eye for eye, tooth for tooth; whatever damage he has done, so let it be done to him."

Jesus, on the other hand, taught in Matt 5: 38–39 –

> "You have knowledge that it was said, an eye for an eye, and a tooth for a tooth: But I say to you, do not make use of force against an evil man; but to him who gives you a blow on the right side of your face let the left be turned."

Magic, Sorcery and Divination

When it comes to magic, sorcery and divination, the Bible clearly applies double standards.

Magic and magicians are condemned in the strongest terms in the Bible and we are informed that people who dabble in these dark arts are headed for the flames of hell. This is what Lev 20: 27 has to say:

> "A man also or a woman that has a familiar spirit, or that is a wizard, shall surely be put to death: they shall stone them with stones; their blood shall be on them."

The Greek word for "sorcerer", as used in Rev 21: 8, is φάρμακος (pharmakos). The English word "pharmacist" is clearly derived from this Greek word. Sorcerers are, therefore, people who mix magic or poisonous potions. These sorcerers deserve to suffer in "the lake that burns with fire and sulphur". According to Rev 13: 13–15, the Antichrist will have magical powers. Acts 19: 19 informs us that new converts to Christianity in Ephesus burned their books containing magical formulae.

The question arises: what exactly is magic and sorcery? Greenwood and Airy give this description: Magic is "the art of using spells to invoke supernatural powers to influence events."[106] The In Encyclopaedia Brittanica, 2010, provides the following definition:

> Magic is "a concept used to describe a mode of rationality or way of thinking that looks to invisible forces to influence events, effect change in material conditions, or present the illusion of change."[107]

Now, one has to ask: how are we to judge the miracles of which we read in the Bible? What are the dozens and dozens of miracles described in the Bible anything but magic and sorcery? A few well-known examples of biblical miracles may be mentioned:

- Moses' brother, Aaron, changed his staff into a serpent, which devoured the staves of the Egyptian sorcerers, which they also had transformed into serpents (Ex 4: 3–4, 30);
- Moses managed to turn bitter water into sweet water (Ex 15: 25);
- Moses caused water to flow from a rock by hitting it with his staff (Ex 17: 5–8);

---

[106] Greenwood and Airy, *Complete Illustrated Encyclopaedia*, 14.

[107] Encyclopaedia Britannica, "Magic".

- The waters of the river Jordan were divided by Joshua to enable the Israelites to cross the river bed on dry land (Josh 3: 14–17);
- The walls of Jericho came tumbling down when the Israelites blew on their horns (Josh 6: 6–20);
- The prophet Elijah multiplied a poor widow's supply of oil and flour (1 Kgs 17: 12–16);
- Elisha, the prophet, caused a heavy axe head to float on water (2 Kgs 6: 5–7);
- Jesus changed water into high-quality wine (John 2: 1–11);
- Jesus walked on water (Matt 14: 25–33);
- Jesus fed a few thousand people with only a few loaves of bread and a few fishes (Matt 14: 15–21); and
- The Gospels tell of numerous occasions where Jesus healed sick people: lepers, blind people, paralyzed people and people possessed of demons. He even brought dead people back to life.

Can these miracles be distinguished from magic and sorcery in any way? I honestly don't think so and I am sure that any other rational human being will agree with me.

Nevertheless, the biblical prohibition of magic and sorcery led to the death of thousands of innocent people during the Middle Ages and thereafter when they were suspected of witchcraft – mostly single elderly females. The ecclesiastical and civil authorities were convinced that they were obeying God's laws by torturing and executing these hapless people.

Divination is another activity condemned by the Bible (Ezek 13: 6–7; Lev 20: 6, 27; Jer 14: 14). What is divination? Park and Gilbert describe this activity in the following terms: Divination is –

> "... the practice of determining the hidden significance or cause of events, sometimes foretelling the future, by various

natural, psychological, and other techniques. Found in all civilizations, both ancient and modern, it is encountered most frequently in contemporary mass society in the form of horoscopes, astrology, crystal gazing, tarot cards, and the Ouija board."[108]

Is it possible to see any difference between divination and the forecasts of the prophets in the Bible? What makes divination different from prophecy as practiced in biblical times? Ahlström describes prophecy as –

"… in religion, a divinely inspired revelation or interpretation. Although prophecy is perhaps most commonly associated with Judaism and Christianity, it is found throughout the religions of the world, both ancient and modern. In its narrower sense, the term prophet (Greek: προφήτης – *prophētēs*, 'forthteller') refers to an inspired person who believes that he has been sent by his god with a message to tell. He is, in this sense, the mouthpiece of his god. In a broader sense, the word can refer to anybody who utters the will of a deity, often ascertained through visions, dreams, or the casting of lots; the will of the deity also may be spoken in a liturgical setting. The prophet, thus, is often associated with the priest, the shaman (a religious figure in primitive societies who functions as a healer, diviner, and possessor of psychic powers), the diviner (foreteller), and the mystic."[109]

There is only one conclusion possible: divination and prophecy are exactly the same activity. We see that clearly in the case of the Magi, wise men and astrologers from the East, who came to look for the

---

[108] Park and Gilbert, "Divination".
[109] Ahlström, "Prophecy".

baby Jesus after reading the signs in the heavens regarding his birth (Matt 2: 1–12). They were nothing but practitioners of divination, yet their activity is portrayed as proof that Jesus really was the Messiah.

What must we make of this? The Bible condemns magic and sorcery on the one hand, but then various biblical figures, including Jesus, performed so-called miracles that cannot be distinguished from magic and these miracles are presented as praiseworthy and as a proof that God was with those people. The Bible rejects divination as evil, but there is a multitude of prophetic utterances with predictions of the future, which amount to oracles. Jesus also predicted certain future events (Mark 13). All this can only mean that the Bible contradicts itself.

The miracles described in the Bible all amount to a suspension of natural laws, which – according to contemporary thinking – is just not possible. In Biblical times, people held to a magical worldview in which natural laws played no role and, therefore, they could believe in all sorts of miraculous and supernatural events. In our time, this magical thinking is still to a certain extent prevalent, especially when one considers, for instance, the success of the Harry Potter stories and films. But sophisticated people of the twenty-first century do not believe in miracles anymore – just as they are not impressed by magic. They usually take the stories of miracles in the Bible with a large pinch of salt and regard them as myths. Alternatively, they offer natural explanations for seemingly miraculous deeds and events.

Divorce

When one reads what the Bible teaches regarding divorce, it is easy to become confused. There are just too many contradictions and inconsistencies.

Deuteronomy 24: 1–4 teaches that it is permitted for a man to divorce his wife "if she find no favor in his eyes, because he has found some unseemly thing in her". Unfortunately, we are not informed what this "unseemly thing" amounts to and it was presumably left to the husband to decide. It is also clear that only men had the right to divorce their spouses – according to this passage in the Bible. Women did not have such a right. A divorced woman, though, was permitted to become another man's wife.

Divorce on account of religious differences was deemed compulsory in Ezra's time. Ezra 10 relates how this leader of the returned exiles in Jerusalem forced those men who had married pagan women to send them and their children away because such marriages were considered a grave sin. However, no consideration was given to these women and their children who suddenly became homeless.

The teachings of Jesus regarding divorce, according to the Gospels, do not tally with the prescriptions in Deuteronomy and the precedent in Ezra. We read in Mark 10: 2–12 that Jesus permits a woman to get a divorce from her husband – in contravention to Deuteronomy. On the other hand, and in contradiction to his own words, he totally disapproved of any form of divorce: "What therefore God has joined together let no man separate" (Matt 19: 6). He added: "Whoever will divorce his wife, and marry another, commits adultery against her. If a woman herself divorces her husband, and marries another, she commits adultery" (Luke 16: 18).

It is not clear how Jesus could condemn remarriage after a divorce as "adultery" if this practice was permitted by Deuteronomy 24.

In Matt 5: 32, Jesus is reported as finding divorce due to adultery to be permissible. According to this text, he was not totally against divorce.

The prophet Malachi, on the other hand, thought that any form of divorce is wrong: "For I am against the putting away of a wife, says the Lord, the God of Israel…" (Mal 2: 16). If God is against anything then, presumably, it is not permitted in any way.

When one reads all these biblical passages it is easy to become perplexed and confused. There is no consistency regarding divorce and the various passages contradict each other.

Oaths

There is no consistency in the teachings of the Bible regarding the taking of an oath. Deuteronomy 6: 13 provides us with clear rules how oaths have to be administered. In other words: oaths are permitted.

On the other hand, Jesus and James taught that any oath was wrong and that anyone who did take an oath was condemned by God (Matt 5: 34–37; Jas 5: 12).

Strange Commands

It happened that certain biblical figures received strange and even absurd commands from God. For instance – the prophet Isaiah was commanded to wander around without clothes for three years:

> "At that time the word of the Lord came to Isaiah, the son of Amoz, saying, Go, and take off your robe, and your shoes from your feet; and he did so, walking unclothed and without shoes on his feet. And the Lord said, as my servant Isaiah has gone unclothed and without shoes for three years as a sign and a wonder to Egypt and Ethiopia, so will the king of Assyria take away the prisoners of Egypt and those forced out of Ethiopia, young and old, unclothed and without shoes, and with backs uncovered, to the shame of Egypt" (Isa 20: 2–4).

One can only wonder whether Isaiah's strange behavior was not perhaps due to something akin to schizophrenia. It is often a symptom of schizophrenia that the sufferer hears voices giving him strange and even absurd commands.

Jesus taught his followers:

> "Therefore, I tell you, don't be anxious for your life, what you will eat, or what you will drink; nor yet for your body, what you will put on. Isn't life more than food, and the body more

than clothing? See the birds of the sky, that they don't sow, neither do they reap, nor gather into barns. Your heavenly Father feeds them. Aren't you of much more value than they?" (Matt 6: 25–26).

This all sounds very pious. We are advised that if we simply rely on God then everything will turn out to be all OK. But one must also ask: where does hard work fit in? Do we really have to follow the example of the birds by waiting upon God to perform miracles and provide us with everything we need? Is it a sign of a weak faith to sow, reap and gather in barns? There is only one conclusion possible: If Jesus was reported correctly, then he didn't understand how the world works and he encouraged laziness.

Fundamentalism and Anti-Evolutionism

Origins
It is necessary to devote some attention to a movement within Christianity known as fundamentalism. This movement takes the Protestant position regarding the infallibility of the Bible to extremes and, thereby, exposes some of the many weaknesses of this religious movement and the conventional view with regards to the Bible.

Christian fundamentalism had its origins towards the end of the nineteenth century in America as a reaction towards Charles Darwin's theory of evolution – which seemed to clash with a literal reading of the creation story in Genesis 1 – and also theological modernism or liberalism. The appellation "fundamentalism" is derived from a series of booklets published in America with the title "The Fundamentals: a Testimony to the Truth" (1910–1915). This movement is of the view that the Bible has to be taken literally in all respects because it is God's Word in human language. This movement is still very alive and active in many churches and movements.

"Scientific Creationism" and "Intelligent Design"

In an effort to counter the theory of evolution, a rival philosophy based on a literal interpretation of the creation myth in Genesis 1 was devised, called "scientific creationism", later renamed "intelligent design" (ID). Theologians who support this movement declare that God created all extinct and existing species of plants and animals separately and that no form of life can develop into something else over time.[110]

Charles Darwin who first formulated the theory of evolution in 1859.

Christian fundamentalists have been accused of doing Christianity a great disservice by disseminating untenable and even ridiculous points of view.[111] That definitely seems to be the case. Their alternatives to the theory of evolution, namely "scientific creationism" or "intelligent design" cannot be proven scientifically and are flatly rejected by the vast majority of biologists and other scientists.[112]

  Richard Dawkins devoted a whole book, *The Greatest Show*

---

[110] Sandeen, "Fundamentalism"; Glick, "Intelligent Design".

[111] Collins, *The Language of God*, 172–79.

[112] Ayala, "Evolution"; Glick, "Intelligent Design"; Graffin and Ohlson, *Anarchy Evolution*, 60–61; Cunningham, *Decoding the Language of God*, 233–45.

on Earth: the Evidence for Evolution, to point out the fallacies, misrepresentations and mistakes of these intellectual constructs and to demonstrate that the theory of evolution is the only scientific theory, which can satisfactorily explain the diversity of life forms on earth.

Jurie van den Heever, retired professor of zoology at the Stellenbosch University in South Africa, declares:

> "The idea of evolution forms the basis of science in general and biology in particular because it explains the development of all life, as well as our presence on the third planet on account of innumerable proven research results of the past 150 years" (*own translation*).[113]

He adds:

> "The enormous quantity of additional and wide-ranging research since 1859 has proved Darwin's basic insights as undoubtedly correct and it is currently an indisputable fact that all life on the third planet is related and that it developed over a period of millions of years, while the planet itself is much older" (*own translation*).[114]

In spite of this, it is amazing that there are still scientists who declare the scientific theory evolution or Darwinism to be a fallacy, due to the fact that it purportedly clashes with the Bible. A good example is Walter Veith, retired professor of zoology and physiology at the University of the Western Cape in South Africa. In his book, *Truth Matters*, he adopts the fundamentalist position on the infallibility of the Bible and rejects the theory of evolution – despite having a Ph.D. in zoology.

---

[113] Van den Heever, *Wat Moet ons met ons Kerk Doen?* xiv.
[114] Van den Heever, *Wat Moet ons met ons Kerk Doen?* 76–77.

According to Carl Zimmer, there is "very little real science" in ID. The claims of ID, that God miraculously created each life form or species independently and separately, cannot be tested empirically and no scientific investigation has ever been able to pinpoint God's supposed intervention in the natural world.[115]

David Mills argues that ID is nothing but religious propaganda; it cannot claim to be a scientific theory since it fails to show through empirical observations or experiments exactly how God intervened to bring the present state of affairs in the universe and on earth about. Supporters of ID simply claim that God was responsible for phenomena for which science at present does not yet have a clear explanation, such as the origin of life on earth. They utterly fail to provide empirical proof for their assertion that God was responsible for the phenomena in question.[116]

Greg Graffin points out that creationists and supporters of ID have, up to date, contributed nothing to further scientific knowledge. All they do is to postulate that the only explanation for gaps in our knowledge of the world is that a particular gap is an indication of God's creative interference in the universe. All they do is to criticize the findings of scientists in an endeavor to "prove" that God must have designed and created the universe, including life on earth. They don't ever perform independent scientific investigations by conducting laboratory work or going on field expeditions.[117]

Mills adds that should sciences, such as physics, arrive at rigorous explanations for everything in the universe – and that is the way science is developing – then there will ultimately be no space left for the God of creationists or ID. When there are no more gaps in our

---

[115] Zimmer, *Evolution*, 403–404.
[116] Mills, *Atheist Universe*, 76.
[117] Graffin and Olson, *Anarchy Evolution*, 60–61.

knowledge, then this God will, inevitably, become redundant and superfluous.[118]

Of all the species that ever lived on earth, 99,9% became extinct. They were unable to adapt to changing circumstances and new challenges and died out.[119] Mills remarks that that is an abysmal failure rate for a God who, according to fundamentalists, created every life form separately." Any watchmaker whose product similarly failed would be dismissed as incompetent."[120] Graffin argues that a divine designer or creator of the world must have been extremely wasteful and even cruel by creating "a tremendous amount of seemingly pointless experiments with living creatures, causing mass extinction and limitless pain and suffering."[121]

Creationists are convinced that God created everything, including man, within the span of a single week, called "creation week" – the seven days of creation of Genesis 1. That implies that Adam and Eve must be exactly one day younger than the dinosaurs and that they were actually contemporaries, just as gorillas and trilobites were supposed to be living at the same time. The geological record shows that this was never the case; no human fossils were ever found together with dinosaur fossils in the same geological strata. Dinosaurs became extinct millions of years before the appearance of man.[122]

David Mills hammers the final nail into the coffin of so-called "creation science" and ID by asking: will any practitioner of these philosophies ever be nominated for a Nobel Prize in science? The answer is, of course, "No". "The intelligent design movement is a congregation of religious fanatics… The rest of the world, including

---

[118] Mills, *Atheist Universe*, 103.
[119] McCarthy and Rubidge, *The Story of Life*, 299.
[120] Mills, *Atheist Universe*, 113.
[121] Graffin and Olson, *Anarchy Evolution*, 135.
[122] Mills, *Atheist Universe*, 118.

the Nobel committee, pays no attention to their faith-based sermons."[123]

That the theory of evolution and the Christian message do not necessarily have to clash has been eloquently argued by eminent Christian scientists, such as Denis Alexander, Francis Collins (the former head of the human genome project), and Leon Rousseau[124], as well as eminent reformed theologians, such as Adrio König.[125]

Professor Joseph Ratzinger, who later became Pope Benedict XVI, wrote:

> "Der Schöpfungsglaube fragt nach dem Daß des Seins als solchen; sein Problem ist, warum überhaupt etwas ist und nicht nichts. Der Entwicklungsgedanke hingegegen fragt, warum gerade diese Dinge sind und nicht andere, woher sie ihre Bestimmtheit erlangt haben …"[126]

This means that the belief in creation and the theory of evolution deal with different aspects of reality and, therefore, need not clash with each other.

The present leader of the Roman Catholic Church, Pope Francis, has a diploma in chemistry, a master's degree in philosophy, as well as a doctorate in theology, and he openly declared that he finds that the big bang theory as an explanation of the origin of the universe

---

[123] Mills, *Atheist Universe*, 253–54.

[124] Denis Alexander, *Creation or Evolutin*; Collins, *The Language of God*; Rousseau, *Die Groot Gedagte*.

[125] König, *Die Groot Geloofswoordeboek*.

[126] Ratzinger, *Schöpfungsglaube und Evolutionstheorie*, 234. ("The belief in creation asks about the 'that' of being as such; its problem is: why is there something and not rather nothing? The idea of development, on the other hand, asks why things are as they are and not something different and how they have received their qualities…")

and the theory of evolution to be compatible with his Christian faith and his belief in a divine creator.[127]

Cunningham, on the other hand, is of the conviction that an established scientific theory, such as evolution, cannot be reconciled with the beliefs of Christians in any way. Christians who find the biblical message of God as creator compatible with the theory of evolution usually argue that God must have guided the various steps in the development of various life forms on earth, while the theory of evolution also provides a complete explanation for this process. One may indeed ask: if the theory of evolution explains the development of life forms on earth satisfactorily and completely, is there still any need for a creator who steered the process? Doesn't the theory of evolution make such a creator totally superfluous?[128]

The Literal Reading of Genesis 1

Although it certainly does seem possible to harmonize the convictions of Christians with the theory of evolution and other scientific findings, according to certain Christian scientists, there are insurmountable obstacles in the path to a full-scale harmonization between this theory and a literal interpretation of Genesis 1 as propagated by "scientific creationism" and ID.

For instance, the very first sentence in the Bible contains a demonstrable error: "In the beginning God created the heavens and the earth" (Gen 1: 1). The Hebrew word for "the heavens" is הַשָּׁמַיִם (ha-shamayim). It may mean the following: "heaven, heavens, sky, visible heavens, abode of the stars, the visible universe, the sky, atmosphere, the abode of God."

If we take "the heavens" to refer to the universe, then it has to be pointed out that the earth and the rest of the solar system did not have their origin "in the beginning", but several billions of years after

---

[127] Biography.com Editors, "Pope Francis Biography".
[128] Cunningham, *Decoding the Language of God*.

the origin of the universe, which happened about 13,7 billion years ago. The solar system, including the planet earth, is merely 4,6 billion years old.[129]

If "the heavens" in Gen 1: 1 refer, on the other hand, to the dwelling place of God, then one is forced to ask: where did God reside before he created everything "in the beginning"? Was he homeless before? Or, if these heavens are part of creation, as Gen 1: 1 assures us, then God, as inhabitant of these heavens, must also be part of creation, which disqualifies him as creator of everything or anything.

Proponents of "scientific creationism" claim that the universe is only a few thousand years old. They base this on the conviction that Adam, who was created on the sixth day of creation, must have lived only about four thousand years before the time of Christ if one calculates the time of his life by using the ages of people mentioned in genealogical lists in the Bible.

Geologists and astronomers have established, though, that the planet earth, together with the solar system, is about 4,6 billion years old. There is ample evidence to prove this. McCarthy and Rubidge declare: "Modern equipment makes it possible to obtain extremely precise ages [for the earth and for rocks], with errors of measurement typically better than one part in a thousand."[130] There can also be absolutely no doubt that the universe as a whole is around 13,7 billion years old – and not only a few thousand years.[131]

One phenomenon that "creation science" cannot explain is the fact that it takes millions and even billions of years for the light and other forms of radiation of distant galaxies to reach earth where astronomers can detect this light and radiation with their telescopes

---

[129] Clark, *The Big Question*, 34, 53.

[130] McCarthy and Rubidge, *The Story of Earth*, 69.

[131] Hawking and Mlodinow, *The Grand Design*, 158–59, 195–97; Clark, *The Big Question*, 29, 37–38; Joubert, *Die Groot Gedagte*, 50, 110; McCarthy and Rubidge, *The Story of Earth*, 60.

and other instruments. For instance: the Milky Way's nearest neighbor of a comparable size, the Andromeda Galaxy, is a mere 2,2 million light years away – a distance that has been measures accurately. In other words: the light from this galaxy needed 2,2 million years to reach us.[132] There is experimental proof that light always travels at a fixed speed of about 300 000 km per second, irrespective of the movement of the light source or the observer.[133] In other words: it is impossible for the universe to be only a few thousand years old if it took 2,2 million years for light from the Andromeda Galaxy to reach us.

"Creation scientists" have come up with the absurd explanation that God created the universe only a few thousand years ago with the appearance of antiquity and with the light waves of these distant galaxies already on their way to earth – an idea that the respected reformed theologian, Adrio König, finds ridiculous and dishonest.[134] This position turns God ultimately into a "deceiver" or a "cosmic trickster" – a position that no "creation scientist", of course, can accept. Francis Collins declares that young earth creationism "has reached a point of intellectual bankruptcy, both in its science and its theology."[135]

There can be no doubt: the stance of "scientific creationism" and ID, namely that we must regard the first chapter of Genesis as an accurate description of how everything was created, creates insurmountable difficulties and has absurd consequences.

The Image of God
Another obstacle in the path of harmonization is the fact that Gen 1: 27 states: "God created man in his own image. In God's image he

---

[132] Clark, *The Big Question*, 23.

[133] Clark, *The Big Question*, 152–55.

[134] König, *Die Groot Geloofswoordeboek*, 393.

[135] Collins, *The Language of God*, 177.

created him; male and female he created them."

What is being meant by "God's image"? The Heidelberg Catechism explains:

> "**Question 6**: Did God then create man so wicked and perverse?
> **Answer**: By no means; but God created man good, and after his own image, in true righteousness and holiness, that he might rightly know God his Creator, heartily love him and live with him in eternal happiness to glorify and praise him."

In other words, Genesis 1 tells us that man was originally without sin; he had "true righteousness and holiness" and he loved God. Man was, therefore, supposed to be a perfectly moral creature. That is, however, not what the geological and paleontological record reveals. Man did not appear on earth as a perfect, sinless creature.

There was a very gradual evolution from a common ancestor with the chimpanzee, through various types of ape-men until modern man eventually appeared. The first modern people, about 200 000 years ago, were by no means pacifists; the record shows that they were violent, aggressive and bellicose producers of various types of weapons, which were not only used for hunting. They were just as aggressive as their more animal-like predecessors.[136] It is, therefore, impossible to determine when "God's image" was supposed to have appeared in mankind – and, also, when this "image" was supposed to have been spoilt by the fall into sin when mankind became "wicked and perverse". There just never was a stage in which mankind was living in "true righteousness and holiness".

Another difficulty is the fact that Gen 1: 11–13 informs us that green plants are supposed to have been created on the third day of

---

[136] Dawkins, *The Greatest Show on Earth,* 187–207; Rousseau, *Die Groot Gedagte,* 297–301; Tuttle, "Human Evolution".

creation. The sun and other celestial bodies only appeared afterwards on the fourth day of creation (Gen 1: 14–19). Biology teaches us that plants cannot grow without the ultraviolet rays of the sun. One may, therefore, ask: how was it possible for these plants to survive without sunlight? Were the plants created as mature specimens, as seedlings or as seeds from which the plants could later grow? One may also wonder: if there was as yet no sun on the third day of creation then there also could not have been a climate conducive for the growing and survival of plants because the temperature must have been far below zero at which temperature no organism can live. Moreover: how were these plants selected and distributed by the supposed creator according to the climate in which they were meant to thrive if there was no friendly climate yet?

Creationists often use the argument of the so-called "irreducible complexity" of certain organs, such as the eye, to declare that God must have designed and created these organs. Biologists have demonstrated, though, that the human eye, for instance, with all its complexities, went through various stages of development in the process of evolution and that every stage was fully functional. We do not need a supernatural explanation for the existence of the eye or for all the other complex biological organs.[137]

According to fundamentalist Christians, we must regard the seven days of creation in Genesis 1 as periods of precisely 24 hours each – and that is what the text seems to imply. A problem, though, is created when Gen 1: 13 is considered –

"There was evening and there was morning, a third day."

One has to ask: how was it possible to measure the first three days of creation week as periods of 24 hours each if the sun only appeared on

---

[137] Graffin and Olson, *Anarchy Evolution*, 60–61; Rousseau, *Die Groot Gedagte*, 217–18; Stenger, *The New Atheism*, 100.

day four? How was it possible that the evening ended the third day off without a sun setting in the west? The length of a day can only be measured by the apparent movement of the sun around the earth. For the Jews, each day ends when the sun sets in the west and the first stars appear. It has to be asked: how was it possible to measure the length of the first three days of creation if no sun purportedly existed during that period?

Only one conclusion is possible: it is not possible to harmonize a *literal* reading of Genesis 1 and the theory of evolution and other scientific insights. They are plainly and utterly incompatible.

These fundamentalists also do not seem to realize that one cannot read Genesis 1 as if it is a scientific report. The structure and language of this chapter point clearly to the fact that it has to be read as a poetical rendering of an article of faith, namely that YHWH, the God of Israel, is the Creator of everything and that the deities of the pagans – the sun, moon, stars, rain, lightning, the seasons, plants, animals and other natural phenomena – are only his creations. The fact that certain phrases in Gen 1 are repeated over and over clearly shows that this chapter has a carefully thought-out structure and a poetical quality; it just cannot be read as a scientific report.

It has to be pointed out that there are no fewer than five creation myths in the Bible: Gen 1: 1–2: 4, Gen 2: 5–25, Job 38: 1–39: 33, Ps 19, and Ps 33. Each of these tells another tale and they differ regarding the order in which the different parts of the world came into being. They all agree, however, on this point: YHWH, the God of the Israelites, is to be seen as the creator of everything. The myths contained in Job and Psalms are clearly poetic in nature and cannot be regarded as scientific reports.

Christian fundamentalists usually make the mistake of confusing the scientific theory of evolution with the philosophy of evolutionism. The theory of evolution is simply the most credible and satisfactory way of explaining why there are so many life forms on earth. A Christian biologist, such as Collins, is able to reconcile his biblical beliefs with his scientific insights.

Evolutionism, on the other hand, is an atheistic school of thought, which teaches that there is no place for a supernatural being called God and that everything in the universe, including its origin, as well as the development of life forms and even civilizations, can be explained from a purely natural perspective. Fundamentalists will do good to keep this distinction in mind.

The two Faces of Fundamentalism

Hyper-Orthodoxy and the Charismatic Movement

Contemporary fundamentalism is the reaction against newer scientific insights, rationality and post-modernism with its motto that we cannot be sure of anything. Fundamentalism has diverged basically into two streams: hyper-orthodoxy and the charismatic movement.[138]

Hyper-orthodoxy tries to restore the old sense of security that reigned in the time when Christianity had all the answers. Adherents of this tendency are more Calvinistic than John Calvin himself and they interpret every text of the Bible literally. For them, the historical creeds of the church are all-important.

The charismatic movement – which includes Pentecos-talism – also takes the Bible extremely seriously. They focus on all the parts that deal with the Holy Spirit and the spiritual gifts, with the result that they flee into a hyper-emotional type of Christianity. They find their certainty primarily in religious experiences – talking in tongues, ecstatic prayers, prophetic utterances, exorcism, dancing and gospel songs – in contrast with the ultra-orthodox believers who find their certainty in the purported infallible utterances of God's Word.

A survey done in European countries found that contemporary Christian fundamentalism can also be attributed to a reaction towards

---

[138] Müller, *Opstanding*, 102.

increasing secularism. Many Christians feel threatened by the fact that the churches are losing members and influence in society and that makes them more vociferous and radical in an effort to boost the reputation of Christianity.[139]

Fundamentalists of all persuasions are very sure that they know exactly what God thinks and what he disapproves of. Certain fundamentalist preachers in America interpreted the attacks on the Twin Towers in New York and the Pentagon in Washington on 11 September 2001 by Muslim extremists as a sign of God's wrath against America where homosexuality is tolerated. Other fundamentalists sanctioned the bombing of abortion clinics in order to sabotage these "abominations" in the eyes of God.[140] They are able to find justification for all their pronouncements and action somewhere in the Bible and, in the process, they ignore other biblical texts where exactly the opposite is to be found.

Theological Warfare in the Reformed Churches

One of the most unpleasant chapters in the history of the church in which I used to be a minister, the Nederduitse Gereformeerde Kerk (Dutch Reformed Church in South Africa) was the campaign by fundamentalists to get rid of Professor Johannes du Plessis who taught New Testament studies at the Theological Seminary in Stellenbosch during the twenties of the previous century.

Professor du Plessis published a monthly magazine called "Het Zoeklicht" (the Searchlight) since 1922 in which he introduced newer theological insights. He had some good things to say about the theory of evolution and declared that Moses could not have written the first five books of the Bible, that the Bible contained historical errors and that Jesus as a human being could not have been omniscient.

---

[139] Achterberg et al., "Christian Cancellation"
[140] Ali, *The Clash of Fundamentalisms*, 283–84.

Some of his colleagues and other influential ministers in the church who were of the fundamentalist and hyper-orthodox persuasion started another theological magazine to counter Het Zoeklicht and they called it "Die Ou Paaie" (The Olden Ways). Month after month articles were published to defend the fundamentalist point of view and to attack du Plessis.

Du Plessis was officially accused of heresy by his opponents and an ugly battle followed. The Synod of 1928 of the church in the Cape Province decided that the presbytery of Stellenbosch should investigate the accusations and subject du Plessis to a disciplinary hearing, after declaring that his views were unacceptable.

To the dismay of his opponents, du Plessis was cleared by the presbytery. His accusers appealed to the synod and a special Synod was convened in 1930 where the appeal was upheld and du Plessis was dismissed from his position. Du Plessis took the matter to court and in 1932 won his case.

Professor Johannes du Plessis

The court found –
- That the Synod was already prejudiced and broke its own rules by deciding beforehand that du Plessis' views were heretical before referring the case to the presbytery of Stellenbosch for investigation; and
- That his teachings did not clash with the confessional creeds of the Dutch Reformed Church.

The Synod of 1932 decided that it could not abide by the court's ruling and reaffirmed its decision to dismiss the professor, although he would receive his salary as if he was still working. Du

Plessis was too weary to start a new court case and he died in 1935, a broken man.

The irony is that Die Kerkbode, the official organ of the Nederduitse Gereformeerde Kerk, declared at the end of the previous millennium in 1999 that du Plessis was the greatest theologian of that church during the twentieth century.[141]

Today, there are three statues of former professors in the garden of the Theological Seminary in Stellenbosch – Nicolaas Hofmeyr, John Murray (the founders of the seminary in 1859) and Johannes du Plessis.

At the time of writing, a schism is threatening in the Nederduitse Gereformeerde Kerk. The General Synod took conflicting decisions regarding the position of gay people during the recent past, until this body was forced by a court decision to allow gay people to occupy offices in the church and to accept marriages (called "civil unions") between gay people in order to comply with the law of the country. Since the Bible condemns homosexual acts between men in various texts, those congregations, which are against the final decisions of the General Synod, threaten with a break-away actions and they refuse to take part in projects of the denomination, withholding money meant for administrative and charitable projects run by the denomination. These congregations feel that the authority of Holy Scripture is being undermined. They also feel aggrieved that various theologians purportedly propagate "liberal" ideas, without being disciplined by the church.

Another Reformed Church in South Africa, the Nederduitsch Hervormde Kerk, a group that separated from the Nederduitse Gereformeerde Kerk in 1853 due to political reasons, experienced a schism in 2011 when a number of congregations decided to form a new body, called "Geloofsbond van Hervormde Gemeentes" (Faith League of Reformed Congregations) as a reaction against the "liberal"

---

[141] Olivier, "Johannes du Plessis".

theology that, according to them, took hold of their denomination. At the time of writing, about 26 independent congregations belong to this league, according to their website. They declare themselves to be loyal to the doctrinal creeds of the church – especially the doctrines regarding the sufficiency of Scripture, the total depravity of the human race, the sacrifice of Jesus on the cross to save sinners, the virgin birth of Christ, his physical resurrection and ascension into heaven and the second coming of Christ.

This type of theological warfare in the Reformed family is not restricted to South Africa. Similar schisms happened in the Netherlands, England, Scotland and America.

This theological warfare in the churches between fundamentalists and more progressive theologians did much to discredit the church in the eyes of many and to undermine the credibility of the church. The desperate efforts of these fundamentalists to stem the flow of newer theological insights is proof of their aversion to honest inquiry and research and they prefer to abide by traditional points of view that can no longer be upheld or rationally defended in the light of honest research.

Flat-Earth Theology

The most extreme fundamentalist absurdity and foolishness is to be found in a movement, which propagates a flat earth on account of a literal interpretation of a number of biblical texts. Garwood, who investigated this movement, writes:

> "Although such creationist organizations recoil from association with flat-earth believers, some general similarities between the two campaigns cannot be overlooked. (. . .) They concur on a number of issues, including the authority of the scriptures as a scientific guide to the natural world, the limitations of a theory-led approach, the duplicity of

conventional scientists, and the impossibility of reconciling orthodox science with the Bible. And just as they have similar foundations and histories, so, too, have they employed similar strategies to promulgate their world-views."[142]

The modern revival of the idea of a flat earth was the brainchild of an American travelling lecturer and quack doctor known by the pseudonym of "Parallax". He was a certain Samuel Birley Rowbotham (1816–1884) and he called his movement "zetetic astronomy."[143]

Rowbotham, and his disciples, based their ideas on the following texts of the Bible:

- Earth is not a globe: Gen 1: 9 – 10; Ps 24: 1 – 2; Ps 86: 6; 2 Pet 3: 5;
- Earth rests on waters: Ex 20: 4; Deut 4: 18; Deut 33: 13;
- Earth is immovable and the sun is in motion: Ps 19: 4–6; Eccl 1: 5; Judg 5: 31; Josh 10: 13;
- Earth is not a planet and is the only material world: Luke 18: 29–30; Matt 12: 32;
- The sun, moon and stars are mere lights: Gen 1: 14–17; Ps 86: 7–9; Job 25: 5; Isa 30: 26; Isa 13: 10; Joel 2: 10; Dan 12: 3; and
- Heaven is above and hell is below: Deut 26: 15; Ps 52: 19; Ps 53: 2; 2 Kgs 2: 11; Mark 16: 10; Luke 24: 51; Isa 14: 15; Prov 15: 24; Ezek 31: 16 – 17; 2 Pet 2: 4; Rev 20: 10, 13–14.[144]

These notions of the flat-earth theology are totally in accord with the Bible. We cannot explain these pronouncements of the Bible as mere

---

[142] Garwood, *Flat Earth*, 356.

[143] Garwood, *Flat Earth*, 36.

[144] Garwood, *Flat Earth*, 363–69.

metaphors – the biblical authors really thought that the earth was a flat disk, floating upon waters, while heaven as the abode of God was just beyond the stars and hell was situated below the surface of the earth. The following biblical statements – only a selection from many more – must be interpreted as an indication of how the poets, prophets, historians and apostles from biblical times saw the cosmos:

- The author of the book of Job informs us in 22: 14 that God "walks on the vault of the sky." That means that he was to be found immediately beyond the dome surrounding the earth and onto which the planets and the other stars are affixed.
- "Isn't God in the heights of heaven? See the height of the stars, how high they are!" (Job 22:12). In other words: God was to be found between or just beyond the stars.
- Ps 19: 4 calls the firmament "a tent for the sun" behind which he hides at night and comes forth in the morning "as a bridegroom coming out of his chamber".
- Isaiah 66: 1 proclaims: "Thus says Yahweh, heaven is my throne, and the earth is my footstool." That means that God occupies the same space as the rest of the cosmos.
- In 1 Sam 2: 8 we are informed: "For the pillars of the earth are Yahweh's, He has set the world on them." Ps 104: 5 adds: "He laid the foundations of the earth, that it should not be moved forever." Psalm 93: 1 and Ps 96: 10 both declare: "The world is also established. It can't be moved." These texts proclaim that the earth is stationary and rests upon pillars. The Bible is silent about the foundations of these pillars.
- Psalm 148: 2–3 contains this call: "Praise him, all his angels! Praise him, all his host! Praise him, sun and moon! Praise him, all you shining stars!" That means that the angels, the host of heaven and the astrological bodies were seen to be the same entities.

- We read in Dan 12: 2–3 – "Many of those who sleep in the dust of the earth shall awake, some to everlasting life, and some to shame and everlasting contempt. Those who are wise shall shine as the brightness of the expanse; and those who turn many to righteousness as the stars forever and ever." In other words: Daniel expected the deceased faithful to gain places in the starry skies.
- In Phil 2: 9–10 Paul quoted a hymn about Christ: "Therefore God also highly exalted him, and gave to him the name which is above every name; that at the name of Jesus every knee would bow, of those in heaven, those on earth, and those under the earth…" John of Patmos likewise wrote that "no one in heaven, or on the earth, or under the earth" was able to open the book in the hand of God (Rev 5: 3). This means that the cosmos was thought to consist of three levels – the heavens, earth and the netherworld.
- The fact that both the Old Testament and the New Testament used one and the same words for "wind", "breath" and "spirit" is an indication that spiritual beings were thought to be composed of a material element, namely air.

It is clear from the preceding biblical quotations that the biblical authors thought about God, heaven, angels and the cosmos in very concrete terms. Their descriptions are not metaphorical, but realistic. God was seen as a material being or entity within the whole of the cosmos, living just beyond the stars – although he was also depicted as the creator of the world.

The fact that most fundamentalists or creationists cannot accept this flat-earth theology must be seen as a tacit acceptance of the results of scientific investigations, which showed without the slightest doubt that the earth is a solid sphere that rotates around its own axis and completes a revolution around the sun in a year's time.

One may then ask: why do they accept these scientific findings, but do their best to refute other established scientific theories, including the so-called big bang theory as an explanation of the origin of the universe and the theory of evolution as an explanation of the diversity of life forms? Isn't that intellectual dishonesty?

Conclusions

The foregoing facts and arguments ought to convince any unbiased reader that the Bible cannot be regarded as a collection of infallible sacred writings inspired by a supernatural being called God or the Holy Spirit. We can confidently conclude on account of solid and irrefutable evidence the following regarding the Bible:

- The Bible's rendering of history is often wrong, contradictory and improbable and one may often find pious fiction presented as historical fact;
- Some authors of writings in the New Testament quoted from the Old Testament to prove a point; these quotations are often out of context, a misrepresentation of the original or even a falsification of the meaning of those Old Testament texts;
- The various parts of the Bible have contradictory ideas regarding the nature of God and of his will for mankind; one often gets the impression that it cannot be the same God who is presented in different parts of the Bible;
- It is not possible to accept certain biblical ideas today; slavery, polygamy and the inferior position of women are nowhere condemned in the Bible – while no sane and rational person will try to defend these practices or views in our time;
- Although the Bible condemns magic and divination, the miracles and prophecies of the Bible cannot be distinguished from these practices;

- Numerous biblical prophecies have never been fulfilled and will certainly never be fulfilled;
- The biblical pronouncements regarding the compo-sition of the cosmos and the place of God inside this cosmos cannot be entertained anymore;
- Certain barbaric practices, such as genocide in the case of the conquest of Palestine by the Israelites, or the execution of adulterers, witches, homosexuals and idol worshippers, are explicitly commanded by the God of the Bible. In our day, these types of executions are deemed to be totally unacceptable and evil; and
- Apart from all this, we cannot always be sure that we know what the original biblical authors wrote; we only have copies of copies of copies of the original writings – containing various copying errors and it is often not possible to reconstruct the original.

There is only one conclusion possible: The Bible, as we have it today, can by no stretch of imagination be regarded as the inspired word of God. It is, rather, a collection of myths, pious deceptions, nonsensical teachings and the record of the hallucinations and delusions of self-appointed holy people.

A God, who is supposed to be the fountain of truth (Ps 117: 2; Rev 15: 3) and whose actions are thought to be perfect and without flaw (Ps 18: 30), would and could never have inspired the Biblical authors to write what they have written and how they have written it. The Bible just does not have the characteristics one would expect from a divinely inspired collection of writings. It is clear that the confessional creeds, cited at the beginning of this chapter, are misleading and misguided regarding the supposed inspiration and credibility of the various Biblical books. The fundamentalist Christians who regard every word and every sentence in the Bible to be infallibly true, maintain an untenable position, which just cannot convince rational, intellectually honest and intelligent people.

More and more people are becoming aware of the facts and viewpoints mentioned in this chapter. The result is that they turn away from Christianity, the church and the Bible in ever increasing numbers. If anybody makes a thorough study of the Bible it is impossible to remain a Christian. The mental gymnastics practiced by many biblical scholars in an endeavor to explain these problems away do not convince people any longer and it is proving increasingly difficult to modernize Christianity without distorting the message(s) of the Bible seriously. One must conclude: Christianity is doomed to become extinct sometime in the future because more and more people do not believe or trust the Bible with its nonsensical, irrational and incredible message(s) and unjust laws anymore.

The foregoing paragraphs have demonstrated amply that the traditional Protestant position, taken to its extreme by fundamentalists, which holds every word and every sentence of the Bible to be infallibly true, leads to absurd, ridiculous and untenable results. Fundamentalism as an intellectual system is doomed to expire, due to its inherent contradictions, just as communism as a political ideology has collapsed.

The eminent German-Swiss theologian, the late Hans Küng, convincingly argued that Protestant fundamentalism got stuck in ancient and medieval paradigms. For him, theology – to be credible and relevant – has to take into consideration contemporary scientific insights, including the theory of evolution. Theology has to be rational and conform to scientific standards, otherwise it will, inevitably, become implausible and unreliable. In other words, fundamentalism does Christianity a disservice with its indefensible notions.[145]

Although Küng endeavored to demonstrate that theology can be a rational scientific activity, it has been shown in chapter 1 of this

---

[145] Küng, "Paradigm Change in Theology", 143–49.

book that Christian theology can only be regarded as a pseudoscience, whatever cloak it wears – fundamentalist, Reformed, Catholic or contemporary. In this chapter it has been demonstrated that theologians cannot agree on what the message of the Bible is and that the Bible can also not be regarded as a divinely inspired collection of writings.

CHAPTER 3

THEOLOGICAL ABSURDITIES

It has already been shown that the Bible cannot be regarded as a collection of writings inspired by the Holy Spirit. All Christian denominations and groups have their character-istic doctrines, which are supposed to be – partly or wholly – based upon the ideas found in the Bible. If the Bible cannot be regarded as a trustworthy guide to know and worship a Supreme Being, then all these doctrines must be suspect, too.

It has to be granted: these doctrines are dear to more or less all Christians. They regard them as a valuable part of their lives and they define the identities of these persons. It is part-and-parcel of their self-images that they accept certain ideas and concepts and they cannot imagine themselves living without these convictions.

In this chapter it will be shown that the most important doctrines held by most Christians are absurd, irrational, characterized by internal contradictions and inconsistencies, in conflict with known and established facts and therefore – said with all due respect – nothing but pious nonsense and superstition. Christianity, with is creeds and doctrines, is doomed to lose more and more adherents who become aware of the incredible and impossible claims of this religion.

Something similar is bound to happen with Judaism and Islam.

Original Sin

The Origin of Sin and Death
The Christian religion in all its permutations was, and still is, obsessed with sin and how man can be saved from eternal punishment by God

in hell for being guilty of a whole range of sins.

At the beginning of the Bible, in Gen 2 and 3, a myth is to be found, explaining the existence of sin, evil, wrong-doing, guilt and shame and the origin of death. God gave the following warning to the first pair of human beings:

> "And the Lord God gave the man orders, saying, 'You may freely take of the fruit of every tree of the garden: But of the fruit of the tree of the knowledge of good and evil you may not take; for on the day when you take of it, death will certainly come to you'" (Gen 2: 16–17).

This pronouncement of God was always interpreted as an explanation why human beings became mortal. Genesis 3 contains the tale of how the snake lured the woman into eating from the forbidden fruit and she offered some to the man as well. Thereafter, God banished them from the garden so as to prevent them from eating from another tree, the "tree of life", through which they could have attained immortality.

There cannot be the slightest doubt that this story is nothing but a myth without any historical foundation. With the knowledge we presently have it can be surely said that death was always a part of life. The geological records show clearly that plants, animals and humans always had a limited life span. Death is certainly not the punishment our ancestors brought upon themselves – and us! – for disobey-ing God; it is simply an inherent characteristic of life that life comes to an end at some point.

Humans, especially males, have a violent tendency encoded within their DNA. They inherited this from their animal ancestors[146] – and definitely not from a mythical pair of humans ages ago who fell for the temptation of a forbidden fruit tree. Karen Armstrong summarized it accurately: "Palaeolithic men were proficient

---

[146] Jones, *In the Blood,* 212–13.

killers."[147] Being evil is part of human nature, although man also has the capacity to suppress this tendency and to act ethically more correctly.

Born as Sinners

When the mythical first pair of human beings, who later got the names of Adam and Eve, fell for the temptation to eat the frut of the forbidden tree, they discovered that they were naked and they hid themselves from God. God did, though, find them and condemned them to work hard to earn a living and women were doomed to a painful process of pregnancy and childbirth.

Protestant creeds declare that all humans, as descendants of Adam and Eve, are born as sinners. The Belgic Confession states:

> **"Article 15: The Doctrine of Original Sin**
> We believe that by the disobedience of Adam original sin has been spread through the whole human race.
> It is a corruption of all nature – an inherited depravity which even infects small infants in their mother's womb, and the root which produces in man every sort of sin. It is therefore so vile and enormous in God's sight that it is enough to condemn the human race, and it is not abolished or wholly uprooted even by baptism, seeing that sin constantly boils forth as though from a contaminated spring."

The Heidelberg Catechism teaches:

> "**Question 7**: Whence then proceeds this depravity of human nature?

---

[147] Armtrong, *Fields of Blood*, 5.

Answer: From the fall and disobedience of our first parents, Adam and Eve, in Paradise; hence our nature is become so corrupt, that we are all conceived and born in sin."

The Westminster Confession teaches something similar in Chapter VI.

Human Embryos
The doctrine of original sin, as formulated above, boils down to the idea that as soon as a man and a woman have had sexual intercourse and the ovum in the woman's womb was fertilized by the man's sperm, a sinful creature is supposed to have been conceived. And since that tiny little creature, consisting of only one fertilized cell, has a sinful nature it deserves to be punished in hell for all eternity should it be aborted and die.

The development of the central nervous system and the peripheral nervous system in the human embryo only starts approximately 18 days after fertilization. A rudimentary brain develops only after six or seven weeks after fertilization.[148] According to the doctrine of original sin, that embryo – with or without a primitive brain and without any form of consciousness – is already condemned to never-ending punishment, should it be aborted and die.

Here it must be asked: will that aborted fertilized ovum or developing embryo suddenly receive a fully developed consciousness when it arrives in hell? Will it endure excruciating feelings of guilt for all eternity for having rejected God and not believing in Jesus Christ, although it never participated in a conscious life during its short stay in the mother's uterus? Did it do anything to deserve this hellish punishment and torture in "the lake of fire and sulphur" (Rev 20:10), apart from the fact that it had sinful people as parents?

---

[148] Zilmer et al., *Principles of Neuropychology*, 116–17.

Of course, according to this absurd Christian doctrine, that microscopic embryo does deserve to be roasted in hell for all eternity. But – can anybody with a little bit of common sense accept this absurdity?

> *It happened more than once during my career as minister of religion that I had to provide pastoral support to a woman who had a miscarriage. For each of these women it was an intense emotional experience. Every one of them asked me whether their unborn baby would go to heaven. If I stayed true to the official Christian doctrine, I should have told them that their babies were destined for hell. I, nevertheless, assured them that since these aborted babies came from believing parents, God will regard these babies as part of his covenant with believers.*

No Accountability

According to the epistles of the apostle Paul, the only way to be saved from eternal damnation is to believe that Jesus Christ died for our sins on the cross. However, there were and are millions of people on earth who never had the opportunity of hearing of Jesus – and they are all supposed to be condemned and to be tortured in hell. Any person with a small measure of sanity will declare this doctrine to be insane. A Christian may retort that these people are not condemned because they never heard of Jesus; they are condemned because they are sinners. But – then one has to ask this Christian: did these people have any control over the fact that they were born at a certain time and place from certain parents? No, of course they had no control whatsoever over these facts. How can they be punished for something for which they were not responsible?

All civilized judicial systems embrace the concept of accountability. If somebody who is accused of a crime is found to be mentally unhinged or retarded that person is deemed not to be accountable for his or her deeds. That person can, therefore, not be punished. Any human being, born from sinful parents, can likewise not be deemed to be accountable for that fact. He or she had absolutely no choice or control regarding his or her conception and birth.

The Bible teaches:

- "For I will give honor to the name of the Lord: let our God be named great. He is the Rock, complete is his work; for all his ways are righteousness: a God without evil who keeps faith, true and upright is he" (Deut 32: 3–4).
- "As for God, his way is perfect: The word of Yahweh is tried; He is a shield to all those who take refuge in him" (2 Sam 22: 31).
- "For the Lord is upright; he is a lover of righteousness: the upright will see his face" (Ps 11: 7).

If God is really the God of justice and righteousness and if whatever he does is always perfect, as these texts maintain, then one can expect him to obey this basic rule of jurisprudence that nobody can be punished if he cannot be held accountable for his actions. But that is exactly what God does, according to the Bible. Should that be the case, he cannot be a perfect, just and righteous God and then he is also not worthy of worship.

It is abundantly clear: the doctrine of original sin leads to absurd and ridiculous consequences, which no rational human being can accept. It militates against all norms of fairness and justice and cannot be reconciled with the idea of a supposedly just and loving God who is deemed to have created that small little embryo or never gave the vast majority of people an opportunity to become Christians.

Mary Without Original Sin
It is official Roman Catholic doctrine that Mary, the mother of Jesus, was born without original sin in order to be a suitable mother for Jesus, the perfect and sinless human being. There is absolutely no biblical

justification for this doctrine, but Catholics rely on old traditions to justify this idea. It is, however, a mystery how especially Mary could have escaped original sin since all other human beings are born that way – with the exception of Jesus who supposedly had no mortal father but was fertilized by the Holy Spirit. She had ordinary parents and she was conceived in the conventional manner, that is, through sexual intercourse. How did her parents succeed in preventing her from being born with a sinful nature? Was some or other mysterious, supernatural and otherwise unknown biological process at work?

Needless to say, Protestants reject this doctrine and many a contemporary Catholic theologian is embarrassed by it.

Morality and Religion

The Bible and Morals

There is a popular idea that morality is based upon religion and that no morality can exist where there is no religion. It has to be granted: the Bible contains a multitude of moral injunctions of which the Ten Commandments are the best known. Many people derive their moral principles from the teachings of the Bible. Church leaders regard themselves as experts on morality and ethics. Councils, synods and church conferences habitually criticize certain social customs or actions of the government of the day as being immoral or unethical.

Paul teaches us in Gal 5: 22–23 that people who have the Holy Spirit in their lives are supposed to exhibit the fruit of the Spirit, namely "love, joy, peace, patience, kindness, goodness, faithfulness, gentleness, and self-control" – all of them desirable and admirable moral attributes or virtues. In other words: one may expect Christians to be moral creatures who do not take part in crime and other unacceptable forms of behavior.

The late Professor Johan Heyns argued that know-ledge of that which is moral or ethical can only be gained from God's special revelation in Holy Scripture.[149] But is that what one finds in reality? Are Christians who read the Bible and believe in Jesus more moral than people without a religious faith? Are atheists and agnostics necessarily immoral and filled with evil? This does not seem to be the case. It can be demonstrated that there are just as many crooks, liars, cheats, hypocrites, adulterers and criminals inside the churches and religious organizations as there are in the world at large.

> *During my ministry, I frequently met wonderful Christian people – honest folks, filled with compassion and moral examples. They enriched my life. But I have also seen many people in the church, including previous colleagues in the ministry, who can only be described as frauds. These previous colleagues lied, they schemed, they cheated on their wives and they saw the ministry as a comfortable job where they did the minimum of work to stay out of trouble, while living in a comfortable parsonage and enjoying the admiration of people for their eloquence. The sincerity of their faith and religious views may certainly be questioned.*

The media regularly carry news regarding the sins of Christian religious leaders – bishops, priests, television evangelists *etcetera*. Because they are supposed to be moral examples (1 Tim 3), their misdeeds make great news. Too many of them have behaved badly – being guilty of pedophilia, swindling people, corruption, adultery, fornication, lying, and so forth. They certainly do not prove that Christians, who are supposed to show the fruit of the Spirit, are in any way better than others. In fact, they discredit Christianity and drive people out of the church in disgust.[150]

Are Christians more law-abiding than unbelievers? This certainly does not seem to be the case.

---

[149] Heyns, *Teologiese Etiek*, 110–34.
[150] Küng, *Can we save the Catholic Church?*

Correlation Between Christianity and Crime Rate

I undertook a statistical analysis to find out whether there was any correlation between the strength of Christianity in different countries and their crime rates. I googled the phrases "Irreligion by Country" and "Crime Index by Country".

Wikipedia provided me with a website containing the results of investigations regarding the importance of religion in all the countries in the world. Another website provided the crime rates of all the countries in the world. I selected all the countries where Christianity historically had a significant foothold and compiled the following table where the importance of religion and the crime rates of these countries are compared. These numbers were fed onto a spread sheet on my computer to provide a statistical correlation between "importance of religion "and the "crime rate" of those countries. I wanted to find out: is the crime rate perhaps lower in countries where the Christian religion is stronger?

In the following table, the first column of numbers gives the percentages of inhabitants of the various predominantly Christian countries who regard themselves as being religious. The second column contains the crime rates of these countries. The website containing the crime rates explains these numbers as follows:

> "To present survey result, we use the scale [0, 100] for values since it is easier to read for users. *Crime Index* is an estimation of overall level of crime in a given city or a country. We consider crime levels lower than 20 as very low, crime levels between 20 and 40 as being low, crime levels between 40 and 60 as being moderate, crime levels between 60 and 80 as being high and finally crime levels higher than 80 as being very high."

Country	Importance of religion	Crime rate
Angola	88	68
Australia	32	42.2
Austria	55	26.3
Belarus	33	30.5
Belgium	33	42
Belize	61.5	62.3
Bolivia	88.5	65.6
Bosnia	66	45.8
Botswana	77	46.8
Brazil	86.5	69
Bulgaria	33.5	43.5
Cameroon	95.5	64.8
Canada	42	37.5
Chile	69.5	45
Colombia	82.5	56.9
Costa Rica	79	63
Cyprus	75	31.6
Czech Republic	20.5	32.9
Denmark	18	25.7
Dominican Republic	86	67.7
El Salvador	83	69.4
Estonia	16	28.1
Ethiopia	91	35
Finland	28	29.6
France	29.5	49.7
Georgia	80	22
Germany	40.5	28.5
Ghana	94.5	49.4
Greece	71.5	41.6
Guatemala	88	79.3
Haiti	75	62,3
Honduras	84	74.9

Ireland	53.5	49.7
Italy	71.5	47.5
Jamaica	70	71.9
Kenya	94	72.6
Kosovo	63.5	46.8
Latvia	39	37.2
Lithuania	41.5	36.7
Macedonia	78.5	36
Mexico	72.5	53.8
Moldova	71.5	49.7
Montenegro	45.5	34.9
Mozambique	86	60.5
Namibia	91.5	55.6
Netherlands	24.5	35.4
New Zealand	33	40
Nicaragua	84	42.4
Norway	20.5	31.2
Panama	88	50
Paraguay	91.5	55.6
Peru	83.5	57.6
Philippines	95.5	43.1
Poland	75.5	33
Portugal	71.5	35.8
Puerto Rico	84.5	67
Russia	33	51.3
Rwanda	95	19.2
Serbia	50.5	43.4
Slovakia	46.5	33.3
South Africa	84.5	78.4
Sweden	16.5	42.1
Switzerland	41.5	26.8
Trinidad & Tobago	92	75.3
Ukraine	45.5	49.4
United Kingdom	26.5	42

United States	65	50.1
Uruguay	40.5	47.2
Venezuela	79	84.7
Zimbabwe	87.5	62.2

The statistical correlation between the two columns[151] was calculated. The computer gave me a surprising result. There is a definite positive correlation between the "importance of religion" in Christian countries and their "crime rate". The calculated correlation is $r = 0{,}563$.

Any correlation above $r = 0{,}5$ is considered to be a significant or strong correlation. A perfect correlation is expressed as $r = 1{,}00$.[152] This correlation means that countries in which the Christian religion is strongest also tend to be the countries in which the crime rate is highest!

I did another statistical computation. From the list of the countries in the table I computed the correlation between the importance of religion and the crime rate only in countries with a westernized culture and I excluded countries from Africa and Asia. The computer gave me a correlation of $r = 0.587$, which is a slightly stronger correlation than the previous one.

In a third computation, I only took the countries where the Protestant variety of Christianity is or was dominant. In these countries a very strong correlation between the importance of religion and the crime rate of $r = 0{,}788$ was found.

In other words: there is a clear tendency for countries where religion doesn't play an important role to have lower crime rates. In countries where the Christian faith is professed by a large percentage of the population – especially Protestantism – the crime rate tends to be higher.

---

[151] Wikipedia, "Irreligion by Country" and "Crime Index by Country".
[152] McCall, *Fundamental Statistics for Psychology*, 120.

The correlation between the strength of religion in predominantly Christian countries and their homicide rate per 100 000 inhabitants per annum, as found in a Wikipedia website[153], was also calculated. The following table gives the numbers:

Country	Importance of religion	Homicide rate per 100 000
Angola	88	10
Argentina	66	5.5
Australia	32	1.1
Austria	55	0.9
Belarus	33	5.1
Belgium	33	1.6
Belize	61.5	44.7
Bolivia	88.5	12.1
Bosnia	66	1.3
Botswana	77	18.4
Brazil	86.5	25.2
Bulgaria	33.5	1.9
Cameroon	95.5	7.6
Canada	42	1.6
Chile	69.5	3.1
Colombia	82.5	30.8
Costa Rica	79	8.5
Cyprus	75	2
Czech Republic	20.5	1
Denmark	18	0.8
Dominican Republic	86	22.1
Ecuador	82	12.4
El Salvador	83	41.2
Estonia	16	5
Ethiopia	91	12

---

[153] Wikipedia, : *"Irreligion by Country"* and *" Homicide Rate per Country"*.

Finland	28	1.6
France	29.5	1
Georgia	80	4.3
Germany	40.5	0.8
Ghana	94.5	6.1
Greece	71.5	1.7
Guatemala	88	39.9
Haiti	75	10.2
Honduras	84	90.4
Hungary	39	1.3
Ireland	53.5	1.2
Italy	71.5	0.9
Jamaica	70	39.3
Kenya	94	6.4
Kosovo	63.5	3.6
Latvia	39	4.7
Lithuania	41.5	6.7
Macedonia	78.5	1.4
Mexico	72.5	21.5
Moldova	71.5	6.5
Mozambique	86	12.4
Namibia	91.5	17.2
Netherlands	24.5	0.9
New Zealand	33	0.9
Nicaragua	84	11.3
Norway	20.5	2
Panama	88	17.2
Paraguay	91.5	9.7
Peru	83.5	9.6
Philippines	95.5	8.8
Poland	75.5	1.2
Portugal	71.5	1.2
Puerto Rico	84.5	26.5
Russia	33	9.2

Rwanda	95	23.1
Serbia	50.5	1.2
Slovakia	46.5	1.4
South Africa	84.5	31
Sweden	16.5	0.7
Switzerland	41.5	0.6
Trinidad & Tobago	92	28.3
Ukraine	45.5	4.3
United Kingdom	26.5	1
United States	65	4.7
Venezuela	79	53.7
Zimbabwe	87.5	10.6

A significant correlation of $r = 0{,}509$ between importance of religion and the homicide rate in these countries was found. That means that there is a tendency for less violence in countries where religion is not so important and that Christian countries tend to be more violent than less religious countries.

Only one conclusion can be drawn from all this: inhabitants of Christian countries tend to be more immoral and more inclined to commit crimes than the people in countries where Christianity has to a certain extent disappeared. There are more criminals in predominantly Christian countries than in more secular countries. In other words: Atheists, humanists, and agnostics generally seem to be more moral and law-abiding and less violent than their fellow human beings who profess to be Christians.

Religion and Compassion

Three studies undertaken by the Department of Psychology at the Berkeley University in the USA during 2012 and involving hundreds of subjects showed consistently that religious people showed less compassion, generosity and willingness to help unfortunate people than people who regarded themselves as non-religious.

Compassion was defined as "an emotion felt when people see the suffering of others which then motivates them to help, often at a personal risk or cost." Generosity was described as "random acts of kindness, such as loaning out belongings and offering a seat on a crowded bus or train."

The researchers came to the following conclusion: "Overall, this research suggests that although less religious people tend to be less trusted in the U.S., when feeling compassionate, they may actually be more inclined to help their fellow citizens than more religious people."[154]

Altruism in Children

Research done with more than 1 000 children between the ages of five and twelve in six countries, namely the United States, Canada, Jordan, Turkey, South Africa and China, supports the idea that a religious upbringing may actually produce children who are less altruistic. Children from parents who were Christians or Muslims were compared to children from non-religious homes by subjecting them to tests to measure their level of altruism or their willingness to share.

It was found that religiously-raised children are less altruistic in the laboratory and the study points to the possibility that a religious home might not have the positive effects expected on the development of morality.[155]

Watching Pornography

In recent years, pornography of any conceivable flavor has become available through the internet. Pornography is the explicit portrayal of sexual acts, including perverted sex. How do Christian men behave in this regard?

---

[154] Anwar, "Highly Religious People".
[155] Turner, "Children with a Religious Upbringing".

The Barna Group in the USA did some research regarding this aspect in 2014. They found that 64% of Christian men watch pornography at least once a month – compared to 65% of non-Christian men. That means that there is no real difference between Christians and non-Christians regarding the habit of watching pornography.[156]

It appears, therefore, that almost two-thirds of Christian men in the USA ignore the following biblical admonitions:

- "Therefore don't let sin reign in your mortal body, that you should obey it in its lusts" (Rom 6: 12); and
- "Put to death therefore your members which are on the earth: sexual immorality, uncleanness, passion, evil desire, and covetousness" (Col 3: 5).

Moral Instinct

Richard Dawkins cites research that shows that the moral instincts between religious believers and atheists do not differ in any significant way. A number of people from both these groups were asked to indicate how they would respond to a set of three moral dilemmas. There was no statistically significant difference between the two groups and all the participants displayed more or less the same moral inclinations. That demonstrates that personal morality is actually independent from religious belief.[157]

Dawkins also noted: "Science, it is true, cannot give you any ethics. Religion can't either." There are many immoral biblical commands and examples of unethical behavior by biblical personages, such as stoning adulterers or keeping slaves. Our ethics is based on a "liberal consensus" and "a consensus of people of good

---

[156] Hallowell, "Shocking Porn 'Epidemic' Stats".
[157] Dawkins, *The God Delusion*, 225–26.

will getting together to discuss it."[158] One can only agree with Marcelo Gleiser who declared: "Believers should accept the fact that one does not need religion to be a moral person."[159]

Apart from the finding that Christians are clearly not the moral stars they are supposed to be, it is also clear that the morality taught in the Bible demonstrates more than one dubious aspect. This will be considered in the paragraphs that follow.

Slavery

All civilized communities nowadays accept that slavery is wrong. Article 4 of the Universal Declaration of Human Rights states:

> "No one shall be held in slavery or servitude; slavery and the slave trade shall be prohibited in all their forms."

It has to be stressed that the Bible totally fails to condemn slavery and only requires of slave owners to treat their slaves humanely. The Old Testament contains a number of provisions on how slaves can be acquired and how they are to be treated (Lev 25: 44–46). It was even permitted for a father to sell his daughter into slavery (Ex 21: 7–11). The Ten Commandments takes it for granted that the Israelites would make use of slave labor (Ex 20: 10, 17).

We have no pronouncement of Jesus on the topic of slavery. Paul required of slaves to obey their masters (Eph 6: 5–9; Col 3: 22–24; see also 1 Pet 2: 18). He had a very good opportunity to condemn the practice of slavery when he wrote a short letter to his friend Philemon. This letter was to be taken back by the runaway slave Onesimos whom he had met in prison. He only required from Philemon to accept Onesimos as a brother in Christ, but he totally

---

[158] Dawkins, "Religion – the Mental Equivalent", 295–96.
[159] Gleiser, "Blind Ambition and Sincere Piety", 182.

failed to ask him to give this man his freedom due to the fact that slavery is cruel and evil.

The failure of the Bible to condemn slavery can be understood against the background of the prevailing moral standards of those days. But if slavery is clearly wrong, why didn't the supposedly inspired biblical authors give any hint of the sort? It is clear: the moral injunctions of the Bible are incomplete and defective. The omniscient God, who supposedly inspired the Bible, must have foreseen that slavery would be condemned as a barbaric and evil practice sometime in the future; why did he not inspire the biblical authors to include this insight in their writings?

Equality of Sexes

The Bible teaches that men and women are not equal. Paul encouraged wives to obey their husbands, while husbands are only exhorted to love their wives (Eph 5: 22–25; Col 3: 18–19). The First Letter of Peter (3: 1–7) admonishes women to obey their husbands, to refrain from wearing jewelry and fine clothes and to win their husbands for Christ by a chaste and sober lifestyle. Women were regarded as part of their husbands' property; after all, a wife is listed in the same breath as her husband's house, his animals and his slaves in the Ten Commandments (Ex 20: 17).

The Bible deals with divorce in various texts. It is clear, though that only a man had the right to send his wife away if he found anything not to his liking in his woman. No woman had this right (Deut 22: 13–19 and 24: 1–4).

Civilized societies nowadays find this inequality of the sexes to be unacceptable. The Universal Declaration of Human rights declares in article 1:

> "All human beings are born free and equal in dignity and rights."

Article 2 states:

> "Everyone is entitled to all the rights and freedoms set forth in this Declaration, without distinction of any kind, such as race, color, sex, language, religion, political or other opinion, national or social origin, property, birth or other status."

Contrary to a popular point of view, the practice of polygamy is absolutely nowhere condemned in the Bible. The Old Testament mentions a few cases of polygamy, but those involved were not criticized for having committed a sin and that state of affairs was depicted as being quite normal, although it seems that most people in biblical times did enter into monogamous unions.

The following cases of polygamy come to mind:

- Jacob, who married two sisters and also had two concubines
- Gideon, who had 70 sons from many wives
- Elkanah, the father of the prophet Samuel, who had two wives
- King David who had several wives
- King Solomon who reportedly had 700 wives and 300 concubines (question: how did he get along with all those mothers-in-law?)

The Heidelberg Confession, likewise, fails to declare a polygamous marriage to be wrong (Heidelberg Catechism, Q & A 108 & 109). The Westminster Confession, in contrast, states in chapter XXIV, par 1:

> "Marriage is to be between one man and one woman: neither is it lawful for any man to have more than one wife, nor for any woman to have more than one husband at the same time."

Theologians usually quote Gen 2: 24 as a justification for a monogamous marriage as being the will of God:

"Therefore, a man will leave his father and his mother, and will join with his wife, and they will be one flesh."

This verse, according to the context, only amounts to a description of the usual state of affairs in those days. It cannot be seen as a command for monogamous marriages.

In civilized societies it goes without saying that marriage consists of only one man and only one woman, who are bonded for life. This is another instance where contemporary morals are better than biblical morals.

It is, therefore, clear that the social ethics of the Bible leaves much to be desired and is rejected with good reason by our modern societies.

The Library of Alexandria

One of the biggest blots on the history of Christianity was the scandalous torching of the huge library of Alexandria in Egypt in AD 391 by Christian fanatics. This library was at that time already in existence for many centuries and contained almost all the books published in antiquity – in many cases, the only copies. These Christian fanatics could not tolerate the fact that the library housed writings they regarded as heretical or blasphemous and, therefore, the whole library had to go up in flames.[160] This was, surely, the greatest tragedy in the history of human civilization and no Christian can be proud of it. It certainly did not contribute to the glory of God.

Immoral Popes

The spiritual leader of the Roman Catholic Church is called the Pope. He is the bishop of the diocese of Rome, the former capital of the Roman Empire. It goes without saying that it may be expected of the

---

[160] Encyclopaedia Britannica, "Alexandria, library of".

holder of this office to be irreproachable in all respects, a role model for all his followers. Unfortunately, that was not always the case.

It has to be granted: the present pope, Pope Francis, is a moral example with his humility, compassion and willingness to listen to people. He refrains from wearing all the expensive and shiny regalia of his predecessors, appearing only in simple white clothing. He doesn't live in the luxurious papal palace with its art treasures and more or less eleven thousand rooms, but in the Vatican's guest house in a simple two-room apartment. He has taken a lenient stance regarding divorce, abortions and homosexual people, but he promised to be hard against priests who are guilty of pedophilia.

The magazine Time chose him as the personality of the year for 2013. He has drawn much criticism from conservative clerics who regard him as a heretic for breaking with tradition.

Pope Francis

Pope Francis' lifestyle is in stark contrast with that of a large number of his predecessors from the so-called dark ages to the time of the Renaissance and thereafter.

Peter de Rosa, a former Catholic priest and professor of theology who wrote a book about the history of the papacy, states the following regarding these popes:

"Many were sons of priests, bishops and popes; some were bastards; one was a widower; another an ex-slave; several were murderers, some unbelievers; some were hermits, some heretics, sadists and sodomites; many became popes by buying the papacy (simony), and continued their days selling holy things to rake in the money; one at least was a Satan-worshipper; some fathered illegitimate child-ren, some were fornicators and adulterers on a grand scale; some were astonishingly old, some even more astonishingly young; some were poisoned, others strangled; worst of all were those who worshipped a granite God. As well as these, many were good, holy and selfless people, and a few martyrs."[161]

De Rosa adds: "Without question, the pontiffs constitute the most despicable body of leaders, clerical or lay, in history. They were, frankly, barbarians. Ancient Rome had nothing to rival them in rottenness."[162] He discusses the lives of these rotten and corrupt spiritual leaders at length in his book and it appears that many were power-hungry despots, narcissists, psychopaths, hedonists and men who revenged perceived wrongs in a cruel way. They called themselves the vicars or representatives of Christ and successors of Saint Peter, but they copied nothing of Jesus' simple lifestyle and service to his fellow human beings.

Pope Alexander VI (Rodrigo Borgia, 1431–1503) was arguably the most corrupt, evil and cruel pope that ever sat on St Peter's throne. He rose to the papacy by outbribing his rivals. He fathered many children by his various mistresses, creating one of them, Cesare, a cardinal. Cesare poisoned his own father by mistake with a potion meant for somebody else.[163]

The power-hungry bishops of Rome established their primacy over their peers by means of a series of forged documents. The most well-known is the so-called *Donatio Constantini,* a document purportedly written by the first Christian emperor, Constantine the Great, in which he granted the primacy over the whole church to bishop Sylvester of Rome, as well as political control over the western

---

[161] De Rosa, Vicars of Christ, 30.
[162] De Rosa, Vicars of Christ, 48.
[163] De Rosa, *Vicars of Christ*, 103–10.

part of the Roman Empire. This document was drawn up around AD 750 or 760 by an unknown person, centuries after the time of Constantine, most probably with the knowledge of the pope of the time. Subsequent popes often used it to settle disputes about their authority.[164]

More forgeries were fabricated during the reign of Pope Gregory VII in the eleventh century. De Rosa reports that "he had a whole school of forgers under his very nose, turning out document after document, with the papal seal of approval, to cater for his every need."[165] Gregory used some of these documents in his battle with Emperor Henry IV, whom he deposed.[166]

Trial of a Cadaver

Perhaps the most bizarre episode in all the history of Christianity happened in AD 897 when the cadaver of a dead pope was taken out of its grave and put on trial. Pope Formosus was the victim of political infighting and his successor, Stephen VI, was forced by the then king of Italy to call a synod of cardinals and bishops to put Formosus on trial. Formosus' cadaver was disinterred and seated on a throne in his papal clothing. He was found guilty of stealing the papal position and he was punished by having his corpse thrown into the Tiber, the river that flows through Rome. A fisherman caught him in his nets a few months later. Stephen VI was himself later imprisoned and strangled to death for staging this farce of a synod.[167]

This is but one episode where the leaders of Christianity acted stupidly and selfishly. There is much more in the history of Christianity about which Christians ought to be ashamed.

---

[164] Encyclopaedia Britannica, "Donation of Constantine".
[165] De Rosa, *Vicars of Christ*, 59.
[166] Encyclopaedia Britannica, "Gregory VII, Saint".
[167] Ontillera, "Vengeance at the Vatican", 14–17.

The Inquisition

Certainly, the darkest chapter in the history of Christianity is the story of the Holy Inquisition, a series of ecclesiastical courts that had to try people suspected of heresy and witchcraft and which were active between the twelfth and nineteenth centuries in Europe and the Americas. As heresy was regarded not only the denial of any of the doctrines of the church, such as the divinity of Christ, but also of adherence to Jewish customs or questioning any pronouncement of the pope.

The origin of the Inquisition can be traced to Pope Lucius III who ordered bishops in 1184 to root out all forms of heresy in their dioceses. Pope Gregory IX appointed special ecclesiastical judges as inquisitors, mostly from the ranks of the Dominican and Franciscan orders and they had jurisdiction over all Christians, except over bishops and their officials. There was no central authority for these judges other than the Pope and his officials. The first manual for the conduct of inquiries onto heresy and how to deal with heretics was issued in 1248.[168]

The normal rules of justice were not followed during these inquiries and trials. Failure to appear at a trial was considered an admission of guilt. Formal charge sheets were mostly not issued to the suspects, they were usually not informed of who accused them and they were not allowed legal representation. Confessions of guilt were often extracted under torture. No appeal against a finding of guilt was possible.

People found guilty were handed over to the civil authorities and they were often incarcerated for life in solitary confinement or burned at the stake. Thousands died in this way. For instance, in Andalusia, Spain, two thousand heretics were burned in 1482 alone. Burning was the prefer-red method of execution because it did not

---

[168] Encyclopedia Britannica, "Inquisition".

entail the spilling of blood, which was deemed to be abhorrent to Catholic clerics. When mitigating circumstances were found, the victim was not burned but strangled. Those who confessed and renounced their heretical beliefs were usually punished less harshly, including imprisonment and confiscation of all their possessions, which left
them destitute.

Even dead people could be subjected to a trial by the Inquisition. If anybody was accused of heresy after having died, his or her body or bones could be dug up, put on trial and then consigned to the flames. Needless to say, the excommunication that went with a verdict of guilt with the authority of the Pope behind it automatically meant that the soul of that person was sent directly to hell, even months or years after his or her death. The belongings of the condemned that were inherited by his or her heirs were also confiscated and the Inquisitors could keep part of the proceeds for themselves; the rest went to the Pope.

No record exists of any accused who was found to be innocent. There were cases, however, where no proof of guilt could be found. Just to be on the safe side, the poor accused was locked up in a dungeon for the rest of his or her life.

The inquisitors, who were bishops and priests, were naturally concerned about the salvation of the souls of those whom they tried, tortured and punished. It was thought that any method justified the end, that is, the salvation of the soul of the suspect. If that person confessed his sins and accepted the doctrines of the church, be it under duress, then that person was saved from eternal damnation in hell – which was, of course, much more important than living a life without persecution, pain and torture.

The members of the Inquisition were convinced that they had biblical authority for doing what they did. After all, the apostle Paul emphatically called the condemnation of God upon those who preached a Gospel that differed from his (Gal 1: 8–9). Various passages in the Old Testa-ment called for the execution of those who were guilty of breaking the Sabbath, adultery, fornication, sodomy, sorcery or idolatry – as was shown in chapter 2.

Moreover, the inquisitors had the promise of the Pope that their good deeds by rooting out heresy would guarantee them a place of honor in heaven.

Inquisitors had papal authority to absolve one another should it happen that they caused accidental deaths or unnecessary pain upon their tortured victims.

The most infamous inquisitor of all times was the Spanish Dominican friar Tomas de Torquemada (1420–1498). During his reign of 15 years more than 114 000 people fell victim to his tender ministrations and 10 220 were consigned to the flames.

Tomas de Torquemada

The Inquisition's reign of terror rendered any resistance to this cruel institution ineffective. People were simply too afraid to speak out against these practices and they rather fled abroad if they thought that they stood a chance of being prosecuted. Only after the Napoleonic wars, in 1818, were these barbaric practices abolished by the Roman Catholic Church.[169]

In our age, we just cannot condone the actions of the Inqui-sition. We find these deeds to be cruel, sadistic, bad, tragically misguided and totally wrong. But our judgment should perhaps not be

---

[169] Encyclopaedia Britannica, "Inquisition, Burning at the Stake and Heresy"; Martinez, "The Spanish Terror:, 64–75; De Rosa, *Vicars of Christ*, 102, 162–78.

too harsh – these people honestly believed that they were serving God and executing his will. They were convinced that they were doing their victims a favor by saving them from the horrors of hell if they repented as well as ridding the holy church of dangerous and despicable heretics and witches.

But we cannot justify their actions, either – even if they earnestly considered themselves to be servants of God who obeyed the Bible, the teachings of the church and the orders of the Pope. What they did was horribly wrong and despicably bad. This is another instance where the moral teachings of the Bible were superseded by more just and rational views of our time.

In the light of all this the following evaluation of the inquisitors by the Catholic Encyclopedia is utterly incomprehensible: "Far from being inhuman, they were, as a rule, men of spotless character and sometimes of truly admirable sanctity, and not a few of them have been canonized by the Church. There is absolutely no reason to look on the medieval ecclesiastical judge as intellectually and morally inferior to the modern judge." However, this encyclopedia does concede that torture was indeed applied: "Curiously enough, torture was not regarded as a mode of punishment, but purely as a means of eliciting the truth." The encyclopedia also had to admit: "Torture was applied only too frequently and too cruelly…"[170]

Peter de Rosa gives this assessment: "It is clear…. that the aim of the Inquisition was to defend not the faith but the papal system."[171]

Protestants were also guilty of killing heretics. For instance, the Spanish theologian, Miguel Servet, was found guilty of heresy and burned alive on 27 October 1553 in the Protestant town of Geneva

---

[170] Catholic Encyclopedia, "Inquisition".
[171] De Rosa, *Vicars of Christ*, 167.

with the approval of the Reformer, John Calvin, although he preferred beheading instead of burning.[172]

Witch Hunts

During the past, but especially during the 14th to 18th centuries AD, when the lives of people were ruled by all sorts of superstitions, people were very easily suspected of witchery or sorcery if they displayed any type of eccentric behavior, suffered from a mental disorder or looked different from their neighbors. Witches and sorcerers were seen as the allies and servants of Satan and, therefore, had to be exterminated. The church got biblical authority for these steps from Deut 18: 9–14, 2 Kgs 9: 22, 2 Chr 33: 6, Mic 5: 12, Gal 5: 20 and Rev 22: 14–15 where sorcery and witchcraft were condemned and the death penalty was ordered by God.

It was one of the tasks of the Inquisition to root out all witches and rid the earth of these instruments of the devil. Protestants, likewise, were guilty of hunting and killing suspected witches.

Since these wretched people were thought to be in cahoots with Satan, they had no rights whatsoever and they could be tortured and killed at will by ecclesiastic and secular courts. It is not possible to calculate today how many thousands of these hapless people were condemned to the stake, but it must be a huge number. It is known that up to half of the populations of certain villages fell victim to this inhuman practice. The pleas for mercy and screams of their victims convinced the inquisitors that they were inflicting pain on Satan himself.

A manual for the treatment of witches was issued by the Inquisition, called the *Malleus Maleficorum* (Hammer of the Witches). It contained fantastic tales of sexual orgies, sexual intercourse with the devil and satanic worship given by people under torture who said anything their tormentors wanted to hear. These tales

---

[172] Encyclopaedia Britannica, "Servetus, Michael".

were dished up as the holy truth, on the same level as in Europe that he almost gained as much power over the credulous and superstitious clergy as the almighty God himself.[173]

It has to be remarked that no case was ever recorded where a single witch or sorcerer was able to use his or her supposed magical powers against the inquisitors or to free themselves from the torture chambers. In no single case did Satan aid any of his alleged followers to harm or stop the ecclesiastical and secular judges after they had been cursed by their victims. The evil powers ascribed to the so-called witches by the Inquisition were therefore purely a case of wishful or delusional thinking. The extreme interest of many inquisitors in the imagined sexual exploits of their victims must have been quite sick or pathological.[174]

Anti-Semitism

The National Socialists in Germany, generally known as the Nazis, are usually credited with anti-Semitism of the worst kind. It is certainly true; the Nazi's put into practice the ideology of Adolf Hitler, assisted by SS-chief Heinrich Himmler, by exterminating the European Jews who were regarded as inferior beings. Both of these gentlemen were Roman Catholics and they only continued what the Church did for many centuries.

A succession of popes throughout the Middle Ages and thereafter took Matt 27: 25 to heart where the crowd of Jews outside the Praetorium of Pontius Pilate during the trial of Jesus is reported to have yelled: "May his blood be on us, and on our children!" These words were undoubtably the invention of the author of Matthew. The Gospels anyway carried an anti-Jewish flavor by depicting the Jewish leaders of the time as Jesus' enemies in order to present Christianity

---

[173] Encyclopaedia Britannica, "Witchcraft"; De Rosa, *Vicars of Christ*, 181–91.
[174] De Rosa, *Vicars of Christ*, 189–90.

in as positive a light to the Roman world after the destruction of Jerusalem in AD 70.

The Encyclopaedia Britannica explains:

> "From St. Augustine in the 4th century to Martin Luther in the 16th, some of the most eloquent and persuasive Christian theologians excoriated the Jews as rebels against God and murderers of the Lord. They were described as companions of the Devil and a race of vipers."[175]

Nevertheless, the popes regarded it as their sacred duty to punish the descendants of the so-called killers of Jesus Christ. Wherever the pope had any political influence, the Jews were herded into ghettos, prohibited from employing Christians and were barred from most professions and crafts. Hygiene was non-existent in these overcrowded ghettos and therefore people easily referred to the "filthy Jews". Untold numbers of them were simply murdered by the Inquisition and others who acted on the wishes of the Church. Jewish children were regularly taken away from their parents and baptized to convert them into Christians and then raised by the Church as Christians.

What these popes and their pious henchmen never took into consideration was that the parents of Jesus, Joseph and Mary, Jesus himself, as well as the apostles of Jesus, were all Jews. The popes, who saw themselves as the successors of St Peter, conveniently forgot that he was a Jew, born and bred in Galilee.[176]

Peter de Rosa points out:

---

[175] Encyclopedia Britannica, "Anti-Semitism+; see also: Gottheil and Kayserling, "Inquisition".
[176] De Rosa, *Vicars of Christ*, 191–203.

"One Christian superstition of the time was that whoever was responsible for baptizing an infidel gained free passage to Paradise."[177]

The anti-Semitism of the Nazi's and others was nothing but a continuation of the actions of the Roman Catholic Church. To make matters worse, Pope Pius XII, who ruled between 1939 and 1958, stayed totally silent regarding the Nazi Holocaust, although he knew about it. After the war, the Vatican and many Roman Catholic clergy even helped Nazi war criminals to escape justice.[178]

The official anti-Semitism of the Roman Catholic Church only came to an end when Pope John Paul II visited the country of Israel in 2000 and apologized for the persecution of the Jews by the Church.[179] With this step, he in effect repudiated the "infallibility" of his predecessors who issued one ant-Semitic bull after the other.

Summary

The preceding paragraphs clearly demonstrate that Christians do not live more moral lives than people who are non-religious. On the contrary, Christians tend to be less law-abiding, more violent and more prone to plain stupid and cruel practices. There is no difference between Christians and non-believers when watching pornography is considered. Children from religious homes are less altruistic than their friends from non-religious homes. The record of the utmost cruelty and insane actions perpetrated by the Church through many centuries did nothing to enhance the public image of the Church.

The history of the Christian church contains many records of commendable actions where suffering was mitigated, where the needy were supported, where the infirm and elderly were provided for and

---

[177] De Rosa, *Vicars of Christ*, 194.
[178] De Rosa, *Vicars of Christ*, 196–201.
[179] Encyclopedia Britannica, "Anti-Semitism".

where education was given. But, on the other hand, there were so many actions unworthy of the followers of Jesus of Nazareth that Christians don't have much to be proud of.

Apart from that, the morals taught in the Bible are often of questionable value and have been shown to be far less acceptable than the insights prevalent in modern secular societies and the values encoded in their legal systems.

The Trinity

The doctrine of the Trinitarian God is deemed to be one of the foundation stones of the Christian faith. What does this doctrine entail? According to the Belgic Confession, this doctrine is to be understood as follows:

> **"Article 8: The Trinity**
> In keeping with this truth and Word of God we believe in one God, who is one single essence, in whom there are three persons, really, truly, and eternally distinct according to their incommunicable properties – namely, Father, Son, and Holy Spirit. The Father is the cause, origin, and source of all things, visible as well as invisible.
> "The Son is the Word, the Wisdom, and the image of the Father.
> "The Holy Spirit is the eternal power and might, proceeding from the Father and the Son.
> "Nevertheless, this distinction does not divide God into three, since Scripture teaches us that the Father, the Son, and the Holy Spirit each has his own subsistence distinguished by characteristics – yet in such a way that these three persons are only one God.

"It is evident then that the Father is not the Son and that the Son is not the Father, and that likewise the Holy Spirit is neither the Father nor the Son.

"Nevertheless, these persons, thus distinct, are neither divided nor fused or mixed together.

"For the Father did not take on flesh, nor did the Spirit, but only the Son.

"The Father was never without his Son, nor without his Holy Spirit, since all these are equal from eternity, in one and the same essence.

"There is neither a first nor a last, for all three are one in truth and power, in goodness and mercy."

It is my experience that few Christians have a clear or accurate idea of what this doctrine entails. This is also true of a significant number of ministers of religion, although they are supposed to accept the creeds as a faithful rendering of scriptural "truths". They often are guilty of the heresy of modalism or Sabellianism – the school of thought that teaches that the Father, the Son and the Holy Spirit are not separate and distinct divine persons, but are only three different names or appearances of the single divine person. But that is not the accepted teaching of the church, which holds that there is only one God, but three distinct divine persons, each with his own role in die heavenly household.

This is a concept that makes sense to few people. Very often, parents teach their young children that Jesus created the universe, although the Bible declares that God the Father is actually the creator. Children are often taught by their parents to pray to "Dear Jesus" and many grown-ups – and even ministers – often pray directly to Jesus, although we find only a single example in the Bible where a prayer was addressed to Jesus (Acts 7: 39). All the other biblical examples of prayers were addressed to God, the Father. I have heard sermons from the pulpit teaching the congregation that the relationship between

Jesus and his followers is akin to the relationship between a father and his children. This idea has the consequence that we have to think of God the Father as actually our heavenly grandfather, since Jesus Christ is his son!

Recently, I listened to a television interview with a well-known sports star. He declared that he was grateful that he got his talents from his "heavenly Father, Jesus Christ".

Article 9 of the Belgic Confession quotes a number of verses from the Old and the New Testament to "prove" the doctrine of the Trinitarian God. There seems to be unanimity amongst theologians in our time that the Old Testament certainly does not contain anything that can be construed as "proof" of this doctrine. The Israelite prophets and other authors of the Old Testament books always thought of God as a single divine entity, without any internal divisions.[180]

The Belgic Confession takes verses from various parts of the New Testament and by combining them artificially, it arrives at a scriptural "proof" that the one God also has three personalities, often taking these texts out of context. The biblical "proof" for this doctrine is, therefore, rather shaky.

It may be added that Jews and Muslims, who also worship the God of Abraham, Isaac and Jacob, can see no justify-cation to think of God as a triune God. For them, God is a single Person. Whenever the Old Testament mentions the "Spirit" of God, it is not a separate divine Person – it is merely a way of speaking of the one God who is thought of as a spiritual being and this expression may just as well be translated as the "mind" of God. The same applies to the New Testament where the names "God" and "Holy Spirit" are often used as synonyms (Acts 5: 3–4).

The doctrine of the Trinity is perhaps the most important intellectual construct of Christianity. Roman Catholics and Protestants are in total agreement regarding this doctrine. Yet, when

---

[180] Boshoff et al., *Geskiedenis en Geskrifte*.

we accept that Jesus was not a divine being and merely a human being, this doctrine falls apart and may just as well to be discarded and scrapped.

It has to be stressed that the doctrine of the Trinity depends largely upon the writings of Paul. He, nevertheless, contradicted this doctrine explicitly in 1 Cor 15: 24–28 where he wrote that Jesus Christ will abdicate his position after Judgment Day and "he will deliver up the kingdom to God the Father." He adds: "When all things have been subjected to him [Christ], then the Son will also himself be subjected to him who subjected all things to him, that God may be all in all." In other words: Jesus Christ cannot be the equal of God the Father if he is to surrender all his power to his Father and is to subject himself to his Father. It is impossible to maintain the doctrine of the Trinity in the light of this passage in Scripture.

Redemption

Redemption Through Faith in Jesus Christ

According to Protestantism, a sinner only has to have faith in Jesus Christ and believe what the Bible promises regarding the forgiveness of sins by God, in order to be saved from eternal punishment in hell.

This is what the Heidelberg Catechism says on this subject:

> "**Question 20**: Are all men then, as they perished in Adam, saved by Christ?
> **Answer**: No; only those who are ingrafted into him, and, receive all his benefits, by a true faith."

> "**Question 21**: What is true faith?
> **Answer**: True faith is not only a certain knowledge, whereby I hold for truth all that God has revealed to us in his word, but also an assured confidence, which the Holy Ghost works by the gospel in my heart; that not only to others, but to me also,

remission of sin, everlasting righteousness and salvation, are freely given by God, merely of grace, only for the sake of Christ's merits."

These thoughts are a repetition of Paul's stance to be found in his letters, namely that we are to be saved through faith. Paul argues, for instance, in Rom 1: 16 – "For I am not ashamed of the gospel of Christ, for it is the power of God to salvation to everyone who believes; to the Jew first, and also to the Greek." He adds: "We maintain therefore that a man is justified by faith apart from the works of the law" (Rom 3: 28).

Thomas Paine argued convincingly that this doctrine doesn't make sense:

> "If I owe a person money, and cannot pay him, and he threatens to put me in prison, another person can take the debt upon himself, and pay it for me. But if I have committed a crime, every circumstance of the case is changed. Moral justice cannot take the innocent for the guilty even if the innocent would offer itself. To suppose justice to do this, is to destroy the principle of its existence, which is the thing itself. It is then no longer justice. It is indiscriminate revenge."[181]

This doctrine boils down to the absurd conclusion that somebody may lead a violent life of vice and crime, but if he repents on his deathbed and accepts Jesus into his heart, two minutes before he breathes his last breath, then his eternal fate is suddenly changed and he is no longer to be barbecued in the eternal flames of hell but, instead, is to receive unending heavenly bliss[182] – or, as somebody put it: he no

---

[181] Paine, *The Age of Reason*, 20.
[182] Mills, *Atheist Universe*, 17–18.

longer has to prepare himself to shovel coals but has to take harp lessons instead.

Redemption Without Faith in Jesus Christ

The letter of James, written by Jesus' brother and successor as leader of the group of Jesus' followers, nowhere advocates the point of view explained in the Protestant creeds quoted above. He indirectly criticizes Paul by declaring: "But do you want to know, vain man, that faith apart from works is dead?" (Jas 2: 20).

The Didache, the oldest piece of Christian literature not included in the New Testament, gives no evidence of having been influenced by Paul's ideas. This document only requires of believers to love God and their fellow human beings in order to please God (see Did 3).

Throughout the Old Testament, the only way to serve God and lead a moral life was to obey God's laws. In Ps 103 we are even told that we can rely on God's love and forgiveness solely on the fact that he is a God of love who shows compassion with fragile human beings. No repen-tance is even required. There is no hint that another person could be punished in the sinner's place in order to effect God's forgiveness.

> *A man who had been recently widowed asked to have a meeting with me. In his church he and his wife, who had cancer, were told that some or other sin in her life prevented her from being healed. They confessed every real and imagined sin in their lives, often with tears streaming from their eyes. His wife, nevertheless and in spite of all their confessions, died. This man's faith in God was severely shattered. I find the stance of his church to be wrong and the treatment he and his wife received to be cruel.*

Anyway, it is a miracle how anybody can think that he will be able to impress God on Judgment Day by declaring that he believed or accepted certain ideas or doctrines. More and more people conclude that the acceptance of certain biblical ideas or concepts will not make the slightest difference to their fate after they have died.

Did Jesus Die for the Neanderthals?

Orthodox Christians believe that Jesus also died for people who lived before his time. The Belgic Confession declares in article 27 that the church of Christ "has existed from the beginning of the world and will last until the end, as appears from the fact that Christ is eternal King who cannot be without subjects." The Heidelberg Catechism teaches the following in Q & A 54 regarding "the holy catholic church of Christ":

> "That the Son of God from the beginning to the end of the world, gathers, defends, and preserves to himself by his Spirit and word, out of the whole human race, a church chosen to everlasting life, agreeing in true faith; and that I am and forever shall remain, a living member thereof."

The implication of all this is that certain number of people "from the beginning of the world" and "out of the whole human race" belong to the universal or catholic church – those who will receive life eternal. The authors of these creeds, of course, did not have the knowledge of paleontology that we have in our time. They had no inkling that human beings evolved from non-human ancestors to become the species of *homo sapiens* that inhabited the world since $\pm 200\,000$ years ago.[183]

In ages gone by, there existed other types of human beings, the best-known being the Neanderthals (*homo neanderthalensis*) who became extinct about 20 000 years ago. That they belonged to the

---

[183] McCarthy and Rubidge, *The Story of Earth,* 290–92; Rousseau, *Die Groot Avontuur,* 146, 295, 301.

human branch of living beings is beyond dispute, although modern humans (*homo sapiens*) and the Neanderthals had a common ancestor that lived more than half-a-million years ago, with the result that we are actually two different species.[184]

The Neanderthals are, nevertheless, to be included in "the whole human race" as mentioned in the Heidelberg Catechism. Did Jesus also die for these human beings? Can some of the Neanderthals be considered to have belonged to the church that existed "from the beginning of the world"?

We may also ask: were the Neanderthals also created in the image of God (Gen 1: 26–27), just as modern human beings? When exactly did the image of God appear during the course of evolution from animal-like beings to human beings? Did the Neanderthals have the need to be saved from their sins?

Should it happen that a lost tribe of Neanderthals be discovered in a remote part of the earth, will they be regarded as part of the human family and enjoy the same human rights as modern humans? Will missionaries try to convince them to adopt Christianity and baptize them?

From all this, it becomes clear that the orthodox Christian view, when taken to its logical implications with the knowledge we now possess, runs into serious difficulties. It is impossible to answer the questions posed above in the positive or the negative because the whole doctrine of redemption does not, in any case, makes sense. After all, it has already been shown that the doctrine of original sin cannot be accepted. This implies that human beings have no real need to be saved from their sins and their sinful human natures.

Do Extraterrestrials Need Salvation?
Very few theologians over the ages gave any attention to the question whether intelligent extraterrestrial beings might fit in with the Chris-

---

[184] Jones, *The Molecule Hunt*, 61; Rousseau, *Die Groot Avontuur*, 133.

tian God's purpose with his creation.

St Augustine thought that it was impossible for extraterrestrials to exist because of the uniqueness of Christ's incarnation.[185] Tom Paine, the rationalist from the eighteenth century, on the other hand, was convinced that there existed millions of other worlds with intelligent beings in the vast universe:

> "Since then no part of our earth is left unoccupied, why is it to be supposed that the immensity of space is a naked void, lying in eternal waste? There is room for millions of worlds as large or larger than ours, and each of them millions of miles apart from each other."[186]

That Paine's reasoning is not off the mark is proved by the fact that astronomers have, since 1992, discovered thousands of planets revolving around neighboring stars. Many of them are of a comparable size to our earth and seem to be habitable. They are in the so-called "Goldy Locks zone" where the temperature seems to be right for liquid water to exist. The SETI ("Search for Extraterrestrial Intelligence") Institute declared in 2020: "Thanks to new research using data from the Kepler space telescope, it's estimated that there could be as many as 300 million potentially habitable planets in our galaxy."[187]

For Paine, this plurality of worlds was an indication that the Christian religion must lead to absurdities:

> "From whence then could arise the solitary and strange conceit that the Almighty, who had millions of worlds equally dependent on his protection, should quit the care of all the rest, and come to die in our world, because, they say, one man and

---

[185] Barrow, *The Artful Universe,* 40.
[186] Paine, *The Age of Reasn,* 40.
[187] SETI Institute, "How Many Habitable Planets are Out There?"

one woman had eaten an apple! And, on the other hand, are we to suppose that every world in the boundless creation had an Eve, an apple, a serpent, and a redeemer? In this case, the person who is irreverently called the Son of God, and sometimes God himself, would have nothing else to do than to travel from world to world, in an endless succession of death, with scarcely a momentary interval of life."[188]

In other words: did Jesus also have to die on millions of others planets for extraterrestrials – that is, should they also be sinful creatures? Or is the death of Jesus on our earth sufficient for the inhabitants of the millions of other planets in the universe? Of course, nobody has the answers to these questions (yet). But should it happen that we manage to contact a civilization vastly superior to our own somewhere in our galaxy, it will certainly have a profound influence on our religious ideas and practices. It is quite possible that these extraterrestrials will tell us that they have not found any evidence for the existence of an intelligent creator of the universe and that there is no need for them to be saved from their sins.

Resurrection, the Last Judgment and Life Everlasting

Resurrection from the Grave
Another Christian doctrine, the idea that there is an existence beyond the grave, contains some more contradictions and unacceptable or absurd notions.

This doctrine has its roots in ancient Mesopotamian religions, the ancient Egyptian religion, the Greek-Roman world view and the Old Testament. All these held that a deceased person's spirit, soul or shadow persisted after death and resided in the underworld in a shadowy existence. Only the most virtuous or most important (such

---

[188] Paine, *The Age of Reason*, 44.

as the Egyptian Pharaohs) could gain a place in heaven, which was conceptualized as a place or condition between or beyond the stars.

The Old Testament gave very little attention to the afterlife and it was merely thought that the dead were to be collected in *Sheol* (Hebrew: שְׁאוֹל), the realm of the dead, somewhere below the surface of the earth – in accordance with Mesopotamian religious thought. In Job 10: 21–22 it is called the "land of darkness" and "the land dark as midnight". When the patriarch Jacob heard of the purported death of his son Joseph, he reportedly exclaimed: ""For I will go down to Sheol to my son [while] mourning" (Gen 37: 35). This realm of the dead was thought to be under the surface of the (flat) earth. Ps 63: 9 locates it in "the lower parts of the earth". The author of Amos 9: 2 thought that it was even possible to "dig into Sheol".

The New Testament, on the other hand, teaches that all deceased believers and unbelievers will be resurrected on Judgment Day. They are then to appear before the judicial throne of either God the Father or Jesus Christ[189], where they will either be condemned to eternal damnation in hell or admitted into unending heavenly bliss. Something like this was also to be found in the ancient Egyptian religion according to which the hearts of the deceased were to be weighed to determine whether they were worthy of a place in the heavens.

The Belgic Confession and the Heidelberg Catechism give the following descriptions of this Christian doctrine:

> **"Article 37: The Last Judgment**
> Finally we believe, according to God's Word, that when the time appointed by the Lord is come (which is unknown to all creatures) and the number of the elect is complete, our Lord

---

[189] The biblical authors are not sure which divine Person is to be the judge on Judgment Day – see Matt 13: 41–43; Matt 25: 31; Acts 17: 30–31; Rom 2:5; Rev 14: 14–20; Rev 20: 13–15.

Jesus Christ will come from heaven, bodily and visibly, as he ascended, with great glory and majesty, to declare himself the judge of the living and the dead. He will burn this old world, in fire and flame, in order to cleanse it.

"Then all human creatures will appear in person before the great judge – men, women, and children, who have lived from the beginning until the end of the world.

"They will be summoned there by the voice of the archangel and by the sound of the divine trumpet.

"For all those who died before that time will be raised from the earth, their spirits being joined and united with their own bodies in which they lived. And as for those who are still alive, they will not die like the others but will be changed 'in the twinkling of an eye' from 'corruptible to incorruptible.'"

"**Question 57**: What comfort does the 'resurrection of the body' afford thee?
Answer: That not only my soul after this life shall be immediately taken up to Christ its head; but also, that this my body, being raised by the power of Christ, shall be reunited with my soul, and made like unto the glorious body of Christ."

These are brave efforts to reconcile conflicting and contradictory messages from different parts of the Bible regarding the resurrection, the last judgment and eternal life.

According to Paul (1 Cor 15: 42–44), believers are to be resurrected – like Christ – with an "imperishable body" and a "spiritual body" (whatever that means). That body and soul are to be "reunited" on resurrection day – as the Belgic Confession and the Heidelberg Catechism contend – is a notion foreign to Paul's way of thinking. He teaches that the dead body of the person in the grave will be transformed into a new spiritual substance that will allow it to enter heaven, because the physical body made of flesh and blood cannot enter the kingdom of God – just as the risen Christ was transformed into a spiritual being before his ascension into heaven (1 Cor 15: 20–23).

In 1 Pet 3: 18 we read that Jesus was "put to death in the flesh, but made alive in the spirit." That means that only his immaterial spirit survived death – and that will also happen to other human beings.

On the other hand, John and Luke tell us that the resurrected body of Jesus was the same visible body with which he wandered the earth before his crucifixion and burial. He invited Thomas to inspect his wounds (John 20: 27). Jesus made a fire to roast some fish, which he handed to his disciples to eat (John 20: 9–13). According to Luke 24: 39–42, the resurrected Jesus assured his disciples that he was not a spirit and he showed them his wounds and invited them to touch him. He enjoyed a meal of roasted fish with them.

These descriptions of Jesus make one wonder: was this resurrected physical body of Jesus, as described in the Gospels, made of perishable stuff? If so, how is it possible that he will survive to return to earth on Judgment Day, centuries after his ascension? If his body was, on the other hand, imperishable as Paul insists, then one may wonder what the chemical composition of it must have been, since it must have differed from all other biological entities known to man. It must have had some sort of a chemical composition, otherwise he would not have been able to digest the fish he had eaten. It is also to be wondered how it was possible to get revived after having suffered horrific wounds and having died due to a severe loss of blood. How did he manage to overcome these and again walk the earth as if his fatal wounds and his bloodless body were trivialities?

We may also ask: did Jesus appear naked or clothed after his resurrection? After all, the disciples found his burial cloth lying in the tomb after he had disappeared (John 20: 7). If he appeared clothed, then where did he suddenly obtain these clothes?

We have only two descriptions of Jesus' ascension into heaven – both by Luke (Luke 24: 50–51 and Acts 1: 9–11). We are told that he drifted or glided off into the air and disappeared behind a cloud, while the disciples stared into the sky. In 1 Pet 3: 21–22 we find an interesting idea, namely that "through the resurrection of Jesus Christ, who is at the right hand of God, having gone into heaven, angels and authorities and powers being made subject to him."

These descriptions are in accordance with the primitive world view, which places heaven as the dwelling of God beyond the clouds and the stars. Various texts in the Old Testament equated the angels with stars, while "the authorities and powers" were seen as astrological constellations or signs, consisting of pagan deities and other monsters (1 Kgs 22: 19; Job 38: 4–8; Ps 103: 20–21; Ps 148: 2–3; Neh 9: 6).

But one cannot help to wonder how Jesus, with his physical body, all of a sudden managed to defy the law of gravity. In which direction and towards which constellation of stars did he disappear? How did he manage not to suffocate since there is no oxygen in outer space?

If we are to believe that the dead are to be resurrected in the same way as Jesus – as depicted in the Gospels – then the dead will also have physical bodies, made of flesh and blood, at their resurrection. This poses a serious difficulty. Dead bodies in graves decompose after a period of time, where they become food for worms and bacteria. Many people who die without being buried are eaten by birds and wild animals. People who drown at sea are consumed by marine creatures. The bodies of certain dead people are cremated and only a small heap of ash remains. After a certain period of time the molecules and atoms, which composed the bodies of these dead people, are recycled into the bodies of other living beings or are scattered over the surface of the earth. The DNA molecules containing the blueprints for the composition of the organism fall apart and their code is lost forever. How is it possible that these scattered molecules and atoms will ever be reassembled to form a reconstituted living body of somebody who died centuries before? There is no way for this to be remotely possible or feasible.

Paul's explanation that resurrected people have "imperishable" or "spiritual" bodies doesn't make sense either. Nobody has ever encountered such an imperishable or spiritual body. Paul also fails to describe the process through which a body of flesh and blood is transformed into a "spiritual body". There is a distinct possibility that Paul thought of this "spiritual body" as composed of a fifth element, the so-called quintessence – apart from the four "ordinary" elements, namely fire, air, water and earth – of which stars and other celestial bodies were supposed to be made, according to the Greek philosopher Aristotle.[190]

If Jesus was resurrected with a physical body, as Luke assures us, and he ascended with this body into heaven, then one must conclude that heaven must also be physical in nature, a locality somewhere in the universe where physical bodies can survive. If that is the case, then one may ask whether God is also a physical being and who must, therefore, inhabit this physical heaven somewhere. The Bible is adamant, though, that God is a spiritual being and that heaven cannot be part of the physical universe (Job 11: 7–9; Ps 139: 7; John 4: 24) – and, therefore, it was not possible for Jesus to ascend into the presence of God in heaven with a body of flesh and blood as Luke makes us believe. Therefore – the Gospel stories just cannot be accepted on this point.

Judgment Day

Judgment Day will be an impossibly crowded event if one takes the biblical accounts thereof seriously. We read in Matt 25: 31–32:

---

[190] Aristotle, *On the Heavens*, Book 1: 9.

"But when the Son of Man comes in his glory, and all the holy angels with him, then will he sit on the throne of his glory. Before him all the nations will be gathered, and he will separate them one from another, as the shepherd separates the sheep from the goats."

Something similar is found in Rev 20: 11–13:

"I saw a great white throne, and him who sat on it, from whose face the earth and the heaven fled away. There was found no place for them. I saw the dead, the great and the small, standing before the throne. Books were opened. Another book was opened, which is the book of life. The dead were judged out of the things which were written in the books, according to their works. The sea gave up the dead who were in it. Death and Hades gave up the dead who were in them. They were judged, each one according to his works."

The United Nations estimated that the population of the earth reached the seven billion mark in 2011.[191] If only the present population of the earth was to appear before the divine throne on Judgment Day and each person had 0,5 m² standing space, then one could have packed 20 000 resurrected people onto a square kilometer. Seven billion people will need 350 000 km² standing space. In comparison, Texas has an area of 690 000 km². That means that all of those who are alive today and who are supposed to attend Judgment Day somewhere in the future will need an area more than half the size of Texas. If one adds all those who have lived and died in the past one will need an area that covers the southern half of the United States of America.

---

[191] United Nations, "Human Development Report 2015".

Will God (or Christ) ever be able to process this vast crowd in a single day? Where will the records of the lives of each one, containing a list of all their sins and crimes, be kept?

Only the first few rows of that vast crowd can be said to be "standing before the throne". The rest will simply be too far away – even hundreds of kilometers away – to be part of the proceedings on that day.

According to Rev 16: 16, Judgment Day will take place at Armageddon – the plain of Jizreel next to the ancient city of Megiddo in Northern Israel. It will, of course, be totally impossible to fit a crowd of billions of people onto that spot.

The story was told to me about an eccentric and autocratic old farmer who ordered his son to bury him on a certain hilltop on his farm after his death. The son did exactly that out of respect and fear for his father, although he needed to drag a pneumatic drill uphill to dig a grave on the rocky hilltop and had to go to great lengths to get his father's coffin safely onto the hilltop and into the grave. The old man's reason for this strange order was that he wanted to have a last look from the hilltop on Judgment Day when he was resurrected from the grave to see whether his descendants had cared properly for his farm in the years following his funeral! His gravestone is to be seen on that hilltop to this day.

Eternal Life

The notion of life everlasting in heaven (or hell) is equally absurd and impossible.

This is what the Heidelberg Catechism has to say on this topic:

> "**Question 58**: What comfort takest thou from the article of 'life everlasting'?
>
> **Answer**: That since I now feel in my heart the beginning of eternal joy, after this life, I shall inherit perfect salvation, which 'eye has not seen, nor ear heard, neither has it entered into the heart of man' to conceive, and that to praise God therein for ever."

According to the Bible, only God is eternal (Ps 90: 2; Heb 9: 14; 2 Pet 3: 8). He supposedly exists outside of time and space and is thought to be without beginning and end. Creation, on the other hand, had a beginning when God created it out of nothing, according to Gen 1:1 and John 1: 1–3, and it must, therefore, also come to an end somewhere in the future (Matt 24: 29–30; 2 Pet 3: 7). Time was created together with the universe and time will again disappear when the universe comes to an end. Should it happen that humans, who are part of creation, enter eternal life after death then it must, of necessity, mean that they are dissolved or absorbed into the eternity of God, otherwise they cannot exist into all eternity. Should that be the case, then it won't be possible to have an individual existence beyond death as the Bible (and the Christian creeds) declares.

On the other hand, if people do exist individually after death into eternity, then it implies that they cannot have had a beginning. Eternity is, per definition, without a beginning and an end. Then it is a puzzle how they could have entered time since in eternity there is no time. It is a mathematical impossibility that there can be any connection between anything finite and infinity/eternity. The mathematical concept of infinity (∞) cannot be used in any computation in which finite numbers appear. One may divide infinity any number of times, subtract from it, add to it or multiply it, but it always stays infinity – except when infinity is divided by infinity, which produces a zero as the result.

Metaphysical infinity, likewise, cannot contain anything finite, such as the finite life of a human being. If people, who exist in time, leave this life through death, then it simply is not possible that they can become eternal or infinite entities, existing in an infinite mode, without beginning and end.

The New Testament abundantly promises eternal bliss for believers and eternal suffering for unbelievers and the ungodly after they have died. This implies that saints and sinners must have existed from eternity to eternity – the same as God. That means that they are, somehow, part of the eternal God. But how a part of God, consisting of the unbelievers, atheists, pagans and sinners, can undergo eternal punishment in hell does not seem to be compatible with the idea of a totally good, just and loving God who supposedly cannot do wrong.

On the other hand, 1 Tim 6: 16 contains the statement that Jesus Christ "alone has immortality" (Greek: ὁ μόνος ἔχων ἀθανασίαν – *ho monon echon athanasian*). If that is the case, then nobody else can hope to gain life everlasting or eternal bliss in heaven. One has to ask: how is it possible that the – supposedly divinely inspired – Bible contains these conflicting and contradictory notions?

Likewise, according to Rev 20: 14, "Death and Hades were thrown into the lake of fire." This amounts to a contradiction since the word Hades is often used in the New Testament for *hell* (Matt 16: 18; Luke 10: 15; Luke 16: 23; Acts 2: 31; Rev 1: 18). This begs the question: how the hell can hell be thrown into hell? Does that mean that hell with its fires will be annihilated and extinguished or abolished on Judgment Day? It must be concluded that the way of depicting the afterlife in Revelation seems to be rather unclear and confused.

The depiction of an existence in heaven by the departed saints in the book of Revelation seems to amount to an absurdity in another sense. One often reads in this book of the hymns being sung by the heavenly beings. Music can only be music if it has a beat – and that presupposes that it needs time to be performed. How can there be music in heaven if there is no time in heaven with its eternity?

These heavenly beings, who sing God's praise and enjoy "eternal joy", supposedly are conscious of their surroundings and of themselves. Consciousness is always consciousness of something. The conscious mind cannot ever be empty – it is always filled with a mixture of sensations, memories and thoughts, otherwise it would amount to unconsciousness. Sensations, memories and thoughts can only exist in time – not in the timelessness of eternity.

> *A colleague of mine, a prison chaplain, more than once told me that he thinks that he is wasting his time with the convicts with whom he is working. Some of them profess to be serious Christians, but he suspects them of being hypocrites who only seek favors from him. Others are visibly antagonistic towards the message he tries to convey and he gets the impression that he will never convince them of their sins. They just don't see the necessity of confessing their transgressions, making peace with God and preparing for Judgment Day.*

The neurologist Oliver Sacks wrote a book with the title, *The River of Consciousness*, in which he argued that consciousness is not an attribute of the brain but a process in which billions of neurons play a role. Sensations and thoughts are mental processes that presuppose time where one moment is followed by another. Memories are always recollections of past events and that also presupposes the passage of time. Oliver Sacks wrote: "Our movements, our actions, are extended in time, as are our perceptions, our thoughts, the contents of conscious-ness."[192]

Therefore, a conscious existence after physical death in heaven or in hell, in eternity, in a state of timelessness, just does not make sense and cannot be possible. The notion of an eternal conscious existence of the individual in an afterlife, whether in heaven or hell, simply cannot be accepted by any sensible and rational person.

The Human Soul

Theologians held long debates regarding the question when exactly a fetus becomes a human being. There are those who contend that the human soul is created at the moment of conception. There are also those who think that the human soul has had a pre-existence before conception and that that soul is united with the embryo at the moment of fertilization. Both ideas are unacceptable.

No neuroscientist of our age will agree with the idea that a human being is comprised of two different elements, namely body and soul. There is no separate soul, apart from the body. The "higher" functions of human beings, namely cognition, the use of language, experiencing emotions, decision-making and being conscious of all this, are all totally dependent upon the all-too physical brain.[193] Neuroscientists also explain that all biological activities, including brain activities, can be described in terms of physics and chemistry. All the processes in brain cells are the result of intricate chemical reactions and electrical currents. Therefore, no immaterial substance, such as a soul, is needed to explain what happens in a brain and when a human being thinks, perceives, experiences, feels, talks and acts.[194]

Psychiatric disorders, such as schizophrenia, depress-sion, bi-polar disorder, autism, epilepsy and dementia can all be explained

---

[192] Sacks, *The River of Consciousness*, 161.
[193] Kolb and Whishaw, *Fundamentals*, 6–8.
[194] Kolb and Whishaw, *Fundamentals*, 82–130.

as disorders of brain anatomy and brain chemistry.[195] One does not need spiritual or supernatural entities, such as demons, to explain these conditions.

Should a person suffer brain damage through an injury, a stroke or dementia, these higher faculties are impaired. When the damage is serious enough, the personality and memories of that person vanish, never to be regained. There just is no possibility that a separate, non-material substance, the soul, can exist apart from the body. There is absolutely no evidence that this soul could have existed before conception, started to inhabit the embryo when conception took place and can survive death.[196]

All the evidence, on the other hand, points to the conclusion that death is final. No part of a person can survive. All that person's memories are stored in the brain – especially in the hippocampus and the temporal lobes.[197] The person's personality, which is comprised of his memories, attitudes, habitual ways of acting and feeling and his mental abilities, is totally dependent upon a functioning brain.

When that person becomes demented through Alzheimer's disease and the brain cannot function anymore, that personality with all its memories disappears – never to reappear. The neurons disintegrate and the stored memories are destroyed.[198] It is totally inconceivable how those memories can survive death when the person is supposed to enter eternal heavenly bliss or unending punishment in hell. How will all those vanished and destroyed information in the memories of a sufferer from Alzheimer's disease or brain damage ever be retrieved after his death?

Neuroscientist Sam Harris puts it succinctly:

---

[195] Kolb and Whishaw, *Fundamentals*, 775–804.
[196] Kolb and Whishaw, *Fundamentals*, 7.
[197] Kolb and Whishaw, *Fundamentals*, 500–06.
[198] Kolb and Whishaw, *Fundamentals*, 800–02.

> "Most scientists consider themselves *physicalists*; this means, among other things, that they believe that our mental and spiritual lives are wholly dependent upon the workings of our brains. On this account, when the brain dies, the stream of our being must come to an end. Once the lamps of neural activity have been extinguished, there will be nothing left to survive."[199]

On the other hand, the Bible teaches us that our memories are supposed to survive death. In his parable of the rich man and the beggar Lazarus, Jesus says that the rich man, who found himself in hell after having died, could remember that he had brothers who were still living and he could even converse with Father Abraham in heaven (Luke 16: 19–31). When Jesus was hanging on the cross, he promised one of the criminals, who was crucified with him, that he would be in Paradise with him as soon as he died that same day (Luke 23: 43). The book of Revelation is filled with scenes of heaven where the blessed beings sing hymns and praise God.

This type of thinking is characteristic of a prescientific age, but cannot be entertained in our time anymore. If these people in heaven, with their immaterial heavenly or spiritual bodies, are supposed to have kept their memories, intelligence and other faculties, then it is a total miracle that all that information could have survived the disintegration of the brain after death. Although information in itself is not material in nature, it needs a material substrate to be stored in the form of connections between brain cells, letters in clay, figures carved in stone, symbols made with ink on paper or electronic traces on a computer's hard drive.

Many people, who regard the "spirit" or the "soul" of a human being as the seat of consciousness and memory, will declare that a deceased spiritual being will also have a consciousness and a memory

---

[199] Harris, *The End of Faith,* 208.

– just as living people. Neuroscience has demonstrated decisively, though, that a consciousness with its memories is totally dependent upon a functioning brain. Should the "spirit" or the "soul" of a departed person continue to exist in some or other higher dimension, than that spirit cannot have a brain because all brains are material in nature. No "spirit" or "soul", therefore, can ever possess consciousness or memories.

Victor Stenger points out that should an immaterial spirit be the seat of consciousness, then it is impossible to explain how a material substance, such as anesthesia or another drug, can cause unconsciousness.[200]

Palmyre Oomen, professor of philosophy at the Eindhoven University in the Netherlands declares – *a la* Aristotle and Aquinas – that the human "soul" is the "form" of the body. This "form" is composed of the organization of the body, *i e* the information regarding its composition, functioning and thoughts. To illustrate his contention that the "soul" may continue to exist after death he uses the example of a letter written in ink on a piece of paper. The contents of that letter may be transferred to a computer and even transferred to other computers via a disc or e-mail and printed out. The message or content of the letter requires "a material basis" to be stored. Oomen concludes: "I do not see any compelling reason why my organizational form, my soul, could not transfer to another carrier or Carrier." Oomen adds, "that everything we do and indeed each particular event in the world is experienced by God and remains preserved in God as its carrier. In this way, events not only come and go in a temporal flux, but they are also everlastingly treasured and summed up...., all of which makes it at least conceivable that they leave more of a 'record' than we ordinarily may think."[201]

---

[200] Stenger, *The New Atheism*, 180.
[201] Oomen, "On Brain, Soul, Self and Freedom", 388–89.

The implications of Oomen's thoughts are twofold. If my "form" can be transferred to another "carrier", it implies reincarnation – which is not a biblical idea. It also implies that God, as the ultimate "Carrier" of information, must also consist of "a material basis" for that information to be stored, which is also not a biblical notion and which is contradicted by Oomen's own ideas.

> *During my time in the ministry, I had to conduct many funeral services for deceased members of my congregations. I used to try to console the bereaved family members with the idea that there is an existence beyond the grave and that loved ones will be united again on the other side. I usually declared that the Bible describes heaven only by means of similes since we cannot really make a mental picture of this wonderful and glorious state. It is possible that I helped the family members to deal with their loss a little easier.*

All the foregoing makes it abundantly clear that the Christian doctrine of the resurrection of the body, Judgment Day and an eternal afterlife in heaven or hell, just cannot be maintained any longer. There are simply too many absurdities, improbabilities and contradictions in this doctrine for it to be acceptable or credible.

Hell and Eternal Damnation

It is a basic Christian doctrine that unrepentant sinners, evildoers, pagans, infidels and unbelievers are to be punished for all eternity in a place or condition called hell. What does the Bible tell us about this place or condition?

The Heidelberg Catechism states in Q & A 52 that Christ will "cast all his and my enemies into everlasting condemnation" on Judgment Day.

It is important to note that the concept of "hell" does not occur in the Old Testament. We do read of "Sheol", the place of the dead or underworld, which is situated somewhere below the surface of the earth (Isa 14: 15). All deceased people go there, irrespective of their lifestyles or their relationship with YHWH, the God of Israel.[202] The poet of Ps 30 cries out in vs 3 and 9:

> "O Lord, you have made my soul come again from the underworld: you have given me life and kept me from going down among the dead. (. . .) What profit is there in my blood if I go down into the under-world? Will the dust give you praise, or be a witness to your help?"

The New Testament, on the other hand, is very explicit: hell, also called the "abyss", is a place below the surface of the earth that is prepared for Satan, his gangs of angels or demons and all godless people (Luke 8: 30–31; Rom 10: 7; Rev 1: 18; Rev 11: 7; Rev 17: 8; Rev 20: 1–3, 13). They will all be condemned on Judgment Day to eternal punishment in "the lake of fire and sulphur" (Matt 25: 46; Rev 19: 20; 20: 10).

This image of hell may have been derived from a volcano, such as Vesuvius, which erupted in AD 79 and a number of other volcanoes in the Mediterranean region. Since volcanoes spew glowing molten lava from below the earth's surface it might have given people in the ancient world the idea that hell with its flames must be somewhere below.

Jesus informs us that hell will also be a place of utter darkness, and he adds that "there shall be the weeping and the gnashing of teeth" (Matt 8: 12). It is difficult to reconcile a hell with huge fires and a hell in utter darkness. It is also difficult to imagine spiritual beings with tear glands and jaws with teeth.

König admits that the idea of eternal punishment for sinners clashes with our contemporary ideas of justice, as well as the notion

---

[202] König, *Die Groot Geloofswoordeboek,* 239; Gaum et al., *Christelike Kernensiklopedie,* 442–43.

that God is a God of love.[203] It is, nevertheless, clear that there cannot be a place below the surface of the earth where the souls of dead godless people are being tortured. The earth is a solid globe. There is also nowhere else in the universe room for such a place. One might perhaps regard the biblical idea of hell as a metaphor for utter loneliness and being abandoned by God after death, the opposite of heavenly bliss in the presence of God. But, as we have already argued, it is not possible for the memories of anybody to be preserved after that person has died and his brain – where these memories are stored – has decayed, decomposed, disintegrated and ceased its actions.

A conscious existence beyond the grave is just not possible, neither in heaven, nor in hell. The notion of eternal punishment in hell contains various contradictions and absurdities and cannot, consequently, be accepted by any right-minded and rational person.

Purgatory

The Roman Catholic Church propagates, in addition, the doctrine of Purgatory. This is supposed to be a place or condition where the souls of deceased believers are being purified to get them ready for heavenly bliss. The souls of the dead are to be kept somewhere in the time between their deaths and Judgment Day or Resurrection Day, when body and soul will be reunited and taken into heaven.

It is, furthermore, taught that the good works of the living may help those who are waiting in Purgatory to lessen their pains during the process of purification. Good works include pilgrimages, the giving of alms or the payment of indulgences and these may be of benefit to deceased family members or other loved ones.

The payment of indulgences was one of the reasons why Martin Luther started the Reformation in the sixteenth century. The popes – especially Pope Leo X – needed money, much money, for the rebuilding of the St Peter's Basilica in Rome and for that reason

---

[203] König, *Die Groot Geloofswoordeboek*, 240.

indulgences were widely sold. This corrupt and superstitious practice was rightly condemned by Luther who argued that if the pope had the power to grant certain favors to the dead against the payment of money, he also had the power to do it without receiving money – which would be much more charitable. Why did he also not use his purported power to redeem all suffering souls from Purgatory instead of only a few?[204]

The dualism between body and soul, as presupposed by this doctrine, is of Greek origin. There is also no scientific proof for this idea.

Superstitions Regarding Heaven and Hell

The official doctrine of the Roman Catholic Church is that there is no salvation outside the church. This doctrine was initially formulated to distinguish between those who have been baptized into the church as believers and those unbelievers and pagans who have not been baptized and are, therefore, outside the church. This doctrine also had the effect that when somebody was excommunicated or banished from the church it was automatically taken for granted that that person was destined for hell.

During the Middle Ages in Europe, when it was assumed that everybody was a Christian and a member of the church – except for a minority of heretics, Jews and witches – people were extremely afraid of ending up in the flames of hell after having died. They had a profound superstitious dread in this regard.

This dread is well illustrated in the story of Emperor Henry IV of the Holy Roman Empire (comprising Germany and Italy in those days) and Pope Gregory VII. Henry's father had insulted Gregory's predecessor and Gregory sought revenge. He accused Henry of meddling in church affairs – which many emperors anyway did. Henry convened a synod in the German city of Worms in response,

---

[204] Duggan, "Indulgence"; Zaleski, "Purgatory".

where it was decided that the Pope's election was invalid. Gregory retaliated by excommunicating Henry and threatening anybody in the Empire who supported Henry with excommunication. Poor Henry got the shock of his life when he heard that he was excommunicated and, therefore, had to forfeit life everlasting in heaven. In order to remedy this disastrous state of affairs and to reverse his eternal fate he travelled in the mid-winter of 1077 over the Alps to the castle of Canossa in Italy where Pope Gregory was staying at the time. He was forced to stand three long days, ankle-deep in the snow, in the courtyard of the castle, clad only in the rags that were thrown at him, before Gregory allowed the frozen and humiliated emperor to appear before him and to beg for forgiveness.

It may be assumed that Emperor Henry's superstitious horror of spending an eternity in hell drove him to this drastic act, although he also wanted to regain his empire. Seven years later, Henry got his revenge by marching on Rome with his army, capturing the city and securing the enthronement of a new pope in the person of Clement III. Gregory died shortly afterwards in 1085 as a lonely exile.[205]

This superstitious dread of hell was certainly not confined to Emperor Henry alone. There are still preachers in our time who try their best to convince people to believe in Jesus as their savior by describing the horrors of hell as their horrible fate, should they refuse or fail to repent and embrace the biblical doctrine of salvation.

Prayer

What Christians Believe
The religious lives of most Christians – and Jews and Muslims – consists for a large part in praying. This is what the Heidelberg Catechism teaches regarding prayer:

---

[205] De Rosa, *The Vicars of Christ*, 62–63; Schmale, "Henry IV".

"**Question 118**: What has God commanded us to ask of him? **Answer**: All things necessary for soul and body; which Christ our Lord has comprised in that prayer he himself has taught us."

The Westminster Confession states in Ch XXI:

"III. Prayer with thanksgiving, being one special part of religious worship, is by God required of all men; and that it may be accepted, it is to be made in the name of the Son, by the help of his Holy Spirit, according to his will, with understanding, reverence, humility, fervency, faith, love, and perseverance; and, if vocal, in a known tongue."

In James 5: 15 we are promised: "And the prayer of faith will heal him who is sick, and the Lord will raise him up."

This all means that Christians are supposed to believe that it helps to pray to God. Is that what experience has confirmed?

Prayer Experiments
Francis Galton, a cousin of Charles Darwin, quoted a statistical analysis done regarding the period between 1758 and 1843 where the life spans of members of European royal families were compared to those of people in other walks of life, such as aristocrats, the gentry, officers of the armed forces and the clergy. He argued that the royal families ought to live longer than other human beings because whole congregations prayed for them publicly every Sunday. The statistics, however, showed the opposite: members of royal houses did not live longer than people in other categories; they even tended to have shorter lives. Galton concludes:

"The prayer has therefore no efficacy, unless the very questionable hypothesis be raised, that the conditions of royal life may naturally be yet more fatal, and that their influence is partly, though incompletely, neutralized by the effects of public prayers."[206]

A big prayer experiment was conducted during 2006 in the USA at a cost of $2,4 million. The leader of the experiment was Dr Herbert Benson, a cardiologist of Boston. Dr Benson and his team monitored 1 802 heart patients in six hospitals. They were divided into three groups:

- Those who were told that they may perhaps be prayed for but received no prayers;
- Those who did receive prayers and were told that they may perhaps be prayed for; and
- Those who did receive prayers and were informed of the fact.

Three congregations in cities elsewhere were tasked with praying for the patients in the second and third groups and they had to ask God for successful heart bypass surgery without complications. The patients were only known by their first names and an initial for their surnames and it was assumed that God would know exactly who were being prayed for. At the end of the experiment, it turned out that there was no difference between the first two groups. The third group, who knew that they were being prayed for, experienced significantly more complications than the other two groups – despite all the prayers on their behalf.[207]

Another prayer experiment was conducted in 2008 in Northern Ireland. About 2 300 high school pupils from Catholic and Protestant schools were tested by the abbreviated Revised Eysenck Personality

---

[206] Galton, *Statistical Inquiries into the Efficacy of Prayer*.
[207] Benson *et al*, "Study of the Therapeutic Effects of Intercessory Prayer"; Dawkins, *The God Delusion*, 62–63.

Questionnaire to ascertain their mental health. They were also asked how often they prayed. It was found that there was a positive correlation between the frequency of prayer and positive mental health on the psychoticism scale. It was found, though, that Catholic pupils who prayed most tended to score higher on the scale for neuroticism.[208]

It may be noted that the positive correlation between the frequency of prayer and the absence of psychoticism is to be expected since high school children seldom suffer from psychoses. Teenagers are, though, more prone to neuroticism. The causal link between frequency of prayer and neuroticism is not clear. Is it a case that children with neurotic tendencies tended to pray more or did the frequency of prayer cause them to become neurotic? However, it is clear that Catholic teenagers in Northern Ireland who prayed more were also those who tended to be more neurotic.

Masters et al. did a meta-analysis regarding intercession-ary prayer (IP). They concluded:

> "There is no scientifically discernable effect for IP as assessed in controlled studies. Given that the IP literature lacks a theoretical or theological base and has failed to produce significant findings in controlled trials, we recommend that further resources not be allocated to this line of research."[209]

Hodge also conducted a meta-analysis of the literature regarding investigations into the efficacy or prayer. He came to the following conclusion:

> "Thus, at this junction in time, the results might be considered inconclusive. Indeed, perhaps the most certain result stemming from this study is the following: The findings are

---

[208] Francis et al., "Prayer and Psychological Health".
[209] Masters et al., "Are there Demonstrable Effects?"

unlikely to satisfy either proponents or opponents of intercessory prayer."[210]

So much for the efficacy and value of prayer!

> *During my ministry in three congregations in the Dutch Reformed Church in South Africa, there were regular prayer meetings in times of drought. South Africa is not blessed with a high rainfall and when the rains stay away farmers suffer. They cannot plant crops and their animals starve. Whenever a drought struck, prayer meetings were held throughout the country in order to convince God to alter the weather patterns and send the rain clouds. I cannot think of any single occasion where these prayer meetings made the slightest difference to the weather patterns. The following story was told to me regarding such a prayer meeting that was to be held on a week day in a town in the Karoo, a semi-desert area in the western parts of South Africa. The minister of the congregation and his family were on their way on foot to the church when they encountered the local rabbi. He enquired why the church bells rang and why everybody was rushing to the church. The minister answered that a prayer meeting for rain was to be held, whereupon the rabbi asked: "But why haven't you brought your umbrellas along?"*

Unfounded Faith in the Power of Prayer

The organization Atheist Republic reported in August 2021: "A 46-year old mother from Toowoomba, Queens-land, Australia, was sentenced to 18 months in jail for child endangerment after claiming God would protect her child. (. . .) The mother calmly insisted that ... since she is a daughter of God, she relied upon and expected that God would heal her daughter. The mother reasoned that she never had to

---

[210] Hodge, "A Systematic Review of the Empirical Literature on Intercessory Prayer", 195.

take her children or herself to the doctor because God has promised to heal them. She was charged with gross negligence in 2019 and was sentenced on July 15th, 2021."[211]

This deluded mother evidently relied on biblical texts such as Jas 5: 15 (quoted above), Ps 91: 5–6, Ezek 34: 16, Hos 6: 1 and Mark 11: 22–23 where the faithful are promised that God will answer their prayers and will cure their illnesses. It is evident that the court did not share in this irrational belief.

Absurd Consequences

If a believer prays, he is confident that the omniscient, omnipotent and eternal God will hear his prayer and grant him his wish or satisfy his need. But – if God is really omniscient, God is supposed to be fully aware of that believer's needs and wishes and what he will say when he prays. One can therefore ask: isn't it a waste of time to pray, since God already knows what he will need in future and how he will ask at that point in time for that need to be satisfied?

If God really is omnipotent, then he is supposed to be able to change the course of history and suspend the operation of natural laws to grant you your wishes when you pray. We don't ever see this happen, though.

Christians pray for rain during a drought or health during illness. The question may, however, be asked: If the drought or the illness were sent by the almighty God with a purpose, will it help to try to convince God that he made a mistake by causing the drought or the illness? The answer to this question cannot but be a "No". If the drought and the illness were God's plan and his will, won't it amount to blasphemy to question his will and his plans? No other answer to this question than a "Yes" is possible. This all means that it is a waste of time to pray and that the very idea of prayer amounts to an absurdity.

---

[211] Atheist Republic, 01.08.2021.

The Apostle Paul gave this instruction: "Pray without ceasing" (1 Thess 5: 17). One can only wonder why this is necessary. Isn't once enough? Or is God so busy elsewhere or deaf that we have to pester him continuously?

The following eloquent comment regarding a huge prayer meeting held on Saturday, 22 April 2017, with evangelist Angus Buchan in South Africa was published online on the news service News24 by one John Aurelius:

> "Is there a godlike omniscient being 'out there' somewhere who is actually listening to you? If he truly was omniscient, all powerful, why would he need you telling him what to do? Don't you think that as an all-powerful god, he would know there was a problem? That he would fix it? Or maybe even, heaven help us, prevent it? I am glad you did not have this massive prayer gathering on Sunday, gods' day of rest... as George Carlin so eloquently put it. Bothering god on his day off... a bit selfish perhaps." [212]

These sarcastic comments are typical of how many people nowadays think.

Incompatible Biblical Ideas

It will be instructive to investigate what the Bible has to say on the subject of prayer.

The following promise was given by Jesus in Mark 11: 24 – "Therefore I tell you, all things whatever you pray and ask for, believe that you receive them, and you shall have them." Something similar is promised in Luke 11: 9 – "I tell you, keep asking, and it will be given you. Keep seeking, and you will find. Keep knocking, and it will be opened to you."

---

[212] John Aurelius, "Praying with Angus".

This was not the experience of the apostle Paul. He was afflicted by a "thorn in the flesh". He reports in this regard: "Concerning this thing, I begged the Lord three times that it might depart from me. He has said to me, 'My grace is sufficient for you, for my power is made perfect in weakness'" (2 Cor 12: 8–9). In other words: he came to the conviction that he had prayed in vain and that he had to continue living with this ailment or problem. This was also the experience of millions of Christians throughout history. They prayed for better health, better fortunes, solutions to their problems, deliverance from dangers, *etcetera*. In the vast majority of cases, nothing happened. Their prayers just went unanswered and the promises of Jesus were not fulfilled.

> *A woman with tears in her eyes consulted me as pastor. She and her husband prayed fervently that she may become pregnant. When she was 38 the miracle happened and she brought their son into this world. They were extremely thankful for God's kindness by granting them their wish. This young man, however, turned out to be a criminal monster and he was serving a prison sentence when his mother came to see me. She asked, "Why is God so cruel to answer my prayers in that way?"*

Psalm 145: 20 contains this promise: "The Lord will keep *all* his worshippers from danger" (*own emphasis*). The Jews who were held in Nazi death camps during World War II prayed daily for deliverance and relied on this promise. Only a small percentage of them survived these camps. One is, furthermore, tempted to ask: how is it possible that the eternal and omniscient God can change his mind when puny human beings ask him to do them a favor?

Because God is supposed to be eternal and unchanging his plans must similarly be eternal and unchanging –

- Psalm 33: 11 informs us: "The counsel of the Lord stands forever, the plans of His heart to all generations."
- In Ps. 135: 6, we read, "Whatever the Lord pleases He does."
- Proverbs 19:21 contains the following: "A man's heart may be full of designs, but the purpose of the Lord is unchanging."
- In Isa. 14: 24, it is written: "The Lord of hosts has sworn, saying, 'Surely, as I have thought, so it shall come to pass, and as I have purposed, so it shall stand.'"
- The Lord says in Is 46: 10, "My purpose is fixed, and I will do all my pleasure."
- Ephesians. 1: 11 tells us that it is God "who works all things according to the counsel of His will."
- Hebrews 6: 17 contains this thought: "So that when it was God's desire to make it specially clear to those who by his word were to have the heritage, that his purpose was fixed, he made it more certain with an oath."

The Bible, on the other hand, also contains the idea that God can, after all, change his mind and that, therefore, he is someone who can hear the prayers of his children and grant them their requests:

- We read the following in Gen 6: 6: "And the Lord had sorrow because he had made man on the earth, and grief was in his heart."
- Exodus 32 tells us about the golden calf which the Israelites worshipped while Moses was on the mountain receiving the Lord's commandments. This awoke God's anger and he told Moses: "I have seen this people, and indeed it is a stiff-necked people! Now therefore, let Me alone, that My wrath may burn hot against them and I may consume them." (Ex. 32: 9, 10.) Moses pleaded with the Lord not to do it. "So the Lord relented

from the harm which He said He would do to His people." (Ex. 32: 14.)

- We read that when king Hezekiah of Judah became seriously ill the Lord sent the prophet Isaiah to him with the message that he had to prepare himself for his forthcoming death. Hezekiah wept bitterly and that made the Lord change his plans. He again sent Isaiah with the following message to Hezekiah: "I have heard your prayer, I have seen your tears; surely I will heal you. On the third day you shall go up to the house of the Lord. And I will add to your days fifteen years." (2 Kgs 20: 5–6)
- Jonah was instructed by the Lord to preach in the city of Nineveh: "Yet forty days, and Nineveh shall be overthrown!" (Jon 3: 4.) The inhabitants of the city, including the king, repented. "Then God saw their works, that they turned from their evil way; and God relented from the disaster that He had said He would bring upon them, and He did not do it" (Jonah. 3: 10).

All these Scriptural quotes make it clear that God can, in fact, change his mind. This begs the question: what are we to believe regarding God? Are his plans immutable and eternal or can they be changed when we pray? The Bible contains both these totally incompatible ideas.

Let's put it this way: if you do manage to convince God that you really need something and he changes his mind by granting you your wish – which he, otherwise, would not have granted – can we still regard God to be an eternal and unchanging God? Furthermore, if he really does change his mind about something, then he must have known beforehand that he was going to change his mind and then it isn't a real change of mind because he actually planned it that way.

In other words: the belief in prayer leads to some absurd, impossible and conflicting consequences.

The only value prayer might conceivably have, is to motivate the person who is praying to do something about his own adverse conditions, in the belief that he can rely on God's help. When he succeeds in solving a problem or overcoming a serious obstacle, he will most probably ascribe that to God's assistance and that will strengthen his belief in the effectiveness of prayer – although his own efforts actually changed his circumstances.

The question may be raised whether it is permissible to pray that God will cause harm to other people. Christians may be inclined to answer that one should not pray for selfish and cruel things to happen. Nevertheless, the pious King David prayed in Ps 69: 24 regarding his enemies: "Let their eyes be darkened, so that they cannot see; and make their loins continually to shake." In other words: he begged God to cause his enemies to become blind and lame!

David also prayed the following with regards to his enemies: "Let their way be dark and full of danger; let them be troubled by the angel of the Lord. (. . .) Let destruction come on them without their knowledge; let them be taken themselves in their secret nets, falling into the same destruction" (Ps 35: 6, 8).

On the other hand, Jesus advised us to love our enemies and do good to them (Matt 5: 43–48). One can only guess what he would have said about David's prayers.

Satan and Demons

Christian Beliefs
The devil, also called Satan or Lucifer, plays an important part in the Christian belief system.

The Heidelberg Catechism and the Westminster Confession mention him numerous times. The Belgic Confession tells us in Article 12:

"**Article 12: The Creation of All Things**
He [God] has also created the angels good, that they might be his messengers and serve his elect.

"Some of them have fallen from the excellence in which God created them into eternal perdition; and the others have persisted and remained in their original state, by the grace of God.

"The devils and evil spirits are so corrupt that they are enemies of God and of everything good. They lie in wait for the church and every member of it like thieves, with all their power, to destroy and spoil everything by their deceptions.

"So then, by their own wickedness they are condemned to everlasting damnation, daily awaiting their torments.

"For that reason. we detest the error of the Sadducees, who deny that there are spirits and angels, and also the error of the Manicheans, who say that the devils originated by themselves, being evil by nature, without having been corrupted."

The conventional Christian view is, therefore –

- That Satan is a fallen angel who rebelled against God;
- That a number of other angels followed him;
- That they became devils and demons after having been expelled from heaven (Jude 1: 6; 2 Pet 2: 4); and
- That he is the source of all evil in the world and it was he, in the form of a serpent, who tempted Adam and Eve in the Paradise to disobey God and eat the fruit from the forbidden tree – thereby introducing sin and death into the human race (Gen 3; Rev 12: 9).

This viewpoint poses serious misgivings. We are repeatedly told in Genesis 1 that God created a perfectly good creation, consisting of heaven and earth. The angels were, therefore, supposed to be part of this perfectly good creation. How was it then possible for some of these perfectly good spirits, who were supposed to serve God, to become rebels and adversaries of God? What could they conceivably gain by challenging the Almighty? It just does not make any sense.

One may furthermore ask: If God is omniscient and he knows the future, why did he bother to create perfectly good beings that would, in any case, later fall into sin and cause so much trouble in his creation? He must have known what would happen when he created Lucifer and the other angels who would turn against him – why didn't he just desist from creating them?

The Old Testament

Satan plays a minor role in the Old Testament and we only encounter him in the post-exilic book of Job.

Christians usually read Genesis 2 and 3 as if Satan is the seducer of Eve, who – in turn – seduces Adam to eat of the forbidden fruit. Shawna Dolansky, however, argues: "Introduced as 'the most clever of all of the beasts of the field that YHWH God had made,' the serpent in the Garden of Eden is portrayed as just that: a serpent. Satan does not make an appearance in Genesis 2–3, for the simple reason that when the story was written, the concept of the devil had not yet been invented."[213]

Christians usually base their identification of Satan with the snake in the story of Adam and Eve on Revelation. Dolansky counters that "although the author of Revelation describes Satan as 'the ancient serpent' (Revelation 12: 9; 20: 2), there is no clear link anywhere in the Bible between Satan and Eden's talking snake."[214]

The book of Job tells the fictitious story of a pious man who suffered many calamities due to the fact that God allowed Satan to test

---

[213] Dolansky, "How the Serpent Became Satan", 4.
[214] Dolansky, "How the Serpent Became Satan", 4.

his steadfastness. It appears that Satan had unlimited access to God and may be considered to have been a member of the heavenly court:

- "Now it happened on the day when the sons of God came to present themselves before Yahweh, that Satan also came among them" (Job 1: 6).
- "Yahweh said to Satan, 'Behold, all that he [Job] has is in your power. Only on himself don't put forth your hand.' So Satan went forth from the presence of Yahweh" (Job 1: 12).

Satan is introduced as a familiar figure without any further explanation. His name in Hebrew is הַשָּׂטָן (*Ha-Shathan*) "The word *Satan* is the English transliteration of a Hebrew word for 'adversary' in the Old Testament."[215]

There is evidence that this figure was adopted into the Jewish religion from the Persian religion, which knew two chief deities, Ahura Mazda (the creator of the cosmos, the father of the pantheon and the source of light and truth) and Ahriman (an evil spirit, the antagonist of Ahura Mazda and the source of darkness and suffering).[216]

Evil spirits are also encountered in the Old Testament. These spirits are not – as is the case in the New Testament – under the reign of Satan, but they are servants of God. We read in 1 Sam 16: 14–15:

"Now the Spirit of Yahweh departed from Saul, and an evil spirit from Yahweh troubled him. Saul's servants said to him, 'See now, an evil spirit from God troubles you.'"

The word used for "spirit" is רוּחַ (ruach), which means "wind, breath, mind, spirit". It is qualified by the word רַע (ra', which means "bad,

---

[215] Encyclopaedia Britannica, "Satan".
[216] Malandra, "Iranian religion."

evil". The word for "trouble" is בעת (ba'at) and it means "to terrify, startle, fall upon, dismay, be overtaken by sudden terror". We read further on that David, the future king and successor of Saul, had to apply music therapy by playing on the harp for Saul in order to lift his spirits.

It may be asked: what were the symptoms of this affliction? A clue is given in 1 Sam 18: 29 and 1 Sam 19: 9–10. These two passages inform us:

- "Saul was yet the more afraid of David; and Saul was David's enemy continually."
- "An evil spirit from Yahweh was on Saul, as he sat in his house with his spear in his hand; and David was playing with his hand. Saul sought to strike David even to the wall with the spear; but he slipped away out of Saul's presence, and he struck the spear into the wall: and David fled, and escaped that night."

The same expression for "evil spirit" is used as in the previous passages.

At this point one may ask: is it possible to diagnose Saul with paranoid schizophrenia, due to his jealousy and suspicions regarding David? That is a real possibility. According to the DSM-5 of the American Psychiatric Association the main symptoms of this condition are delusions, hallucinations, disorganized speech and irrational suspicions. The suicide risk of sufferers is high.[217] It is, therefore, not a surprise that Saul committed suicide in the end (1 Sam 31).

A tentative diagnosis of schizophrenia in Saul is confirmed by 1 Sam 19: 24 –

---

[217] American Psychiatric Association, *DSM-5*, 99–104.

"He also stripped off his clothes, and he also prophesied before Samuel, and lay down naked all that day and all that night. Why, they say, is Saul also among the prophets?"

In Saul's case, his mental disorder – whether it was schizophrenia or something else – was attributed to an evil spirit because people in those days had no inkling of the functioning of the human brain and the human mind and they had to find a supernatural cause for Saul's strange behavior.

It has to be stressed at this point: the evil spirit that we encounter in the case of Saul was sent by God – not by Satan. This, however, does not seem to make sense; how was it possible for God, supposedly the source of all goodness, to employ an evil spirit to torment the king of Israel, his anointed son?

According to 1 Kgs 22: 21–23, God sent "a lying spirit" to cause a number of prophets to utter false prophecies. This text, likewise, contains the idea that evil spirits were in God's service and that they did not come from Satan. This text, anyway, seems irrational. Why would God, supposedly the source of all goodness and truth, deliberately cause prophets to pronounce false prophecies? It just does not make sense.

The New Testament

The word "devil" (Greek: διάβολος – *diabolos*) occurs 35 times in the New Testament and the name "Satan" (Greek: Σατανᾶς – *Satanas*, a literal transcription of the Hebrew name) is used 36 times.

Perhaps the most well-known episode in which this figure appears is the story of Jesus' temptation in the desert after he had been baptized by John. The original story in Mark, the oldest and shortest Gospel, appears in Mk 1: 12–13. We are only briefly told that Jesus stayed 40 days in the desert where he was tempted by Satan. The version of this episode in the other two Synoptic Gospels (Matt 4: 1–11 and Luke 4: 1–13) is much more detailed. This expanded story seems to be part of Q, the oldest report we have regarding Jesus' actions and words.[218] The fact that both Mark and Q – independent sources – contain reports regarding Jesus' temptation, leads to the conclusion that something of this sort really must have happened.

In these stories, we are informed that Jesus stayed without food for 40 days during his stay in the desert. When he became hungry, he was tempted by the devil who promised him various favors, should Jesus worship him. The only source for this story must have been Jesus himself since there were no independent eyewitnesses of these events. He must have related it at a later stage to his followers, from whom the authors of Mark and Q must have collected it. There is, therefore, no independent corroboration for the veracity of all the supernatural events described in Matthew and Luke.

We find the following Greek words to describe Satan:

- διάβολος (*diabolos* – a calumniator, false accuser, slanderer)
- πειράζων (*peirazon* – someone to test one maliciously, to craftily put to the proof one's feelings or judgments)

If Jesus stayed 40 days in the heat of the desert without food and water, he most probably would have succumbed to heatstroke or hyperthermia. Young describes the effects of this condition as follows:

> "Initially, there is a mild impairment of cognitive function including judgment, followed by a more profound acute confusional state. This may progress to a delirium with agitation, increased sympathetic nervous activity, and hallucinations."[219]

---

[218] Mack, *The Lost Gospel,* 82, 174–175, 179; (see also Chapter 2).
[219] Young, "Hypothermia", 611.

It is, therefore, most probable that Jesus became confused or hallucinated while fasting, in which Satan seemed to appear to him. For him, it would have been a very real experience, while we know today that a heatstroke can have a profound effect on the brain and its functioning, often causing hallucinations. Although it is probable that Jesus spent some time alone in the desert where he fasted, this appearance of the devil to him would, therefore, not have been a real historical event; it would merely have been the product of a temporarily malfunctioning brain.

In Luke 10:18, Jesus is reported as saying: "I saw Satan having fallen like lightning from heaven."

Satan is seen in the New Testament as the adversary, one who opposes another in purpose or act, the name given to the prince of evil spirits, the inveterate adversary of God and Christ. In Matt 12: 24 we again read of the Devil: "But when the Pharisees heard it, they said, 'This man does not cast out demons, except by Beelzebul, the prince of the demons.'" It is remarkable that the Devil is given the name of *Beelzebul* (Greek: Βεελζεβούλ) in this passage, since that was the name of a pagan deity in the Old Testament (2 Kgs 1: 2, 6, 16). We are informed that he is called "the prince of the demons".

Demons and demonic possession are often men-tioned in the Gospels and Acts. The Greek word for "demon" is δαιμόνιον (*daimonion*), and it means a spirit, a being inferior to God, superior to men, or evil spirits or the messengers and helpers of the devil. It is clear from Matt 4: 24 that any disease or malady for which no explanation could be given was regarded in those days with its primitive and pre-scientific world view as a case of demonic possession:

> "The report about him went forth into all Syria. They brought to him all who were sick, afflicted with various diseases and

torments, possessed with demons, epileptics, and paralytics; and he healed them."

It is necessary to explain the Greek words used in this passage:
- κακῶς (*kakos* – miserable, to be ill);
- νόσος (*nosos* – disease, sickness);
- βάσανος (*basanos* – torture, torment, acute pain)
- δαιμονίζομαι (*daimonizomai* – to be under the power of a demon)
- σεληνιάζομαι (*seleniazomai* – to be moon-struck or lunatic; to be epileptic)
- παραλυτικός (*paralytikos* – paralytic, disabled, weak of limb)

From this it is clear that in those days all sorts of diseases were seen as being caused by demons; being possessed by a demon was simply used as a synonym for being ill or suffering pain. In our time, we have enough medical knowledge to know that no disease is caused by a demon or that epilepsy is not caused by the moon or the moon goddess, Selene. There are natural explanations for all sorts of aches and pains, fever, epilepsy, paralysis *etcetera*. We don't need demons or spirits to explain medical and psychiatric conditions.

Paul reminds his readers that they are embroiled in a battle: "For our wrestling is not against flesh and blood, but against the principalities, against the powers, against the world's rulers of the darkness of this age, and against the spiritual hosts of wickedness in the heavenly places" (Eph 6: 12).

The Greek word for "in the heavenly places" (ἐπουράνιος – *epouranios*), tells us where these "spiritual hosts of wickedness" have their abode, namely in heaven. The literal meaning of this word is "heavenly, existing in heaven, of heavenly origin or nature". This word is derived from the Greek word for heaven, οὐρανός (*ouranos*). Heaven in this context may denote the heaven of clouds, the starry heaven or the abode of God and angels beyond the stars. It does seem as if Paul is not quite clear how he has to see these wicked spirits: do they come from God in heaven or are they servants of Satan? Do they reside in the air, the space above earth where the clouds and the stars are, or are they to be found in God's dwelling place beyond the stars? In which of the three heavens do they stay? It is not certain how he sees them and it appears that his thinking on this matter was rather confused.

Summary

It appears from the preceding that there is no clear-cut and consistent teaching in the Bible on how one is to understand the devil or Satan and demonic forces.

One has to remember that the Bible originated in the ancient Middle East where the authors and editors of the various biblical books were exposed to various pagan religions. All these religions were populated by pantheons of any number of gods. Natural phenomena, like rivers, trees, clouds, lightning, the sun, the moon, the stars and planets, the ocean and mountains were thought to be inhabited by spirits or gods. People had no inkling that there are, in fact, scientific or natural explanations for all observed phenomena and they thought that unseen agencies were lurking behind everything experienced in this world.

The primitive world view of the Bible, where heaven was thought to be a physical place beyond the stars and where hell and the abode of the dead was thought to be beneath the surface of the earth (Rev 20: 1–3, 10), cannot be entertained by people of our age anymore. The belief in spirits, demons, angels and the devil is, likewise, an outdated primitive way of looking at the universe.

Where the Bible provides us with perplexing and conflicting messages about Satan and demons, we are to conclude that the biblical authors did not describe any reality to us. They had to use imagined supernatural entities – spirits, demons and Satan – as explanatory agencies to make sense of a very confusing world, filled with suffering, injustice, evil, pain, illness and malice.

Parapsychology and Supernatural Phenomena

There is a discipline called parapsychology, which endeavors to investigate abnormal and supernatural phenomena, such as clairvoyance, telepathy, telekinesis, reincarnation and the possible influence of spiritual beings on human beings and earthly events. Although the first investigations of this sort already started during the 1880's, no real progress has been made up to date, despite thousands of attempts to prove the reality of psychic phenomena. The scientific world is very skeptical regarding the purported findings of the practitioners of parapsychology and criticize their lack of rigorous scientific methods to reach their findings, their biased way of interpreting vague and ambiguous data and their lack of acceptable or convincing theories to explain the data they are supposed to gather. No known and accepted scientific theories can account for the so-called findings of these investigations.

Parapsychology must, therefore, be regarded as a pseudoscience – in the same league as palmistry, astrology, and phrenology[220].

All this amounts to the conclusion that there is no scientific proof for the existence of spiritual beings such as angels or demons. Demonic possession is not recognized by the psychiatric and psychological communities as real conditions and so-called cases of demonic possession can always be explained as real psychological or psychiatric disorders.[221]

In other words: there are no devils and no demons and no evil spirits. Satan can, at utmost, be regarded as a personification of all that

---

[220] Stenger, *The New Atheism*, 182–83; Encyclopaedia Britannica, "Parapsychological phenomenon".

[221] American Psychiatric Association, *DSM-5*.

is evil, bad, horrible, wrong and cruel. That evil exists is beyond dispute. That an evil personality from a supposedly spiritual world is ultimately responsible for all the suffering, crime, injustice and pain in this world cannot be accepted. Evil can be adequately explained as the result of human nature, which includes greed, selfishness, malice, aggression, cruelty, dishonesty, superstition and ignorance.

Exorcism

Unfortunately, grievous harm is often being done when people with genuine medical and psychological disorders are subjected to exorcism, a serious form of mental torture. They get the promise from these exorcists that their problems and maladies will vanish – and when no lasting cure is effected, their cancer, heart disorder, festering wounds, arthritis, depression, anxiety, dementia, bipolar disorder, psychosis or phobias just get worse.

> *I have witnessed more than one exorcism session in a charismatic church where imaginary devils or demons are being chased out of people suspected of harboring one or more of these evil spirits. There is much shouting at the devils to scare them away, laying on of hands, anointing with olive oil, singing, ecstatic and loud prayers (as if God is deaf), dancing and other bizarre rituals. All this amounts to great theatre and entertainment for those who believe in this type of nonsense. Scenes like these reminded me of the prophets of Baal who were locked in a contest with the Prophet Elijah to show which deity was the true God, Baal or YHWH. The prophets of Baal called with loud voices to him for many hours and even cut themselves with blood gushing from their bodies – all to no avail (1 Kgs 18: 26–29).*

Conclusion

To conclude: all the Christian doctrines discussed in this chapter have been shown to be riddled with inconsistencies, contradictions, absurdities, improbabilities and impossible claims. No educated person of the twenty-first century can accept these irrational and misguided mental constructs anymore.

When scrutinized objectively, the Christian faith does seem to be rather strange, irrational and filled with superstitions – the same as the religions of the ancient world. It becomes apparent that the whole of the traditional Christian religion with all its doctrines lacks any credibility.

The various theological "schools" all try to even out all these inconsistencies and absurdities in order to formulate a more or less coherent intellectual system. However, they do not achieve this and that is the reason why these "schools" differ so much form each other. The confusing and irrational pronouncements to be found in the Bible may lead to any number of competing and mutually exclusive theological systems.

At this point, one is inclined to ask: why are so many people on earth religious? Why do so many people believe in God or gods, in spirits and in an afterlife? The next chapter will deal with these questions.

CHAPTER 4

RELIGION EXPLAINED

Initial Explanations

A Definition of Religion

Although Christianity is the most successful religion in history, it is, nevertheless, one of a wide range of religions in the world. That begs the question: why are people religious? Why do people worship God or the gods?

Religion is an almost universal phenomenon in humanity. No known civilization from the past or the present has had atheistic or agnostic foundations. At present, the percentage of the world's population that can be regarded as agnostics and atheists is relatively small – although this percentage is definitely increasing (see chapter 1).

But one has to ask: why are not more people atheists or agnostics and skeptics? How did it come about that most world religions have existed for centuries and even millennia?

Before all these questions can be answered, it may perhaps be profitable to get a general description of the phenomenon of religion. Religion can be described or defined as –

> "... human beings' relation to that which they regard as holy, sacred, spiritual, or divine. Religion is commonly regarded as consisting of a person's relation to God or to gods or spirits. Worship is probably the most basic element of religion, but moral conduct, right belief, and participation in religious institutions are generally also constituent elements of the

religious life as practiced by believers and worshipers and as commanded by religious sages and scriptures."[222]

Since overt atheism, agnosticism and religious skepticism only became possible in the Western World during the eighteenth century with the advent of the age of enlightenment and democracy, there were various attempts to explain the roots or origins of religion. The explanations of four well-known atheists of the nineteenth century are briefly presented here:

Ludwig Feuerbach

The German philosopher, Ludwig Feuerbach (1804–1872), attained notoriety for his atheism and materialism. His dictum, "*Man ist was er ißt*" (man is what he eats), became famous.

He wrote extensively about religion and criticized Christianity. For him, God is a mere fantasy and nothing but an outward projection of man's inner nature. Religion can be explained as man's awareness of infinity.[223]

Karl Marx

Karl Marx (1818–1887), whose philosophy, dialectical materialism, became the intellectual foundation for communism, was influenced by Feuerbach, as well as by the idealism of Hegel.

Marx saw history as a series of phases, consisting of clashes between social classes.

---

[222] Encyclopaedia Britannica, "Religion".
[223] Encyclopaedia Britannica, "Feuerbach, Ludwig".

During the capitalistic phase, a minority of capitalists has control over all the means of production, while the worker class suffers in poverty. These poor workers seek solace in religion, which promises a better afterlife.

He called religion the "opium of the masses", the drug that makes them forget their misery. Religion will, however, become superfluous when the workers' class will be able to remove all class distinctions through a revolution and create a socialist paradise.[224]

Friedrich Nietzsche

Friedrich Nietzsche (1844–1900) became famous for his slogan: "God is dead". According to him, life in itself is meaningless and people endeavor to find meaning in life by inventing a god, a supernatural being who rules the cosmos and had a purpose with each person's life. When it became apparent, though, that life can become meaningful without religion, people decided to kill God.[225]

Sigmund Freud

The founder of psycho-analysis, Sigmund Freud (1856–1939), gave a psychological explanation for religion. He explained belief in a deity as meeting the needs for a projected father-figure, who served to embody the cultural ideals of control and manipulation.

Freud was critical of the potential for faith to be used as a denial of emotional health, and suggested that the more mature person should face his fate without recourse to an imagined divine personage, which

---

[224] Feuer and McLellan, "Karl Marx".
[225] Magnus, "Nietzsche, Friedrich".

amounts to escapism.²²⁶

He was of the opinion that the participation in religious ceremonies is nothing but an "obsessional neurosis". Religion and an obsessional neurosis are, according to him, both the products of feelings of guilt due to the repression of sexual instincts.²²⁷

Evaluation

The theories of Feuerbach, Marx, Nietzsche and Freud were little more than educated guesses, which did not rest on any solid scientific empirical evidence. Their insights, that religion satisfies certain human needs may, though, be seen as a valuable contribution. This idea will be pursued later in this chapter.

Personification

Detection of Patterns and Agents

The most persuasive explanation for the phenomenon of religion is to be found in the fact that the human brain is hard-wired to personify all phenomena encountered in the world. This tendency is coupled to a propensity to detect patterns and to ascribe human volition and motives to non-human phenomena – animals and inanimate objects.

Shermer points out that the human brain is programmed to detect patterns because the individual's safety may depend upon it. This faculty is so fine-tuned that humans often detect patterns where there are none. We see faces in the clouds, we hear voices when the wind blows, we detect dangers where there are none and we imagine regularities when there is nothing of the sort.²²⁸

It was found that when people were given L-Dopa, the medication used for patients with Parkinson's disease and which

---

²²⁶ Helsel, "Faith", 315.
²²⁷ Freud, *The Origins of Religion*.
²²⁸ Shermer, *The Believing Brain*, 50–86.

increases the levels of the neurotransmitter dopamine in the brain, the tendency to detect patterns where none existed, was enhanced. This mechanism is related to the fact that an overproduction of dopamine due to the use of certain drugs, such as cannabis, may lead to hallucinations – often with a religious content – and even psychosis.[229]

In addition, we have the propensity to regard non-human phenomena as "agents" – entities with a will, intentions, purposes and even a mind. Natural phenomena and processes such as the stars, the ocean, mountains, trees, lakes, lightning, procreation, rain, animals, *etcetera* are regarded as beings endowed with invisible spirits – just as humans regard themselves as being comprised of body and spirit. The world is, therefore, haunted by spirits, demons, ghosts, angels and gods. Our brains are also hard-wired to imagine and detect all sorts of "presences" – ghosts, spirits, angels and other supernatural agents – during abnormal circumstances, such as extreme cold, lack of oxygen, danger, exhaustion or sleep deprivation. This phenomenon occurs especially during a near-death experience or an out-of-the-body experience when the person suffers from anoxia, a lack of oxygen.[230]

According to Dawkins, humans tend to assign purpose to inanimate objects. This is how our brains were programmed by evolution. We had to be ready at all times to face predators and other dangers or to flee. There was no time to make sure what the intentions of the predator was and it had to be assumed that it had the purpose of making a meal of us. Immediate action was, therefore, necessary. Likewise, purpose was automatically ascribed to inanimate objects, just to be on the safe side.[231]

A manual of neuropsychology explains that the brains of primates, humans included, contain so-called mirror neurons, which enable them to have empathy with others, to mimic the others' behavior

---

[229] Shermer, *The Believing Brain,* 120–21.
[230] Shermer, *The Believing Brain,* 87–110.
[231] Dawkins, *The God Delusion,* 183–84.

and to read and understand their intentions and emotions. This is the underlying neurological structure for personification. "The attribution of intentions to others is so automatic in people that we humans seem compelled to attribute intentions and other psychological motives to nonhumans and even to abstract animations."[232]

This all explains why primitive people experienced natural phenomena as being inhabited by spirits and having the same emotions and motivations as themselves. This explains why pagan religions devised gods for every aspect of the world – the ocean, the sky, the moon, the sun, starry formations, the weather, fertility, *etcetera*.

The human tendency to anthropomorphize animals and inanimate objects is especially visible in children. They are easily entertained by fictional animals in cartoons and stories. Characters such as Donald Duck, Mickey Mouse, Winnie the Pooh and numerous other animals and even animated robots such as R2D2 are part and parcel of contemporary Western culture. Of course, ducks, mice, teddy bears and robots cannot talk and think as we do, but these human characteristics are attributed to these characters and especially children experience them to be credible. The same mechanism was at work when people created spirits and gods inhabiting natural phenomena.

The ultimate act of personification, seeking patterns and looking for agents, occurs when humans ascribe a soul or a spirit to the world or the universe as a whole. This is how a single God must have been invented.[233]

Gerald Benedict finds that "fertility goddess cults" are probably "the earliest religions of which we have evidence in the form of artifacts and artwork." He adds that early religions deified "most, if not all aspects of nature." This form of religion is called "animism" since all elements of nature were seen as being animated by spirits.[234]

---

[232] Kolb and Whishaw, *Fundamentals*, 582.
[233] Shermer, *The Believing Brain*, 165.
[234] Benedict, *The God Debate*, 15, 17–18.

Grayling writes that there is a certain evolutionary process visible in the development of gods. It started when people saw spirits in all natural phenomena. When understanding of natural phenomena grew, these spirits became gods on mountain tops, such as Olympus or Mount Sinai. When people became even more sophisticated, the gods on the mountain tops were relocated to the sky into a hypothetical heaven.[235]

In our time, relics of this tendency are still part of our culture. The ancients identified the visible planets with certain deities and we have retained their names in their Latin translations (Mercury, Venus, Mars, Jupiter and Saturn). The ancients also identified the constellations in the starry sky with mythical figures and we still use their Greek and Latin names (*e.g.,* Andromeda, Perseus, Orion, Hercules, the Twins [Gemini] or Castor and Pollux, Leo, Pegasus, Coma Berenices and Sagittarius).

Natural-born Dualists

Dawkins reminds us that research has shown that humans, and especially children, are natural or instinctive dualists and teleologists. We experience the "me" inside ourselves as being different from our physical bodies and regard it as something immaterial or spiritual since it cannot be localized precisely. We see ourselves, therefore, as composed of two different elements, body and soul – a duality.[236]

We also tend to assign purpose (Greek: τελος – *telos,* goal, purpose) to everything in the world – hence teleology, the tendency to look for purposes. If we assign a purpose to the universe as a whole, we easily think that it was created for God's pleasure.

Shermer agrees with Dawkins. He quotes statistics to show that a majority of Americans believe in an afterlife, including heaven and hell. He explains that this belief is connected to the fact that human

---

[235] Grayling, *The God Argument,* 36.
[236] Dawkins, *The God Delusion,* 180–81.

beings are "natural-born dualists". They experience their inner core, their "ego", their self-consciousness, as something different from their bodies. They believe, therefore, that they are composed of a body and a soul or spirit, that they are a duality. They also find it difficult to imagine a time when this soul or spirit will not be somewhere and, therefore, they are convinced that there must be an afterlife. Humans also possess the faculty of imagination and it is easy to imagine an existence after physical death in a wonderful heaven.[237]

According to Benedict, the fear of death must have been a powerful impulse for the development and power of religion. People were always aware of the temporary and fragile nature of life and they had various myths regarding an existence beyond the grave.[238] He adds that –

> "we can reasonably conclude that human beings have always had the need to believe in something other than themselves, but in a way that fosters an understanding of the nature and meaning of life. Until relatively recently, this need to believe and understand has been determined by the struggle to survive physically, and it remains so in the world's poorer countries."[239]

People who have experienced an out-of-the body experience or a near-death experience very often experience hallucinations with a religious character and they believe that they have had encounters with God, Jesus, deities, angels, deceased loved ones and other supernatural entities.[240] The reports of their visions must certainly have fed and enhanced the belief in an afterlife in all civilizations.

---

[237] Shermer, *The Believing Brain*, 143–45.
[238] Benedict, *The God Debate*, 19–21.
[239] Benedict, *The God Debate*, 24–25.
[240] Cunningham, *Decoding the Language of God*, 210.

This state of affairs must also be the reason why adherents of so many animistic religions revere and interact with their ancestors. They are convinced that these ancestors, although in the grave, are actually still around and can influence events in the world of the living.

Dreams

All people dream several times every night; they just don't always remember their dreams.

In pre-scientific ages, people regarded dreams as the wanderings of their spirits through strange places and experiencing bizarre events. Often, these dreams were seen as prophetic in nature or as predictions of the future. Martin is convinced that dreams played a major role in the origins of religion. People saw their dreams as an indication of a spirit world filled with gods, demons and deceased loved ones or ancestors. These were, after all, the beings they encountered during their dreams.[241]

The dreams of several biblical characters were interpreted as revelations from God. The following examples come to mind:

- Jacob (Gen 28: 10-12);
- Laban (Gen 31: 24);
- Joseph (Gen 37: 5);
- Pharaoh (Gen 41: 1-13);
- Samuel (1 Sam 3);
- King Solomon (1 Ki 3: 5);
- King Nebuchadnezzar (Dan 2: 1-13);
- Joseph (Matt 1: 19-20 & 2: 13);
- The wise men from the East (Matt 2: 12); and
- Mrs Pontius Pilate (Matt 27: 13, 19).

---

[241] Martin, *Counting Sheep*, 188–90.

Scientific investigations since the fifties of the previous century have demystified the phenomenon of dreaming. Dreams were found to be simply products of the brain, occurring in man and higher animals. They happen several times per night during so-called rapid-eye-movement (REM) sleep and they are a mechanism the brain uses to sort through memories, consolidating important recollections and deleting irrelevant memories, to process unpleasant feelings and to deal with problems.[242]

> *During the years of my active ministry, I often had to console those who had lost loved ones through death. They very often declared that they still felt the presence of those who had departed and that they regularly dreamt of them. This certainly is a natural neurological mechanism to help the individual come to grips with a serious loss. These feelings and dreams confirmed their belief that their loved ones were not really gone – they have only "passed on" to the "other side".*

In other words: there is nothing supernatural about dreams and they are certainly not divine communications or excursions or expeditions of the spirit of the sleeper. They explain, though, why people are "natural-born dualists" and inclined to believe in gods, spirits and an existence beyond the grave when their wandering "spirits" meet deceased loved ones or other beings during the night.

Altered States of Consciousness

Hallucinations
Hallucinations may be "defined as perceptual experiences that occur in the absence of external sensory input. They can emerge in any of the sensory modalities and arise from a wide range of conditions as well

---

[242] Kolb and Wishaw, *Fundamentals,* 769–70; Martin, *Counting Sheep,* 99–104, 241–54.

as in different states of normal consciousness."[243] They may be caused by psycho-tic disorders, such as schizophrenia or bipolar disorder, by hallucinogens (psychedelic drugs), hypnosis, brain injuries, anoxia, epilepsy, malnutrition and dehydration.

These hallucinations are caused by an overproduction of the neurotransmitters dopamine or serotonin and their effects are often ascribed to the influence of a demon or a spirit. During hallucinations the distinction between reality and fantasy becomes blurred and the person has the belief that he experiences something real, although the visions he sees or the voices he hears are simply the effect of his altered state of consciousness on the brain.[244]

A strong case can be made that certain biblical figures had hallucinatory visions or revelations – including Jesus of Nazareth.

Jesus and the Biblical Prophets

Jesus spent forty days in the desert without food and drink. This incident has to be explored in more detail.

Jesus departed for the desert after having been baptized by John and saw the heavens opened, while experiencing the presence of the Holy Spirit. During this time, where he tried to make sense of the events surround-ding his baptism, he reportedly experienced temptations by Satan, but afterwards was cared for by angels (Mark 1: 9–12; Matt 3: 13–4: 11; Luke 3: 21–22; Luke 4: 1–13).

This period of forty days must be greatly exaggerated. Nobody can survive more than ten days without water, especially not in a hot desert environment where Jesus experienced these temptations.[245] The period of forty days is rather a symbolic number, a reminder of the

---

[243] Hoffman et al., "Transcranial Magnetic Stimulation", 500–01.

[244] Goetz, "Hallucinogens", 503–04; Temes, *Hypnosis*, 35–36, 49–50; Clark et al., *Pharmacology*, 104.

[245] Craighead and Nemeroff, *The Corsini Encyclopedia*, 1587; Swaab, *Wij Zijn ons Brein*, 247; Encyclopaedia Britannica, "Dehydration".

forty years the Israelites purportedly had spent in the desert after escaping from Egypt. It is also a reminder of Moses who reportedly stayed forty days on the mountain without eating and drinking, while receiving God's commandments (Ex 34: 28).

Anyway, if Jesus fasted for an extended period of time and consequently suffered from malnutrition, as well as becoming dehydrated, it is very possible and highly probable that he experienced hallucinations of a religious nature, in which he struggled with demonic forces, had encounters with angels and which he regarded as a confirmation of his calling from God to establish the kingdom of God in Israel – in other words, a theocracy, free from Roman oppression.

The "angels" who cared for him afterwards were quite likely Bedouins who found the disoriented, dehydrated and undernourished Jesus somewhere in the desert and nursed him back to health.

These experiences must have so real for Jesus that he afterwards told his friends and disciples about it – and the compilers of the Gospels must have collected these stories from people who heard it from Jesus or from his friends or disciples.

We read in the book of Genesis that the patriarch Abram (later called Abraham) held various conversations with God. We must ask: was he hearing voices in his head – just as people with schizophrenia often do? These voices even told him to sacrifice his own son, Isaac – which must be classified as a case of a religious delusion, coupled with serious child abuse (Gen 22).

Moses, the Israelite lawgiver, received a number of revelations from God. The best-known example is his solo meeting with God on Mount Sinai where he received the Ten Command-ments – that is, to say, if the receipt of the Ten Commandments happened as reported.

The first six chapters of his book record the prophet Isaiah's early ministry and visions of God, who sat on his throne and was surrounded by seraphim – hybrid human-animal-bird figures – which is typical of people who hallucinate.

Ezekiel, the priest, received the call to become a prophet during a vision "in the thirtieth year, in the fourth month, on the fifth day" — perhaps July 31, 593 BC. He, likewise, had visions of strange beings, which he interpreted as revelations from God.[246]

Graham Hancock quotes Beny Shanon, professor of psychology at the Hebrew University of Jerusalem, who theorized that the prophet Ezekiel had these visions while under the influence of psychoactive substances. Shanon experimented himself with such substances and claims to have had similar experiences.[247]

The prophet Daniel had strange visions or dreams while asleep. In chapter 7 of his book, he describes hideous beasts and a vision of God on his throne. Chapter 8 mentions a ram and a goat fighting, but also a vision of God. Daniel reports that these visions made him sick. According to chapter 10 he fasted for three weeks and then had more visions of God and of the archangel Michael. Other prophets from the Old Testament claimed to have had direct contact with God, who ordered them to convey certain messages to the Israelites.

John of Patmos, the prophet who wrote the book of Revelation, probably also experienced altered states of consciousness while having visions. He repeatedly had an experience of being "in the Spirit" (Rev 1: 10; Rev 4: 2; Rev 17: 3; Rev 21: 10). His altered form of consciousness could not have been a trance in which he became unconscious – it must only have been a light form of hypnosis that enabled him to concentrate strongly on his visions.

Something similar seems to have happened with Muhammad, the prophet of Islam. The description of his first revelation or vision on mount Hira on the night of 17 Ramadan AD 610, as given by Karen Armstrong, makes it clear that he saw and heard an angel, that he fell trembling on the ground and that he was overcome by fear for the unknown god, Allah. He later repeatedly had similar visions.

---

[246] Rylaarsdam, "Biblical Literature".
[247] Hancock, *Supernatural*, 517–19.

According to Muslims, these were genuine supernatural events, but it might equally well have been a series of trances with hallucinations. After all, Armstrong relates that Muhammad had the habit of praying and meditating on the mountain before his first vision and that he had clear dreams of Allah appearing to him.[248]

Possible Explanations

How are these visions and revelations of the prophets to be explained? Biblical prophets, it seems, had visions and revelations, which "may be induced by a variety of techniques: by meditation, by mystico-magical formulas and gestures ..., by music ..., by drumming, dancing, or the ingestion of intoxicants or narcotics."[249]

Ahlström writes:

> "The nature of prophecy is twofold: either inspired (by visions or revelatory auditions), or acquired (by learning certain techniques). In many cases both aspects are present. The goal of learning certain prophetic techniques is to reach an ecstatic state in which revelations can be received. That state might be reached through the use of music, dancing, drums, violent bodily movement, and self-laceration. The ecstatic prophet is regarded as being filled with the divine spirit, and in this state the deity speaks through him. Ecstatic oracles, therefore, are generally delivered by the prophet in the first-person singular pronoun and are spoken in a short, rhythmic style."[250]

Religious ecstasy may be described as –

---

[248] Armstrong, *The Battle for God,* 82–89.
[249] Encyclopædia Britannica, "Prophet".
[250] Ahlström, "Prophecy".

"the experience of an inner vision of God or of one's relation to or union with the divine. Various methods have been used to achieve ecstasy, which is a primary goal in most forms of religious mysticism. The most typical consists of four stages: (1) purgation (of bodily desire); (2) purification (of the will); (3) illumination (of the mind); and (4) unification (of one's being or will with the divine). Other methods are: dancing (as used by the Mawlawīyah, or whirling dervishes, a Muslim Ṣūfī sect); the use of sedatives and stimulants (as utilized in some Hellenistic mystery religions); and the use of certain drugs, such as peyote, mescaline, hashish, LSD, and similar products (in certain Islamic sects and modern experimental religious groups). Most mystics, both in the East and in the West, frown on the use of drugs because no permanent change in the personality (in the mystical sense) has been known to occur.

"In certain ancient Israelite prophetic groups, music was used to achieve the ecstatic state, in which the participants, in their accompanying dancing, were believed to have been seized by the hand of Yahweh, the God of Israel, as in the case of Saul, the 11th-century-BC king of Israel."[251]

Due to all these observations it seems likely that near-death experiences and out-of-the body experiences (NDE's and OBE's) may also be responsible for the altered states of consciousness in biblical figures – as well as adherents of other religions. These experiences can be caused by anoxia, the electrical stimulation of the temporal lobes of the brain and certain drugs, such as LSD and ketamines. During these events, people very often have religious experiences in which they "see" a bright light, God, Jesus or other deities or spirits, while receiving messages from these beings.[252]

---

[251] Encyclopaedia Britannica, "Ecstasy".
[252] Cunningham, *Decoding the Language of God*, 210.

It may even be argued that no genuine religious vision or revelation ever occurred. Those persons who supposedly had contact with a deity or a supernatural being merely experienced hallucinations, delusions or other altered states of consciousness, such as intoxication by a drug, an OBE or NDE, a trance (hypnosis), a psychosis, dehydration or epilepsy – all the products of chemical and electrical processes in the brain.

In ages gone by, quite a number of people must have recovered from a NDE in which they had experiences or hallucinations, which they then interpreted as being spiritual in nature. Their reports to their friends, family and others must have convinced people of the reality of an afterlife and that gods and spirits exist.

> *My deceased mother, who was very religious, had an OBE when she was in her fifties. She fainted one day after a stay in hospital, due to blood loss. During this time, she had a vision of God and of heaven. Fortunately, I was at home at that time and could pick her up and carry her to her bed, where she regained consciousness. This episode influenced her life profoundly and she constantly longed to re-experience that heavenly bliss.*

William Temple (1881–1944), who was archbishop of Canterbury during the last two years of his life, is reported as saying:

> "If you talk to God you are praying; if God talks to you, you have schizophrenia."[253]

Thomas Paine was of the opinion that "prophesying is lying professionally", since nobody is able to verify or confirm the revelations or visions of a prophet.[254]

---

[253] Humphreys, *In God we Doubt*, 219.
[254] Paine, *The Age of Reason*, 129.

Evidence of Prehistoric Visions and Trances

In his book, *Supernatural*, Graham Hancock argues that ancient cave paintings in Europe, depicting strange beings, as well as more recent rock paintings of the San in South Africa, were all done by shamans after having experienced altered states of consciousness. During these states, they had visions of spiritual beings – which must have formed the basis or origin of various religious ideas and systems. These states or trances could be achieved by the use of psychedelic drugs derived from various plants, as well as chanting, dancing, dehydration and sleep deprivation.[255]

Hancock argues that the ingestion of psychedelic drugs, which produced these visions with a religious content, must be related to the increased production of the neurotransmitters dopamine and serotonin in the brains of those who experienced these trances. He adds that these trances or altered states of consciousness enabled the participants to get access to real or genuine religious experiences and alternative realities, which were not simply hallucinations.[256]

The fact that the shamans of various ages experienced very similar visions may be due to the way the human brain is hard-wired, but it is also proof for him that they all had access "to the same otherworlds and spirits" and with "alternative realities."[257]

According to him, there is evidence that the ancient Greek mystery religion, practiced at Eleusis, was based upon the ingestion of a potion containing an ingredient akin to LSD, which induced religious visions in those who participated in its rituals.[258]

Mike Pitts cites research that suggests that people who lived at the time when structures such as Stonehenge in Britain were being built, about 5 000 years ago, knew "altered states of mind", which

---

[255] Hancock, *SupernaturL,* 163–65, 497, 563–64.
[256] Hancock, *Supernatural,* 519, 577.
[257] Hancock, *Supernatural,* 567, 577.
[258] Hancock, *Supernatural,* 524–25.

could have been induced by various types of herbal drugs or other means. Signs of this are contained in the artistic designs found on pottery from that age, which are typical of the patterns seen during trances.[259]

Graham Phillips has the interesting hypothesis that the "burning bush", which Moses saw and where he encountered God must have been the weed *datura stramonium* – also known as "thorn apples."[260] This does not seem to be too far-fetched. This plant, which originated in India and was used as a medicine for epilepsy and for inducing religious experiences due to its hallucinatory ingredients such as scalopomine, was well-known through-out the ancient world. It grows mostly in dry areas, including the Sinai Peninsula.[261]

The burning bush that Moses encountered while tending the flocks of his father-in-law, is described as follows in Ex 3: 2 –

> "And the angel of the Lord was seen by him in a flame of fire coming out of a thorn-tree: and he saw that the tree was on fire, but it was not burned up."

Phillips speculates that the text of this verse got altered with its transmission and editing through the ages and that the "burning" experienced by Moses must have been due to the fact that the chemicals in the seeds and the leaves of this bush cause the tongue to feel burnt and that a burning sensation is also experienced throughout the body. Moses' encounter with God may, therefore, have simply been the hallucinations he got by chewing the seeds or brewing the leaves.[262]

Experiments with psilocybin, the active ingredient in "magic mushrooms", with terminally ill cancer patients, led to "remarkable"

---

[259] Pitts, *Hengeworld*, 235–36.
[260] Phillips, *The Moses Legacy*, 276–78.
[261] Seebauer, "Datura stramonium"; Arnett, "Jimson Weed".
[262] Phillips, *The Moses Legacy*, 276–78.

results. A single high dose of this drug caused a long-lasting effect on the state of mind of these patients – as well as in healthy persons. This drug lifted their depression and despair in the face of death and helped them to experience their lives as meaningful. Dr Stephen Ross, director of addiction psychiatry at NYU Langone Medical Centre explained that psilocybin activates a sub-type of serotonin receptor in the brain. "Our brains are hard-wired to have these kinds of experiences – these alterations of consciousness. We have endogenous chemicals in our brain. We have a little system that, when you tickle it, it produces these altered states that have been described as spiritual states, mystical states in different religious branches."[263]

Religious experiences may also be caused by electrical stimulation of the brain (such as during a thunder storm) or by a lack of oxygen (such as during an epileptic fit). When certain parts of the brain are surgically removed, these experiences disappear.[264]

Whether these people really did make contact with an alternative or spiritual reality is, of course, another matter. Benedict correctly remarks that arguments for the existence of God relying on religious experiences may be convincing for those who had them, but due to the fact that they are "subjective and incapable of validation", they may not convince skeptics.[265]

Revelations
Thomas Paine had the following comment regarding the idea of divine revelations through the Holy Scriptures:

> "It is a contradiction in terms and ideas to call anything a revelation that comes to us at second hand, either verbally or in writing. Revelation is necessarily limited to the first

---

[263] Carbonaro et al. *"Magic Mushrooms"*.
[264] Stenger, *The New Atheism,* 180.
[265] Benedict, *The God Debate,* 110.

communication. After this, it is only an account of something which that person says was a revelation made to him; and though he may find himself obliged to believe it, it cannot be incumbent on me to believe it in the same manner, for it was not a revelation made to me, and I have only his word for it that it was made to him ... When I am told that the Koran was written in Heaven, and brought to Mahomet by an angel, the account comes to near the same kind of hearsay evidence and second hand authority as the former. I did not see the angel myself, and therefore I have a right not to believe it."[266]

In other words: we only have the word of prophets and other seers that God spoke to them; there is no independent corroboration or objective evidence that such a revelation ever occurred.

Supernaturalism

A Plurality of Supernatural Forces

Human beings in primitive societies tried to make sense of the world in which they lived. They had no rational explanations for a range of natural phenomena. They, therefore, saw these phenomena as the result of magical or "supernatural" forces – deities, spirits and demonic forces. This is also the stance taken by biblical authors.

Man in a pre-scientific age had no idea what the nature of natural phenomena and forces were. Nobody had a rational explanation for lightning, rain, the heat of the sun, the phases of the moon, solar and lunar eclipses, the tides of the ocean, how plants could grow from seeds, how new life could be created through the act of copulation, various illnesses, the nature of the stars, *etcetera*. The only explanation for these phenomena could only be that they must have a

---

[266]Paine, *The Age of Reason*, 3.

"supernatural" origin, that gods, spirits or even demons and magicians were responsible.

Something of this nature, for instance, is to be found in Psalm 77. The poet was initially rather depressed and went through a crisis of faith; he felt that God had forgotten him. But then he experienced a thunderstorm and that restored his faith in God. In other words: for him the violent storm was a manifestation and affirmation of God's power and presence.

The word "supernatural" was placed in quotation marks above on purpose because people in ancient times did not see a discontinuity between nature and anything outside of or above nature. For them, the whole cosmos was one interconnected system.

Deities, spirits and demons were part and parcel of everyday reality, although they were invisible or ungraspable; they simply belonged to parts of the cosmos over which humans had no control. In those times, people had no idea how natural forces worked or that natural laws operated throughout the universe. For them, the whole cosmos was under the influence of the gods who could do whatever they liked.

In our secularized civilization we don't see a thunderstorm anymore as a supernatural or magical event. All educated people know that lightning flashes are merely discharges of high voltage static electricity. We know that the heat of the sun is produced by nuclear explosions inside the sun where hydrogen is converted into helium; the sun is not a deity or a supernatural entity. We know that a solar eclipse happens when the moon moves in front of the sun and blocks the sun's light.

Jackson agrees with Sir James Frazer who divided human history into three ages: the age of magic, the age of religion and the age of science. Advanced civilizations on earth have entered the age of science where people of higher intelligence are seeking rational explanations for all phenomena. This was preceded by the age of religion during which everybody in the civilized world adhered to some or other religion, especially the more sophisticated religions such as Judaism, Christianity, Islam, Buddhism or Hinduism, but also the paganism of the ancient Babylonians, Egyptians, Greeks and Romans. The decay of the age of religion in the West can be seen in the tendency that the more intelligent university students do not enter the ministry anymore, but are choosing other professions. The first age, the age of magic, is characterized by polytheism and animism, the explanation of all natural forces as the result of the use of magic by sorcerers, witches, gods and spirits. This age still lingers on in primitive societies in remote spots on earth, but certain aspects of this age were incorporated into the age of religion.[267]

Mithen cites many instances where archaeologists unearthed the remains of people from the Stone Age and investigated the rock art of ancient humans. They concluded that these humans, who lived millennia ago, must have had a belief in magic, spirits and other supernatural beings, as well as an existence beyond the grave – an elementary form of religion. It seems probable that some individuals must have claimed a special connection with the spirit world and were regarded as shamans or sooth-sayers. We have no way of knowing exactly what these people believed, but it could have been something similar to contemporary societies of hunter-gatherers.[268]

Monotheism

That the ancient Israelites came with the idea of a single God (in other words: monotheism), was rather revolutionary in those days when polytheism was the rule. Some Greek philosophers, such as Aristotle and Cleanthes, though, also had a notion of a single creator of the world. Aristotle called him the "unmoved mover" and "final cause" of

---

[267] Frazer, *The Golden Bough*, 932; Jackson, "Man, God and Civilization", 147–49.
[268] Mithen, *The Prehistory of the Mind*, 198–202.

the world.[269] Various animistic religions also harbor the notion of a single supreme god who created everything, but who isn't involved with the day-to-day affairs of men. For them, the spirits of the ancestors are much more important.[270]

According to Thomas Paine, Christianity does not differ in essence from pagan religions:

> "It is curious to observe how the theory of what is called the Christian Church, sprung out of the tail of the heathen mythology. A direct incorporation took place in the first instance, by making the reputed founder to be celestially begotten. The trinity of gods that then followed was no other than a reduction of the former plurality, which was about twenty or thirty thousand. The statue of Mary succeeded the statue of Diana of Ephesus. The deification of heroes changed into the canonization of saints. The Mythologists had gods for everything; the Christian Mythologists had saints for everything. The church became as crowded with the one, as the pantheon had been with the other; and Rome was the place of both."[271]

One may add: since nobody in our time still believes that gods such as Osiris, Isis, Ra, Zeus, Hera, Aphrodite, Jupiter, Venus, Marduk, Baal and Astarte ever existed and were only human inventions, why do people still believe in the ancient Israelite divine being, YHWH? Isn't he also simply a mythological figure, the same as the other deities?

---

[269] Van Baaren, "Monotheism"; Kenny, "Aristotle".
[270] Van Baaren, "Monotheism".
[271] Paine, *The Age of Reason*, 4–5.

Human Needs Satisfied

Human beings, like all life forms, have certain needs that have to be satisfied for them to survive. These needs can be divided into physical or biological needs, psychological needs and spiritual needs. These needs serve as motivators and determinants of human behavior. If a person has some or other need that has to be satisfied, he is moved to do something about the matter.

One reason why religion has survived so long is that it managed to satisfy some or most of these human needs. A short description of these various needs is necessary before it can be explained how religion satisfies these needs.

Physical Needs
Physical or biological needs are obviously the need for nourishment, water, sleep and rest, oxygen, protection against the elements, warmth and movement or exercise. Nobody can stay alive if these needs are not satisfied.

Psychological Needs
There is no consensus among psychologists with regards to the nature of the psychological needs of humans. The categorization that follows, however, seems to be useful. One can deem psychological needs to include the following (in order of importance): the need for identity, the need for stimulation and the need for security. Many people would like to add the need for love; that may, however, be seen as a combination of all three above-mentioned needs.[272] These needs have to be explained in more detail:

---

[272] Ardrey, *The Territorial Imperative*, 358–70.

The Need for Identity

The need for identity means that every human being would like to be recognized as an individual, as a unique person with human dignity. He needs to receive recognition for work well done, to be regarded highly and to be respected by others.

Identity is coupled to a person's history, his *past*, the road along which he has travelled to reach the present and the factors in his past that made him the person he has become. People retain memories of their achievements, disappointments, trauma, failures and successes – and these memories of past events shape their present identity, personality and self-image.

An individual's identity is largely dependent upon the people and groups to which he belongs: his life partner, his family, his friends, his group of colleagues, his church and his neighborhood. With these people and within these groups he has a certain status and performs a certain role.

His identity is coupled with his address: the piece of the earth that he calls home. This is where he is king of his castle. People who do not have a property of their own find it difficult to settle down. Who wants to be bound to a rented apartment on the tenth floor?

It is important for every human being to have a positive identity and self-image, to be respected and to have his human dignity recognized.

The Need for Stimulation

The need for stimulation is connected to the way the human brain is hard-wired. We all avoid boredom and a lack of stimulation like the plague. This is why life is so difficult for elderly people, invalids and patients; they have nothing to occupy themselves with.

People will even suppress their need for security in favor of stimulation. That is why so many people exchange a somewhat safe existence in rural areas for the excitement of city lights and squatter camps. People engage in certain relationships – even dangerous ones –

on account of the excitement they experience, even though this may endanger their safe relationships.

Love between people of the opposite sexes wanes when excitement and stimulation disappear from the relationship.

The need for stimulation and excitement is concerned with the *present*. People want to make the most of the moment in which they are living, including having religious experiences.

The Need for Security

The human need for security is fairly obvious. It is reassuring to know where you stand with people, especially with a life partner. A person may toil at a tedious job for many years, as it holds out the promise of a secure existence. A person's address also gives security; if there is a "place under the sun" he can call his own he more readily feels safe and secure, and he will – if needs be – fight to keep it his own.

This need is focused on the *future*. People dislike unpleasant surprises and they need to know what they can expect from tomorrow and next year.

The need for security often clashes with the need for stimulation. This may be the source of much stress.

Spiritual Needs

The highest needs of a human being – his spiritual needs – are his needs for meaning in life and for freedom and responsibility.

It is important for every person to experience that life makes sense. Viktor Frankl has demonstrated convincingly that people are prepared to endure extreme difficulties and hardship as long as it makes sense.[273] Rossouw declares that the question regarding the meaning of life is "the most critical question" that anyone can pose. This question deals with "the humanity of man", and when he seeks an answer

---

[273] Frankl, *Man's Search for Meaning*, 6.

without success, he "arrives at an existential crisis" (*own translation*).[274]

It cannot be denied that a great deal of the suffering that people have to endure appears to them to be meaningless and irrational. Christians and other believers are convinced that life and everything connected to it only makes sense if they can experience it in relationship with God.

It may be argued that this need for meaning in life flows from the fact that human beings are rational beings – apart from the fact that they are also emotional beings and beings who act upon their urges and instincts. They seek a reason for their suffering and misfortune that makes sense, that is rational or logical.

A sane human being is able to make decisions freely. Accordingly, he also has the need to put this freedom into practice. This need means that he seeks to have control over his own life. If he gets caught up in circumstances where this control becomes impossible, then the result is frustration and a feeling of powerlessness.

The down-side of human freedom is responsibility. A person must always be able to justify his decisions towards society and himself in the light of his own ethical principles. A normal human being is endowed with a conscience and it is unpleasant to be plagued by a bad conscience. Therefore, people find it best to practice their freedom of choice with responsibility – unless they are pathological liars and cheaters.

Satisfaction of Human Needs by Religion

A very important reason why religions of all sorts have survived through the ages is the fact that religion is able to satisfy most or all of the psychological and spiritual human needs.

---

[274] Rossouw, *Die Sin van die Lewe*, 6.

It can be said that religion fulfills the following three functions: It helps the believer –

- To discover meaning in life;
- To live according to moral norms and standards; and
- To receive social support.[275]

Shermer puts it this way:

> "Religion is a social institution that evolved to rein-force group cohesion and moral behaviour. It is an integral mechanism of human culture to encourage altruism ... and to reveal the level of commitment to cooperate and reciprocate among members of a social community. Believing in God provides an explanation for our universe, our world, and ourselves; it explains where we came from, why we are here, and where we are going. God is also the ultimate enforcer of the rules, the final arbiter of moral dilemmas, and the pinnacle object of commitment."[276]

It has already been argued that human beings seek meaning in life. Religion usually provides in this need. In the Christian religion this is being done by means of sermons, Bible study groups, pamphlets and religious books that explain the message(s) of the Bible and the doctrines of the church. Van den Heever theorizes that this search for meaning lies at the root of all forms of religion; the initial naive explanations of prescientific people needed the presence of gods and spirits as an explanation for natural phenomena, as well as the vicissitudes of life.[277]

---

[275] Louw, *Pastoraat en Ontmoeting,* 66; Meadow and Kahoe, *Psychology of Religion,* 5.

[276] Shermer, *The Believing Brain,* 186.

[277] Van den Heever, *Wat Moet ons met ons Kerk Doen?* 1–2.

Grayling reminds us that most people are too lazy or unable to think for themselves and that they need an institution, like the church, to do their thinking for them and provide them with a ready-made world view to make sense of life and the world. That is one of the reasons why religion has survived so long.[278]

The opposite is actually also true. Many people with religious backgrounds have found that the doctrines of their churches or religions do not make sense anymore. They have been exposed to so many points of view through the media that they regard Christianity, Judaism or Islam as hopelessly outdated and they rather embrace humanism, naturalism, rationalism, agnosticism or even atheism to provide them with meaning in their lives.

Religion also provides norms and standards for good and right behaviour for believers. In the Bible, one finds, for instance, the Ten Commandments with certain prescriptions for good and moral behaviour. This provides in the need for freedom and responsibility. People are challenged to make certain decisions and they have to respond to the dictates of their consciences.

Religious communities are usually geared to provide social support for those in need. There are usually mechanisms or institutions for helping the destitute, the poor, the grieving and the lonely. The human physical and psychological needs are, therefore, taken care of.

> *I had a conversation with a woman in her forties. She grew up in a very religious home, but has turned her back on the church. She says that she cannot believe how much nonsense was pumped into her head through the years and how much fear was generated within her when she thought about all the purported sins she had committed.*

---

[278] Grayling, *The God Argument,* 160.

A recent study in the USA showed that women who regularly attend religious meetings tend to enjoy better health and live longer than women who don't go to church. The report states:

> "The researchers looked at data from 1992–2012 from 74,534 women who participated in the Nurses' Health Study. The women answered questionnaires about their diet, lifestyle, and health every two years, and about their religious service attendance every four years. The researchers adjusted for a variety of factors, including diet, physical activity, alcohol consumption, smoking status, body mass index, social integration, depression, race and ethnicity.
>
> "Compared with women who never attended religious services, women who attended more than once per week had 33% lower mortality risk during the study period and lived an average of five months longer, the study found. Those who attended weekly had 26% lower risk and those who attended less than once a week had 13% lower risk. The study also found that women who attended religious services once per week or more had a decreased risk of both cardiovascular mortality (27%) and cancer mortality (21%)."

It was theorised that the health benefits from the attendance of religious meetings were due to the fact that the participants got social support, were part of a happy crowd, were encouraged to desist from unhealthy practices, such as smoking and excessive drinking and that their psycho-logical needs were being satisfied.[279]

The need for identity is satisfied within a religious community. The individual feels part of a group and experiences himself as a child of God. Especially charismatic groups provide in the need for stimulation and excitement with their ecstatic singing, speaking in

---

[279] Medical Brief, 19.05.2016.

tongues, dancing and rituals such as healing or exorcism. The need for security is satisfied when a believer is reassured that he is a child of God, that his eternal fate in heaven is guaranteed and that he can rely on the support of other members of the group when experiencing distress.

Most believers regard their religion as an important aspect of their lives and they feel offended when others make disparaging remarks regarding their convictions. Their religious beliefs define their personal identity to a large extent and, therefore, they will resist any effort to convince them that what they believe could be wrong. They also distrust those who have turned their backs on religion and even regard them as dangerous. They continue believing what they believe simply because they *want* to believe it and they just cannot imagine themselves embracing an alternative belief system.

In secularized societies, religion does not seem to satisfy the psychological and spiritual needs of people any longer. It may be accepted as a truism that happy people are people whose needs are satisfied and that unhappy people are those whose needs are frustrated. An experiment involving 331 students in Germany, a largely secularized country, found that there was no evidence for a relationship between religiosity and happiness, as measured by appropriate psychometric instruments.[280] In other words: it does seem as if non-religious people in a secularized society have the same capacity for happiness as religious people and that they experience life to be meaningful and fulfilling, despite the lack of a religious faith.

Oracles

Ancient Oracles
The existence of oracles through the ages aided in the continued existence of all types of religion. People were always interested to

---

[280] Francis et al., "The Relationship Between Religion and Happiness".

know what the future would bring and what the advice of the gods in certain circumstances was – and oracles provided in that need.

The ancient Greek oracles – especially the Oracle of Delphi – are well known. Robert Temple investigated the histories of these oracles and concluded that most of them amounted to a "pious fraud". Clients who came for information about the future or advice from the gods were often drugged before they encountered the priest(ess), sybil or seer – which brought them into a confused state during which they were highly suggestible. Many a pronounce-ment of the oracles was extremely ambiguous and could be interpreted in any way. Many seers also used drugs to induce an altered state of consciousness during which they experienced hallucinations, which were seen as messages from the gods. The priests or seers operating the oracles became rich since their clients paid much for the "privilege" to consult the gods.

Ancient oracles around the Mediterranean Sea were connected to each other by a network of carrier-pigeons, which could bring news in the form of messages tied to their legs from far-away places – the outcomes of battles, the death of kings, *etcetera* – within a day, long before this news reached that place through conventional means, namely through official couriers and other travelers. That enabled the oracle to "predict" certain events before they became known through other, more conventional, means.[281]

Temple gave a detailed description of the very ancient Oracle of the Dead at Cuma, on the Bay of Naples in Italy. This oracle, which was closed down in the time of emperor Augustus, consisted of a network of tunnels to simulate the Underworld (Tartarus) where the souls of the dead were supposed to be kept. There was even a make-believe Styx, the river over which the souls of the dead had to be taken in a boat to reach their destination. People who consulted this oracle were kept in isolation for three days while they were being drugged, before they were led deeper into the tunnels where they encountered

---

[281] Temple, *Netherworld*.

the Sybil or Pythia, as well as people playing the parts of dead spirits, who responded to their enquiries.[282]

There can be no doubt that these oracles helped to keep religious superstitions alive – not only in the pagan world, but also in Israel.

Biblical Oracles

The Hebrew word for "oracle" (הַדְּבִיר – *ha-debir*) occurs 21 times in the Old Testament – of which 1 Kings 6–8 contain eleven examples. It is usually translated as "inner chamber" or "holiest of holies" when used in conjunction with the temple of Solomon. In other words, the innermost chamber of the temple, which was only visited once per year by the high priest, was seen as an oracular chamber.

Various examples of prophets or seers are mention-ed in the Bible and there are certain similarities between them and other ancient oracles:

- Joseph, who later became prime minister of Egypt, was able to interpret dreams and forecast a future famine (Gen 40–41).
- We read at the end of the book of Deuteronomy: "There has not arisen a prophet since in Israel like Moses, whom Yahweh knew face to face" (Deut 34: 10).
- The Israelite high priest wore an "ephod" at times to predict the future (Ex. 28: 6–8; 39: 2–5). Part of this garment was an apron called the "Urim and Tummim", which could be used for divination, probably by casting the lot.[283]
- The best-known example of an oracle was the prophet, Samuel. He was supposed to have been called to become a prophet through a series of dreams while still a young boy (1 Sam 3). When Saul, the future king of Israel, looked for stray

---

[282] Temple, *Netherworld,* 3–162.
[283] Encyclopaedia Britannica, "Ephod".

- asses of his father, he in the end consulted Samuel when the animals could not be found. He was prepared to pay for Samuel's services – just as happened at pagan oracles (1 Sam 9: 6–25).
- Another oracle was the witch of En-Dor whom King Saul consulted to get into touch with the spirit of the deceased Samuel. We read that Saul almost fainted in the end, due to the fact that he hadn't eaten for a few days. It is possible that this Sybil kept him in a waiting room for a length of time, in order to prepare him for the séance (1 Sam 28: 3–29) – just as happened in other pagan oracles of the time.

There are those who cite this last episode as a proof that contact between the living and the dead is possible. Jesus would not have agreed. In the parable of the rich man and Lazarus, he explained that it was not possible to send anybody from the dead with a message to the living (Luke 16: 19–31). It is, anyway, extremely likely that the witch only pretended to call Samuel's spirit up from the Underworld.

There can be little doubt that other prophets of the Old Testament saw themselves as oracles. The last prophet of the Old Testament, Malachi, explicitly called his message an "oracle of the Lord" (מַשָּׂא דְבַר־יְהוָה – *massa' debar YHWH*) (Mal 1: 1).

All these oracles in Israel must have aided in furthering the worship of YHWH, the Israelite deity.

The Greek word for "oracle" (λόγιον – *logion*) is used in four instances in the New Testament. It may also mean a "brief utterance" – doubtless because divine oracles were generally brief. In 1 Pet 4: 11 we read: "If any man speaks, *let him speak* as the oracles of God…" The other three examples refer to prophecies in the Old Testament.

The New Testament also contains examples of oracles or prophets. Jesus is surely the best-known example. Shortly before his death, he purportedly predicted the downfall of Jerusalem and linked this event to Judgment Day (Matt 24 and 25). The prophet Agabus is mentioned twice (Acts 11: 26; Acts 21: 10). He predicted future events, just as other oracles.

Credulous People

Graham Phillips argues convincingly that many an oracle or religious charlatan has abused the human tendency to be credulous. A good example is the originator of the cult of The Church of Jesus Christ of Latter-Day Saints – the Mormons – namely a certain Joseph Smith. He purportedly found some golden plates, written in "Reformed Egyptian" (whatever that is), which he claimed he translated with the aid of special stones provided to him by an angel. These plates were seen by nobody else. They contained – as Smith claimed – the story of a group of Israelites who fled from Palestine to North America and whose descendants were to be found amongst the native Americans or Indians. This story became the so-called Book of Mormon. He managed to gather a number of followers, whom he convinced of his ideas. Since they encountered much resistance from other folks, they moved away and eventually ended up in Utah.[284]

Smith's contention that the North American Indians are the descendants of ancient Israelites has been thoroughly disproved by archaeological and genetic studies. It has been shown conclusively that all the original inhabitants of the Americas came from eastern Asia during ice ages when the Bering Strait between Siberia and Alaska dried up and formed a land bridge between the continents.[285] And yet, there are thousands of people who disregard this evidence and continue to believe Smith's stories. Many other examples of similar cults and sects can be mentioned.

The human need for meaning in life was already mentioned. Most unsophisticated people are not able to discover meaning in their lives on their own and they often believe the rantings and ravings of

---

[284] Phillips, *The Moses Legacy,* 16–68.
[285] Jones, "Shocking Decline of Christianity?" 137–145.

eloquent self-proclaimed seers, prophets, preachers and holy men since their ideas do seem to make sense or seem to provide answers to problems these people have.

Many an Old Testament prophet, whose books are contained in the Bible, could have been of this type. They all claimed to have been called by God to proclaim a message – but no independent verification of that calling is, of course, to be found. Yet, they managed to convince a number of credulous people that their messages were genuine, with the result that their writings were accepted as holy scripture.

There are still many credulous people around today who believe what they are told by their church, temple, synagogue or mosque. What they hear satisfies their need for meaning in life – although these messages often contain improbabilities, impossible claims, incredible stories and plain nonsense. They believe all this, simply because they want to believe it and in the absence of a credible alternative. In many cases, these seers, prophets, preachers and holy men are cynics who do not even believe their own messages, although they know how to convince people of the ideas they proclaim.

Rich Oracles and Pastors

These seers, prophets, preachers and holy men often managed to amass much wealth. I once heard somebody say: "There's money in religion. You only have to know where to dig." That does seem to be the case.

For example: According to the Forbes ranking, the ten richest Christian pastors in the world as of 2021 were the following persons –

1. David Oyedepo (Nigeria) – net worth: $200 Million
2. T.D Jakes (USA) – $147 Million
3. Chris Oyakhilome (Nigeria) – $50 Million
4. Joel Osteen (USA) – $40 Million
5. Enoch Adeboye (Nigeria) – $39 Million
6. Creflo Dollar (USA) – $27 Million
7. Kenneth Copeland (USA) – $25 Million

8. Benny Hinn (USA) – $25 Million
9. (The late) T.B. Joshua (Nigeria) – $10 Million
10. Joseph Prince (Singapore) – $5 Million.[286]

In 2009 the Mail & Guardian reported that the Rhema Bible Church in Randburg, South Africa, had an annual income of R100 million ($6,6 million) of which the senior pastor Ray McCauley – who was divorced twice and married three times – received a large cut, prompting many people to accuse him of leading the life-style of a millionaire.[287]

The daily newspaper, The Citizen, revealed in 2016 that bishop-for-life Barnabas Leganyane, leader of the largest church in Southern Africa, the Zion Christian Church, has several sources of income. Apart from copious offerings by church members, he receives income from a funeral scheme, a motor insurance scheme and a transport business he owns.[288]

All this is in stark contrast to Jesus who famously said: "The foxes have holes, and the birds of the sky have nests, but the Son of Man has no place to lay his head" (Luke 9: 58). These holy men seem to follow the examples of ancient Greek oracles, which also became stinking rich – instead of living as Jesus and the apostles did.

The Bible as an Oracle
During my ministry I often encountered people who used their Bibles as oracles. Whenever they had to make a difficult decision, they would scour the Bible for a message that could give them an idea of how God would have liked them to proceed under those circumstances – as if God inspired the Bible with their specific problems in mind.

---

[286] Rich Updates, 2021, "10 Richest pastors in the world".
[287] Tolsi, "For Church and Country"; Mail & Guardian, 20.03.2009.
[288] The Citizen, 17.02.2016.

There were also those who would pray before consulting the Bible and ask God to guide them to an appropriate verse in the Bible to help them in their difficulties. They would then open the Bible at a random page and point a finger at any random verse – in the hope that that verse would give them the guidance they needed – almost as if they used the Bible as a gambling machine to deliver a lucky number.

It is clear that people who use the Bible in this manner do not differ in any fundamental way from those ancient people who consulted "professional" oracles and seers. However one regards the Bible, it is clear that the authors of the various biblical texts never intended their literary creations to be used in this manner.

Rituals and Ceremonies

When one visits a Christian church service on a Sunday, a Muslim prayer meeting on a Friday or a Jewish synagogue on a Saturday, one is bound to find people engaging in all sorts of rituals and ceremonies – readings, prayers, sermons, singing and so forth.

In Christian churches one will, in addition, find baptisms, the celebration of the Eucharist or Lord's Supper, the recital of the apostles' creed, the induction of new members, *etcetera*. Roman Catholics also go to confession regularly and they make the sign of the cross on their bodies at appropriate times. In charismatic churches one may expect dancing, prophetic utterances, speaking in tongues, exorcism and faith healings.

Muslims regard it as a sacred duty to visit the holy city of Mecca at least once during their lifetimes, especially during the festival of Ramadan. A whole program of rituals is to be followed. In addition, Muslims attend regular prayer services, especially on Fridays.

Jews make much of the festival of Passover to celebrate the liberation of the ancient Israelites from slavery in Egypt. They also have a number of other feasts, such as the Jewish New Year.

All these religions celebrate weddings and funerals with certain rituals and ceremonies.

These actions, obviously, convey meaning to the believers. They are symbolic acts to commemorate certain historical events or to give expression to their beliefs and hopes. These actions strengthen the feeling of community between the members of a Christian congregation, mosque or synagogue and affirm that they share the same belief system, ideals and values.

Although some of these rituals and ceremonies may seem strange to the uninitiated, it is accepted by all that they have meaning and that the participants are strengthened in their beliefs and that they are convinced that they are performing actions and movements that are pleasing to God. The believers even have the conviction that God is present at their ceremonies and meetings – albeit in an invisible way.

It is clear that these rituals and ceremonies help to keep religion alive.

There is reason to believe that people who perform rituals in all sorts of religions do so in the belief that they were able to influence the gods, natural forces such as the weather and the actions of other people with their actions. If they do not achieve the desired result, it is because they have committed some or other mistake or sin while performing the rituals and that that displeased the gods.

One cannot but help to ask: are all these ceremonies, rituals and spiritual gymnastics really pleasing to God – should he exist? Does he need or want to be worshipped? Most Psalms and hymns are meant to glorify God and thank him for his love and deliverance – as if he needs to be reminded thereof. Does it help to earn God's favor by singing hymns and reciting prayers in which his purported perfect qualities are extolled? Does it help to flatter God in order to receive his blessings?

Furthermore: does it make God feel good when people celebrate the Eucharist or undertake a pilgrimage to Mecca? Did he enjoy the ritual slaughter of animals at the Jerusalem temple? Is God an egoist or narcissist who has to be reminded of his wonderful qualities whenever people pray or sing hymns?

One may be sure that any sane and rational person will agree that God – should he exist – has no need for all these rituals, ceremonies, spiritual gymnastics and gyrations. The answer to all the questions above must be "No". Believers, nevertheless, persist with their traditions and they will find it a sacrilege if anybody should question any of these actions or traditions.

Freud had it partly correct when he called religious activities the result of an "obsessional neurosis". There is indeed a certain element of obsessivity or compulsivity connected to all these rituals and ceremonies. The fact that they are repeated over and over again make them familiar to the adherents of a certain group and help them to feel secure and at home when attending a gathering with their fellow believers.

Religion in all its permutations has managed to survive through the ages, partly due to the fact that believers participate in rituals and ceremonies. Without these, religion will lose much of its appeal. It is, on the other hand, also true that more and more people don't feel the need to participate in all sorts of actions, which they see as meaningless and empty and, therefore, they abandon all ties with religion.

Summary

All the preceding arguments and facts make it clear that there are rational explanations for the fact that religion has endured so long on earth. But that does not mean that there is necessarily any truth in religion. It has already been shown that the Bible contains incredible and ridiculous teachings and that important dogmas of Christianity cannot be sustained and entertained anymore.

Churches and religious organizations continue to propagate their messages through all the mass media but more and more people realize that this propaganda does not make sense anymore. The power of religion over people is slowly, but surely, being eroded by better education, by more information about the advances of science and by people being repulsed by scandals in the churches and religious organizations.

I can clearly remember that I had to deliver a sermon in front of a congregation during my final year at theological seminary as part of being examined. I chose the following text from the Bible for this sermon:

> "If Christ has not been raised, then our preaching is in vain, and your faith also is in vain." (1 Cor 15: 14).

This pronouncement of Paul can certainly still be applied to our time and our present situation. This book – and numerous others – have concluded that Jesus of Nazareth, the Christ, never survived his crucifixion. If this essential element of the Christian faith has fallen away, then the rest of this faith is also doomed to be discarded. It has been shown that other elements of the Christian faith, namely –

- The divine inspiration of the holy scriptures;
- Man's sinful nature that condemns him to everlasting punishment in the flames of hell;
- The virgin birth of Christ;
- The atonement for our sins by Jesus' death on the cross;
- The promise of life everlasting in the presence of God for the faithful;
- The doctrine of the divine trinity;
- The idea that an evil personage, Satan, exists as an adversary of God; and
- The power of prayer –

certainly do not survive rational and honest scrutiny and investigation.

Just as people of our age cannot any longer accept the cosmology of the biblical authors – a flat earth, the abode of God and the angels just beyond the stars and an underworld below the surface of the earth – the rest of the legends, myths and doctrines of the holy scriptures are also increasingly being regarded as part and parcel of an ancient and outdated world view that doesn't make any sense anymore. More and more people have come to the conclusion that one can lead a meaningful, happy and moral life without any religious faith.

One does not need to be a prophet or clairvoyant to predict the end of Christianity, some or other time. There are enough signs that point in that direction, including the cold, hard numbers of statistics. The same fate awaits Judaism and Islam.

The contents of this book mat be disturbing to many believers because it has been shown that many of their cherished beliefs cannot be upheld any longer and that the belief systems of their churches, synagogues or mosques are nothing but antique superstitions.

It has to be granted: during the past many churches and religious organizations have done much to improve the lives of untold numbers of people by their charitable initiatives, by insisting on ethical behavior in all walks of life and providing education. These bodies deserve the gratitude of humanity.

But that it is not to say that their dogmas, creeds, and belief systems are to be accepted without question by people of the 21st century. By now, it ought to be clear a religious faith doesn't rest on solid evidence and ought to be discarded. The inevitable outcome will be that religious communities will wither, shrink and even die.

BIBLIOGRAPHY

Editions of the Bible
Passages from the Bible are quoted from the "World English Bible" as found on a CD with the title *The Bible Collection, Deluxe Edition*, and published by ValuSoft, a division of THQ Inc, Waconia MN, 2002.

The above-mentioned CD also contains the Hebrew text of the Old Testament and the Greek text of the New Testament, as well as "Strong's Complete Greek and Hebrew Lexicon". Other lexica utilized are mentioned under the heading of Other Literature.

In addition, the following editions of the biblical text in the original languages were consulted:

Elliger, K. and Rudolph, W. eds. *Biblia Hebraica Stuttgartensia*. Deutsche Bibelgesellschaft: Stuttgart, 1997.
Nestle, E. and Nestle, E. eds. *Novum Testamentum Graece*. Deutsche Bibelstiftung: Stuttgart, 1981.

The text of the ancient Greek translation of the Old Testament, the so-called *Septuagint (LXX)*, was downloaded from the following website:
https://www.academic-bible.com/en/online-bibles/septuagint-lxx/read-the-bible-text/

Other Literature

Abbott, G. "Burning at the Stake". In *Encyclopædia Britannica*, 2010.

Achterberg, P. et al. "A Christian Cancellation of the Secularist Truce? Waning Christian Religiosity and Waxing Religious Deprivatization in The West". *Journal for the Scientific Study of Religion*, Vol. 48, No. 4 (Dec., 2009), 687–701. http://www.jstor.org/stable/40405663.

Ahlström, G.W. "Prophecy". In *Encyclopædia Britannica*, 2010.

Alexander, D. *Creation or Evolution, Do we Have to Choose?* Oxford: Monarch, 2008.

Ali, Tariq. *The Clash of Fundamentalisms: Crusades, Jihads and Modernity*. London: Verso, 2003.

American Psychiatric Association. *Diagnostic and Statistical Manual of Mental Disorders, Fifth Edition: DSM-5*. Washington: American Psychiatric Publishing, 2013.

Aminoff, M.J. ed. *Encyclopaedia of the Neurological Sciences*. New York: Elsevier Science, 2003.

Anon. *Crime Index by Country 2015*.
http://www.numbeo.com/crime/rankings_by_country.jsp

----. "Fewer Religious People in SA – Survey". *News24*, 09.11.2015
http://www.news24.com/southafrica/news/fewer-religious-people-in-sa-survey-20120810.

----. "'I'm not About to Die,' Malawi's President Tells Nigerian 'Prophet'". *The Telegraph*, 16.03.2016.
http://www.telegraph.co.uk/news/worldnews/africaandindianocean/malawi/12192933/im-not-about-to-die-malawis-president-tells-nigerian-prophet.html

----. "Nigeria: TB Joshua – 'Fake' Prophets, Pastors 'Worsening' Poverty Levels in Malawi". *News24 Wire*, 12.01.2017.
http://allafrica.com/stories/201701100456.html

----. "Rhema Rakes in Millions". *Mail & Guardian*, 20.03.2009. http://mg.co.za/article/2009-03-20-rhema-rakes-in-millions.

----. "Religious Service Attendance and Death Risk in Women". *Medical Brief*, 18.05.2016. http://www.medicalbrief.co.za/archives/religious-service-attendance-and-death-risk-in-women/ .

Anwar, Y. "Highly Religious People are Less Motivated by Compassion than are Non-Believers". *Berkeley News*, 30.04.2012. http://news.berkeley.edu/2012/04/30/religionandgenerosity/

Aquilecchia, G. "Bruno, Giordano". In *Encyclopaedia Britannica*, 2010..

Ardrey, Robert. *The Territorial Imperative: A Personal Inquiry into the Animal Origins of Property and Nations*. London: Collins, 1970.

Armstrong, Karen. *A History of God: From Abraham to the Present, the 4000-Year Quest for God*. London : Mandarin, 1994.

----. *Fields of Blood: Religion and the History of Violence*. London: Vintage, 2014.

----. *Muhammad : A Biography of the Prophet*. London: Phoenix, 2001.

----. *The Battle for God Fundamentalism in Judaism, Christianity and Islam*. London: Harper Collins, 2001.

----. *The Bible: The Biography*. London: Atlantic, 2007.

Arndt, W.F. and Gingrich, F.W. *A Greek-English Lexicon of the New Testament and Other Early Christian Literature*. Chicago: University of Chicago Press. 1957.

Arnett, A.M. "Jimson Weed (Datura Stramonium) Poisoning". *Clinical Toxicology Review,* Dec 1995, Vol 18 (No 3). https://www.erowid.org/plants/datura/datura_info5.shtml

Atheist Republic, "Polish Archbishop Bans Children from Visiting Priest's Homes Alone." 21.02.2022. https://mail.google.com/mail/u/0/?tab=rm&ogbl#inbox/FMfcgzGmtXJFVVrMxbxglQSsQvCNFJnB

Aurelius, John. "Praying With Angus". *News14*, 25.04.2017. http://www.news24.com/mynews24/praying-with-angus-20170424

Ayala, F.J. "Evolution". In *Encyclopaedia Britannica*, 2010.

Baines, J.R. "Egyptian Religion". In *Encyclopædia Britannica*, 2010.

Barna, G. and M. Hatch. *Boiling Point: It Only Takes one Degree*. Ventura CA: Regal, 2001.

Barrow, J.D. *The Artful Universe: The Cosmic Source of Human Creativity*. London: Penguin, 1997.

Belgic Confession, The.
http://gksa.org.za/pdf/eng%20documents/belgic%20confession.pdf

Benedict, G. *The God Debate: A New Look at History's Oldest Argument*. London: Watkins, 2013.

Benson, H. et al. "Study of the Therapeutic Effects of Intercessory Prayer (Step) in Cardiac Bypass Patients: A Multicenter Randomized Trial of Uncertainty and Certainty of Receiving Intercessory Prayer". *Am Heart J.* 2006 Apr; 151(4):934-42.
http://www.ncbi.nlm.nih.gov/pubmed/16569567

Biography.Com Editors. *Pope Francis Biography.*
https://www.biography.com/religious-figure/pope-francis

Boshoff, W. et al. *Geskiedenis en Geskrifte: Die Literatuur van Ou Israel*. Pretoria: Protea, 2008.

Callahan, T. *Secret Origins of the Bible*. Altadena, Ca: Millennium, 2002.

Carbonaro, T.M. et al. "Magic Mushrooms Lift Depression in Cancer Patients". *Medical Brief,* 7 December 2016.
http://www.medicalbrief.co.za/archives/magic-mushrooms-lift-depression-cancer-patients/

Catholic Encyclopedia,1914. "Inquisition".
http://www.newadvent.org/cathen/08026a.htm

Clark, P. et al. *Lippincott's Illustrated Reviews: Pharmacology*. Baltimore: Wolters Kluwer Health, 2012.

Clark, S. *The Big Questions: The Universe*. London: Quercus, 2010.

Collins, Francis. *The Language of God: A Scientist Presents Evidence for Belief*. London: Pocket, 2007.

Craffert, P.F. "Die Nuwe Hervorming – Wat, Waaroor, Waarheen?" In *Die Nuwe Hervorming,* edited by P. Muller. Pretoria: Protea, 2002.

Craighead, W.E. and Nemeroff, C.B. *The Corsini Encyclopedia of Psychology and Behavioral Science, Volume 4*. New York: John Wiley and Sons, 2002.

Cunningham, G.C. *Decoding the Language of God.* New York: Prometheus, 2010.

Dawkins, Richard. "Good and Bad Reasons for Believing". In *How Things are: A Science Tool-Kit for the Mind*, edited by J. Brockman and K. Matson, K. London: Phoenix, 2001.
----. "Religion: The Mental Equivalent of a Computer Virus." In *Secrets Of Angels & Demons*, edited by D. Burstein and A.de Keijzer. London: Orion, 2005.
----. *The God Delusion*. London: Bantam, 2006.
----. *The Greatest Show on Earth: The Evidence for Evolution*. London: Bantam, 2009.
----. *The Selfish Gene*. Oxford: Oxford University Press, 1976.
De Klerk, Willem. *Die Vreemde God en sy Mense*. Cape Town: Human & Rousseau, 1999.
De Rosa, Peter. *Vicars of Christ: The Dark Side of the Papacy*. London: Bantam, 1988.
Dolansky, S. "How the Serpent Became Satan : Adam, Eve and the Serpent in the Garden of Eden". *Biblical Archaeology*, 04.08.2016. http://www.biblicalarchaeology.org/daily/biblical-topics/bible-interpretation/how-the-serpent-became-satan/
Dreyer, T.F.J. *Poimeniek, 'n Pastorale Oriëntasie*. Pretoria: HAUM, 1981.
Drummond, J.G. "Who is Satan? The Many Forms of The Devil in the Bible. *Biblical Archaeology,* 11.10.2016. http://www.biblicalarchaeology.org/daily/biblical-topics/bible-interpretation/who-is-satan/?mqsc=e3887930&utm_source=whatcountsemail&utm_medium=bhddaily%20newsletter&utm_campaign=ze7a5vz00
Duggan, L.G. "Indulgence". In *Encyclopaedia Britannica*, 2010.
Ehrman, Bart D. *Misquoting Jesus:The Story Behind who Changed the Bible and Why*. New York: Harper Collins, 2005.
Encyclopaedia Britannica, 2010. "Alexandria, Library of". Chicago: Encyclopædia Britannica, 2010.
----. "Cro-Magnon". Chicago: Encyclopædia Britannica, 2010.
----. "Dehydration". Chicago: Encyclopædia Britannica, 2010.
----. "Didache". Chicago: Encyclopædia Britannica, 2010.
----. "Donation of Constantine". Chicago: Encyclopædia Britannica, 2010.
----. "Divation". Chicago: Encyclopædia Britannica, 2010.

―――. "Ecstacy". Chicago: Encyclopædia Britannica, 2010.
―――. "Ephod". Chicago: Encyclopædia Britannica, 2010.
―――. "Gnosticism". Chicago: Encyclopædia Britannica, 2010.
―――. "Hades". Chicago: Encyclopædia Britannica, 2010.
―――. "Hebrew Language". Chicago: Encyclopædia Britannica, 2010.
―――. "Heresy". Chicago: Encyclopædia Britannica, 2010.
―――. "Magic". Chicago: Encyclopædia Britannica, 2010.
―――. "Prophet". Chicago: Encyclopædia Britannica, 2010.
―――. "Resurrection". Chicago: Encyclopædia Britannica, 2010.
―――. "Servetus, Michael". Chicago: Encyclopædia Britannica, 2010.
―――. "University". Chicago: Encyclopædia Britannica, 2010.
―――. "Witchcraft". Chicago: Encyclopædia Britannica, 2010.
Fairchild, M. *Christianity Today: General Statistics and Facts of Christianity.* http://christianity.about.com/od/denominations/p/christiantoday.htm
Feiler, B. *Where God was Born: A Journey by Land to the Roots of Religion.* New York: William Morrow, 2005.
Finkelstein, I. and N. Silberman. *The Bible Unearthed: Archaeology's new Vision of Ancient Israel and the Origin of its Sacred Texts.* New York: Simon and Schuster, 2002.
Firet, J. *Het Agogisch Moment in het Pastoraal Optreden.* Kampen: J.H. Kok, 1968.
Francis, L. et al. "Prayer and Psychological Health: A Study Among Sixth-Form Pupils Attending Catholic and Protestant Schools in Northern Ireland". *Mental Health, Religion & Culture* **11** (1): 85–92. Doi:10.1080/13674670701709055.
Francis, L.J. et al. "The Relationship between Religion and Happiness among German Students. *Pastoral Psychology*, Vol 51, No 4, March 2003: 273–283.
Frazer, J.G. *The Golden Bough: A Study in Magic and Religion.* London: Macmillan, 1971.
Freud, Sigmund. *The Origins of Religion.* Harmondsworth: Penguin, 1985.
Galton, Francis. "Statistical Inquiries Into the Efficacy of Prayer". *Fortnightly Review* Vol. 12, 125–35, 1872.

http://www.galton.org/essays/1870-1879/galton-1872-fortnightly-review-efficacy-prayer.html

Garwood, Christine. *Flat Earth: The History of an Infamous Idea*. London: Pan, 2008.

Gaum, Frits. et al., eds. *Christelike Kernensiklopedie: CKE*. Wellington: Lux Verbi, 2008.

Gleiser, M. "Blind Ambition and Sincere Piety" In *Secrets of Angels & Demons,* edited by Burstein, D. and A. de Keijzer. London: Orion, 2005.

Glick, T.F. 2010. "Intelligent Design (ID)". In *Encyclopædia Britannica*, 2010.

Goetz, C.G. "Hallucinogens". In *Encyclopedia of the Neurological Sciences*, edited by M.J. Aminoff. Elsevier Science, 2003, 503–04.

Gottheil, R. and M. Kayserling. "Inquisition (Called also Sanctum Officium or Holy Office)". In *Jewish Encyclopedia*, 1906. http://www.jewishencyclopedia.com/articles/8122-inquisition

Graffin, Greg. and S. Olson. *Anarchy Evolution: Faith, Science and Bad Religion*. New York: Harper Collins, 2010.

Grayling, A.C. *The God Argument: The Case Against Religion and for Humanism*. London: Bloomsbury, 2014.

Greenwood, S. and R. Airey. *The Complete Illustrated Encyclopaedia of Witchcraft & Magic*. London: Hermes House, 2007.

Hallowell, B. *Shocking Porn 'Epidemic' Stats Reveal Details about Christian Consumption: 'A Very Real Addiction' that can 'Spiral Out Of Control'*. http://www.theblaze.com/stories/2014/08/28/shocking-statistics-about-porn-epidemic-and-christian-consumption-a-very-real-addiction-that-can-spiral-out-of-control/

Hancock, Graham. *Supernatural: Meetings with the Ancient Teachers of Mankind*. London: Century, 2005.

Harris, S. *The End of Faith: Religion, Terror and the Future of Reason*. London: The Free Press, 2005.

Harrison, P. "Narratives of Secularization: Introduction". *Intellectual History Review*, 27 (2017), 1–6. https://www.academia.edu/30890303/narratives_of_secularization_introduction

Hawking, Stephen and L. Mlodinow. *The Grand Design: New Answers to the Ultimate Questions of Life.* London: Bantam, 2011.

Heidelberg Catechism
  http://www.reformed.org/documents/heidelberg.html

Helsel, P.B. "Faith". In *Encyclopedia of Psychology and Religion*, edited by D.A. Leeming et.al. New York: Springer Science+Business Media, 2010, 315–17.

Kenny, Sir Anthony J.P. "Aristotle". In *Encyclopaedia Britannica*, 2010.

Luschnig, C.E. & Luschnig, L.J. *The Teaching of the Twelve Apostles: A Gre Reader with Introduction and Notes.*
  http://www.worldwidegreek.com/downloads/didache.pdf

Magnus, B. "Nietzsche, Friedrich". In *Encyclopaedia Britannica*, 2010.

Malandra, W.W. "Iranian Religion". In *Encyclopædia Britannica*, 2010.

Heyns, Johan Adam. *Teologiese Etiek: Deel 1.* Pretoria: N.G. Kerkboekhandel Transvaal, 1982.

Heyns, J.A. and W.D. Jonker. *Op Weg met die Teologie.* Pretoria: N.G. Kerkboekhandel, 1974.

Hill, J.P. "Faith and Understanding: Specifying the Impact of Higher Education on Religious Belief. *Journal for the Scientific Study of Religion* (2011) 50(3):533–551.
  https://www.academia.edu/3376024/faith_and_understanding_specifying_the_impact_of_higher_education_on_religious_belief?auto=view&campaign=weekly_digest

Hodge, Charles. *Systematic Theology, Volume 1.* London: Thomas Nelson, 1871.

Hodge, D.R. "A Systematic Review of the Empirical Literature on Intercessory Prayer". *Research on Social Work Practice* 2007; 17: 174.
  http://rsw.sagepub.com/cgi/content/abstract/17/2/174

Hoffman, R.E. et al. "Transcranial Magnetic Stimulation of Left Temporal Cortex and Medication-Resistant Auditory Hallucinations. *Arch Gen Psychiatry,* Vol 60, January 2003: 49–56.
  http://www.neuro.hk/img/tmshallucinationsschizophrenia.pdf

Humphrys, J. *In God we Doubt: Confessions of a Failed Atheist.* London: Hodder and Stoughton, 2007.

Jackson, J.G. *Man, God and Civilization*. New York: Kensington, 2001.
Jones, A. "How Will the Shocking Decline of Christianity in America Affect the Future of this Nation?" http://www".infowars.com/how-will-the-shocking-decline-of-christianity-in-america-affect-the-future-of-this-nation/
Jones, M. *The Molecule Hunt: Archaeology and the Search for Ancient DNA*. London: Penguin, 2001.
Jones, S. *In the Blood: God, Genes and Destiny*. London: Flamingo, 1997.
Josephus, Flavius. *The Wars of the Jews, or History of the Destruction of Jerusalem*. Translated by W Whiston. Project Gutenberg E-Book, 2009. . Https://www.gutenberg.org/files/2850/2850-H/2850-H.Htm#Link6noteref-20
Joshua, T.B. "Trump: You Need Spiritual Understanding to Interpret my Prophesy". *Punch*, 13.11.2016. http://punchng.com/trump-you-need-spiritual-understanding-to-interpret-my-prophesy-tb-joshua/
Joubert, Gideon. *Die Groot Gedagte: Abstrakte Weefsel van die Kosmos*. Cape Town: Tafelberg, 1997.
Karasavvas, T. "Only 11 Tribes of Israel? Controversial Findings Reveal Danites Might not be Sons of Israel but Sons of Greece. *Ancient Origins,* 13 December http://www.ancient-origins.net/news-history-archaeology/only-11-tribes-israel-controversial-findings-reveal-danites-might-not-be-021113.

Kolb, B. and I.Q. Whishaw. *Fundamentals of Human Neuro-psychology*. New York: Worth, 2009.

König, Adrio. *Die Evangelie is op die Spel*. Wellington: Lux Verbi, 2009.
----. *Die Groot Geloofswoordeboek*. Vereeniging: Christelike Uitgewersmaatskappy, 2006.
----. *Ek Glo die Bybel – Ondanks al die Vrae*. Wellington: Lux Verbi, 2002.
----. "Teologie". In I.H. Eybers, et al. *Inleiding in die Teologie*, 1–30. Pretoria: NG Kerkboekhandel, 1978.

Küng, Hans. *Existiert Gott?* München: Piper, 1978.

―――. "Paradigm Change in Theology: a Proposal for Discussion", In *Paradigm Change in Theology: a Symposium for the Future*, edited by H. Kung and D. Tracy. New York: Crossroad, 1989.

―――. *Can we Save the Catholic Church? We can Save the Catholic Church*. London: William Collins, 2013.

Kuyper, A. *Encyclopaedie der Heilige Godgeleerdheid, Deel Drie*. Amsterdam: J.A. Wormser, 1894.

Louw, D.J. *Pastoraal en Ontmoeting: Ontwerp vir 'n Basisteorie, Antropologie, Metode en Terapie*. Pretoria: RGN, 1993.

Mack, B.L. *The Lost Gospel: The Book of Q & Christian Origins*. Shaftesbury: Element, 1994.

Martin, D. "2030: The Year Britain will Cease to be a Christian Nation with the March of Secularism. *Daily Mail*, 03.03.2012. http://www.dailymail.co.uk/news/article-2109488/2030-the-year-britain-cease-chrsitian-nation-march-secularism.html

Martinez, D.M. "The Spanish Terror". *National Geographic History*, Vol 1, No 6. Jan/Feb 2016: 64–75.

Masters K.S. et al. "Are There Demonstrable Effects Of Distant Intercessory Prayer? A Meta-Analytic Review". *Ann Behav Med*. 2006 Aug; 32(1): 21–26. http://www.ncbi.nlm.nih.gov/pubmed/16827626

Matlala, A. "Where ZCC Finances Come From". *The Citizen*, 17.02.2016.

McCarthy, T. and B. Rubidge, B. *The Story of Earth & Life: A Southern African Perspective on a 4.6-Billion-Year Journey*. Cape Town: Struik, 2005.

Meadow, M.J. and R.D. Kahoe. *Psychology of Religion*. New York: Harper & Row, 1984.

Malamat, A. "Let My People Go and Go and Go and Go: Egyptian Records Support a Centuries-Long Exodus". In *Ancient Israel in Egypt and the Exodus,* edited by M. Warker. Washington: Biblical Archaeology Society, 2012.

Malina, B.J. *On The Genre and Message of Revelation: Star Visions and Sky Journeys*. Peabody Mass: Hendrickson, 1995.

Martin, P. *Counting Sheep: The Science and Pleasures of Sleep and Dreams*. London: Flamingo, 2002.

McCall, R.B. *Fundamental Statistics for Psychology*. New York: Harcourt, Brace and World, 1970.

Metz, J.B. *Glaube in Geschichte und Gesellschaft: Studien zu einer Praktischen Fundamentaltheologie*. Mainz: Matthias Grünewald, 1984.

Mills, D. *Atheist Universe: The Thinking Person's Answer to Christian Fundamentalism*. Berkeley, CA: Ulysses, 2000.

Mithen, S. *The Prehistory of the Mind: A Search for the Origins of Art, Religion and Science*. London: Thames and Hudsons, 1998.

Müller, Julian. *Opstanding*. Wellington: Lux Verbi, 2006.

Muller, R.A. *The Study of Theology: From Biblical Interpretation to Contemporary Formulation*. Grand Rapids: Zondervan, 1991.

Oden, T.C. *Pastoral Theology: Essentials of Ministry*. San Francisco: Harper & Row, 1982.

Onfrey, M. *In Defence of Atheism: The Case Against Christianity, Judaism and Islam*. Translated by Jeremy Leggatt. London: Profile, 2007.

Olivier, A. *Die Lewe en Werk van Johannes du Plessis : 'n Kort Oorsig*. https://www.google.co.za/?gws_rd=ssl#q=prof+johannes+du+plessis

Ontario Consultants on Religious Tolerance. *The Virgin Birth (Conception) of Jesus*. http://www.religioustolerance.org/virgin_b1.htm

Ontillera, A.R. "Vengeance At The Vatican: The Cadaver Synod". *National Geographic History*, Vol 1, No 6, Jan/Feb 2016: 14–17.

Oomen, P.M.F. "On Brain, Soul, Self and Freedom: An Essay in Bridging Neuroscience and Faith". *Zigong*, Vol 38, No 2, June 2003: 377–92.

Origenes Adamnatios. *Contra Celsum*. http://www.documentacatholicaomnia.eu/03d/0185-0254,_origenes,_contra_celsus,_en.pdf

Ott, Heinrich. *Die Antwort des Glaubens: Systematische Theologie in 50 Artikeln*. Stuttgart: Kreuz, 1973.

Paine, Thomas. *The Age of Reason*. Reprint, London: Freethought, 1880.

http://www.gutenberg.org/files/3743/3743-h/3743-h.htm

Pannenberg, Wolfhard. *Theology and the Philosophy of Science*. Translated by F. Mcdonagh. London: Darton, Longman & Todd, 1976.

Park, G.K. and R.A. Gilbert. "Divination:. In *Encyclopædia Britannica*, 2010.

Pew Research Center. *Global Christianity – A Report On The Size And Distribution Of The World's Christian Population.*
http://www.pewforum.org/2011/12/19/global-christianity-exec/

————. The Global Religious Landscape, 18 December 2012.
http://www.pewforum.org/2012/12/18/global-religious-landscape-exec/

————. US Public Becoming Less Religious. http://www.pewforum.org/files/2015/11/201.11.03_rls_ii_full_report.pdf

————. Measuring Religion.
https://www.pewforum.org/2021/01/14/measuring-religion-in-pew-research-centers-american-trends-panel/

Phillips, G. *The Moses Legacy: The Evidence of History*. London: Sidgwick & Jackson, 2002.

Pitts, M. *Hengeworld*. London: Arrow, 2000.

Ratzinger, Joseph. "Schöpfungsglaube und Evolutionstheorie" In *Wer ist das Eigentlich – Gott?* Edited by H.J. Schultz, München: Kösel, 1969.

Rich Updates 2021. *10 Richest Pastors In The World & Net Worth 2021 [Forbes Ranking]*
https://richupdates.com/richest-pastors-in-the-world/

Rossouw, H.W. *Die Sin van die Lewe*. Cape Town: Tafelberg, 1981.

Rousseau, Leon. *Die Groot Avontuur: Wondere van die Lewe op Aarde*. Cape Town: Human & Rousseau, 2006.

Rylaarsdam, J. C. et al. "Biblical Literature". In *Encyclopædia Britannica*, 2010.

Sacks, Oliver. *The River of Consciousness*. London: Picador, 2017.

Sandeen, E.R. "Fundamentalism, Christian". In *Encyclopædia Britannica*, 2010.

Schmale, F.-J. "Henry IV". In *Encyclopaedia Britannica*, 2010..

Seckler, M. *Im Spannungsfeld von Wissenschaft und Kirche: Theologie als Schöpferisches Auslegung der Wirklichkeit.* Freiburg: Herder, 1980.

Seebauer, U. *Datura Stramonium.*
http://www.arscurandi.ca/stram.html

SETI Institute. *How Many Habitable Planets Are Out There?*
https://www.seti.org/press-release/how-many-habitable-planets-are-out-there

Shermer, Martin. *The Believing Brain: From Ghosts and Gods and Conspiracies – How we Construct Beliefs and Reinforce Them as Truths.* New York: St Martin's, 2011.

Schilling, H.K. "The Threefold Nature of Science and Religion". In *Science and Religion: New Perspectives on the Dialogue,* edited by I.G. Barbour. London: SCM, 1968.

Shanks, H. *The Dead Sea Scrolls–Discovery and Meaning.* Biblical Archaeology Society, 2007.
http://c795631.r31.cf2.rackcdn.com/dead_sea_scrolls_discovery_and%20_meaning.pdf

Statistics South Africa. *Census 2001: Primary Tables South Africa Census '96 And 2001 Compared: Report No. 03-02-04 (2001).* Pretoria: Statistics South Africa.

Stenger, V.J. *The New Atheism: Taking a Stand for Science and Reason.* New York: Prometheus, 2009.

Stichting Pieterskerk Leiden, 2015.
http://www.pieterskerk.com/nl/

Stoker, Herman.G. *Beginsels en Metodes in die Wetenskap.* Johannesburg: Boekhandel De Jong, 1969.

Stone, H.W. *The Word of God and Pastoral Care.* Nashville: Abingdon, 1980.

Sundkler, Bengt G.M. *Bantu Prophets in South Africa.* Cambridge: James Clark & Co, 2004.

Swaab, D. *Wij zijn ons Brein: van Baarmoeder tot Alzheimer.* Amsterdam: Uitgeverij Contact, 2010.

Temes, R. *The Complete Idiot's Guide to Hypnosis.* Indianapolis: Alpha, 2000.

Temple, R. *Netherworld.* London: Arrow, 2003.

The Way? *How Many Christian Denominations Worldwide?* https://theway21stcentury.wordpress.com/2012/11/23/how-many-christian-denominations-worldwide/

Thomas, R. "The Israelite Origins of the Mandaean People". *Studia Antiqua*, 5.2, Fall 2007.

Tolsi, N. "For Church and Country". *Mail & Guardian*, 13.11.2009. http://mg.co.za/article/2009-11-13-for-church-and-country

Turner, V.S. "Children With a Religious Upbringing Show Less Altruism: a Controversial Study with a Surprising Finding". *Scientific American*, 09.02.2016. http://www.scientificamerican.com/article/children-with-a-religious-upbringing-show-less-altruism/ Van Den Heever, Jurie. *Wat Moet ons met ons Kerk Doen?* Cape Town: Naledi, 2017.

Tuttle, R.H. "Human Evolution". In *Encyclopædia Britannica*, 2010.

United Nations. "Universal Declaration of Human Rights, 1948". Reprinted in *Encyclopaedia Britannica*, 2010.

United Nations. *World Population Day, 2015.* http://www.un.org/en/events/populationday/.

United Nations Development Plan. *Human Development Report 2015: Work for Human Development.* http://hdr.undp.org/sites/default/files/2015_human_development_report.pdf

Van Baaren, T.P. "Monotheism". In *Encyclopædia Britannica*, 2010.

Van Huyssteen J.Wentzel. *Teologie as Kritiese Geloofsverantwoording: Teorievorming in die Sistematiese Teologie*. Pretoria: RGN. 1986.

Veith, Walter J. *Truth Matters*. Delta: Amazing Discoveries, 2002.

Ward, Keith. *Is Religion Irrational?* Oxford: Lin Hudson, 2011.

Westminster Confession of Faith, The. https://epc.org/wp-content/uploads/files/1-who-we-are/b-about-the-epc/wcf-modernenglish.pdf

"What is the Best Thing About the Easter Long Weekend? Survey Done By The Online News Service". *News24*, 18.04.2017.

http//www.news24.com/

Wikipedia. "Datura Stramonium".

https://en.wikipedia.org/wiki/datura_stramonium
—―—. "Irreligion".
http://en.wikipedia.org/wiki/irreligion
—―—. "Irreligion by Country",
http://en.wikipedia.org/wiki/importance_of_religion_by_country
—―—. "List of Countries by Intentional Homicide Rate".
http://en.wikipedia.org/wiki/list_of_countries_by_intentional_homicide_rate
—―—. "Major Religious Groups".
http://en.wikipedia.org/wiki/major_religious_groups
Wright, N.T. "The Self-Revelation of God in Human History: A Dialogue on Jesus with N.T. Wright". In A. Flew. *There is a God: How the World's Most Notorious Atheist Changed his Mind.* New York: Harper Collins, 2007.
Young, G.B. "Hyperthermia". In *Encyclopedia of the Neurological Sciences*, edited by M.J. Aminoff. Elsevier Science, 2003, 610–12.
Zaleski, C. "Purgatory". In *Encyclopædia Britannica*, 2010.
Zillmer, E.A. *Principles of Neuropychology.* Belmont CA: Wadsworth, 2008.
Zimmer, C. *Evolution.* London: Arrow, 2003.
ernenglish.pdf

Picture Credits

Introduction
The Theological Seminary, Stellenbosch – established in 1859.
http://www.sun.ac.za/english/news-media/photos

Chapter 2
Charles Darwin
https://za.pinterest.com/louis2396/charles-darwin/

Venus of Willendorf.
http://donsmaps.com/willendorf.html

Prof Johannes du Plessis
https://af.wikipedia.org/wiki/John_du_Plessis

Gravestone on a hilltop
Private collection of the author

Chapter 3
Pope Francis
http://en.radiovaticana.va/news/2016/06/01/pope_francis__pray_for_your_clergy_this_jubilee_for_priests/1233935 (retrieved 13.02.2017)

Tomas de Torquemada
https://www.janapetken.com/tomas-de-torquemada-the-grand-inquisitor/

Chapter 4
Karl Marx
http://infed.org/mobi/karl-marx-and-education/

Sigmund Freud

https://www.jacobinmag.com/2020/05/sigmund-freud-red-vienna-analytic-therapy-psychoanalysis

www.ingramcontent.com/pod-product-compliance
Lightning Source LLC
Chambersburg PA
CBHW050344230426
43663CB00010B/1976